MOSCOW
AND THE GOLDEN RING

K L M Royal Dutch AIRLINES

To Eleanor, Moshka and Jane

ACKNOWLEDGEMENTS

Phil and Barb Penningroth; Carlichka 'Gospodin' Gottlieb; Dr. Brockman, Patrushka Lanza, Leonard and Gorsky; Lyoni Craven; 'Bashkaus' Bill; Ted Steinberg; Anatoly Valushkin and Svetlana Romashkova; Dr. Barbara Stephens; John Porterfield; Richard Neill; St. Petersburg Circus—Sonin and Natasha; Vladimir Uspensky; Sasha, Tanya & Andrei—The Frishkadelkamis; Richard Bangs; Larissa Vilenskaya; Bob Liljestrand; Val Ossipov; Robert Trent Jones, II & Gudren; Steve Robertson & Jim McCutcheon; Dominique Jando; Gene Sawyer; Sloane, Stephen, Buddy & Mary Beth; William Garson; Richard Burgi & Gus; Lori; Jan Appleton; Nikulin & The Moscow Circus; Schneer; The Staub Family; Yuko, Ari & Aidan; Andy and Hank; Margareta, Wouter, Fleur & Peter; Angliisky Misha, Nadiya, E.J. & Anna; Linda Jassim; Karen, Tom, Connie & Dustin; Peggy Burns; Robert & Alexandra Baker and Middlebury College; Tovarishi Magnus Bartlett, Anna Claridge & Sally-Ann Imémé. In special memory of Mek Morsey, Brian Seeholzer, Matt Valensic, Babushki Anna & Evelyn and Dyedushki Mitro & Milford; Anna Akhmatova, sobaka Victoria von Ruppach; koshki Harry & Nicholas I—and a hearty spasibo to all those who helped in THE BIG CABBAGE—BOLSHAYA KAPUSTA!!!

Author

Masha Nordbye is a writer and film producer who has travelled through more than 70 countries, and was one of the first women to ever stand atop the North Pole. She has worked and travelled throughout the former Soviet Union on a regular basis over the past twenty years. Her Russian films include *National Geographic's* 'Voices of Leningrad' and 'Inside the Soviet Circus'; PBS's 'Villages of the North'; Disney's *Mickey Mouse goes to Moscow*; The Discovery Channel's *Bashkaus: Hard Labor in Siberia*, about rafting across southern Siberia; 20th Century Fox's *Back in the USSR*; and ABC's *The Power of the Russian Psychics*. Nordbye has travelled across the country with the Russian Circus many times, and helped organize the Moscow Circus' American Tour in 1989. She is currently producing a number of documentaries on Russia and is also the author of three other books. She resides in Los Angeles, California.

Photographer

Patricia Lanza has been a freelance and contract photographer for the National Geographic Society for many years, with over 700 photos to her credit. She contributed to the book *A Day in the Life of the Soviet Union* and provided the still photography for the *National Geographic* film 'Inside the Soviet Circus' and the travel book *St Petersburg*, and photographed the US tours of the Moscow Circus. Exhibitions of Lanza's photographs have been mounted at Radio City Music Hall and the Lincoln Center in New York and at the Chevron Gallery in San Francisco. She divides her time between Los Angeles and New York.

MOSCOW
AND THE GOLDEN RING

Masha Nordbye

Photography by Patricia Lanza

British Library Cataloguing-in-Publication Data
A catalogue record for this book is available from the British Library

Distribution in the United Kingdom, Ireland and Europe by Hi Marketing Ltd, 38 Carver Road, London SE24 9LT, UK

Grateful acknowledgement is made to the authors and publishers for permissions granted:
Stanford University Press for
The Travels of Olearius in Seventeenth Century Russia, edited and translated by Samuel H Baron, © 1967 the Board of Trustees of the Leland Stanford Junior University

Harvard Univeristy Press for
Moscow Diary by Walter Benjamin, edited by Gary Smith and translated by Richard Sieburth, © 1986 by the President and Fellows of Harvard

Ardis Publishers for
'The Barsukov Triangle,' from *The Two-Toned Blond and Other Stories* by Nina Katerli, edited by Carl R Proffer and Ellandea Proffer, © Ardis 1984

Grove Weidenfeld Inc for
Heart of a Dog by Mikhail Bulgakov, translated by Mirra Ginsburg

Peter Owen Ltd for
Adventures in Czarist Russia by Alexandre Dumas, edited and translated by Alma Elizabeth Murch

Excerpt from *In Plain Russian* by Vladimir Voinovich, translated by Richard Lourie, translation © 1979 by Farrar, Straus and Girous, Inc, reprinted by permission of Farrar, Straus and Giroux Inc and Georges Borchardt Inc

Editor: Stefan Cucos
Illustrations Editor: John Oliver
Maps: Tom Le Bas and Bai Yiliang
Design: Teresa Ho
Cover Concept: Raquel Jaramillo and Aubrey Tse
Excerpts: Andrew Coe
Photography by Patricia Lanza with additional contributions by Cary Wolinsky, Trillium Studios 86–7, 90, 94–5, 98, 99, 102; Masha Nordbye 114, 140 (bottom left), 141 (bottom right), 167, 183, 186, 187, 230–31, 238, 258–59; Patrick Lucero 5, 78–9, 122, 132, 133; Carolyn Watts 107, 162, 163; John Oliver 274

Produced by Twin Age Ltd, Hong Kong
Printed in Hong Kong by Sing Cheong Printing Co Ltd

St Basil's Cathedral, Red Square

Contents

Residence and church combined, Vladimir

The hourly changing of the guards at Lenin's tomb during the Soviet era

Introduction

On with the journey!...
Russia! Russia!
When I see you... my eyes
are lit up with supernatural power. Oh, what a
glittering, wondrous infinity of space....What a
strange, alluring, enthralling, wonderful world!

Nikolai Gogol

Perhaps no other destination in the world has captured the traveler's imagination as much as Russia. Throughout the centuries, its visitors have reported phenomenal and fanciful scenes: from golden churches, bejeweled icons and towering *kremlins* to madcap czars, wild Cossacks and prolific poets. Russia was, and remains, an impressive sight to behold. A travel writer in the early 20th century remarked that Russia's capital, Moscow 'embodied fantasy on an unearthly scale... Towers, domes, spires, cones, onions, crenelations filled the whole view. It might have been the invention of Danté, arrived in a Russian heaven.'

By the 1600s, Russia was already the largest country in the world. The massive conquests deep into the Siberian wilds by Ivan the Terrible and Peter the Great had created a territory larger than the Roman Empire with the richest resources on Earth. It was so vast that in 1856, when American Perry McDonough Collins arrived in Irkutsk to propose a railway line to link the country, it took him nearly a year to cross the 3,500 miles to St Petersburg. He had to change horses over 200 times.

After the 1917 Bolshevik Revolution, the countries bordering Russia fell into the Soviet Union's domain. The USSR became the world's largest nation with 15 republics stretching across 11 time zones and two continents, Europe and Asia. Its borders encompassed one-sixth of the planet's total land area with a population of 290 million speaking 200 languages and dialects. Even today, it is impossible to take in the diversity of the entire country during one, two or even three visits. However, there is no better way to learn about the Russian character and way of life than taking a trip to Moscow and its neighboring area of the Golden Ring.

On the historic day of December 21, 1991, after seven decades of Communist rule, the Soviet Union collapsed. The attempted coup in August 1991 was the catalyst that led to the dissolution of one of the most oppressive regimes in history. As one defender of a new and non-totalitarian government exclaimed: 'I have lived through a revolution, two world wars, the Siege of Leningrad and Stalin, and I will not tolerate another takeover; let the people be in peace!' In its place was established the Commonwealth of Independent States (CIS), or the *Soyuz Nezavysimeekh Gosudarstv (SNG)*.

Moscow is the Commonwealth's largest city and the capital of its largest State, the Russian Federation, which stretches from Moscow to Siberia. With nearly 150 million people and 130 nationalities and ethnic groups, Russia is truly the core of the Commonwealth. Moscow is the center of politics, industry and culture, the heart of this giant nation and the source of the Russian spirit, or *dusha'*. The Russian poet Alexander Pushkin wrote of his first trip to Moscow: 'And now at last the goal is in sight: in the shimmer of the white walls...and golden domes, *Moskva* lies great and splendid before us...O *Moskva* have I thought of you! *Moskva* how violently the name plucks at any Russian heart!'

The true enchantment of Moscow begins in the city center, where you can gaze upon the gilded domes of the palaces and churches of the former czars, rising up from within the old protective walls of the Kremlin. From the citadel, paths lead out to the fairy-tale creation of Ivan the Terrible, St Basil's Cathedral, which looms up from the middle of *Krasnaya Ploshchad*, Red Square. *Krasnaya* is an old Russian word meaning both red and beautiful. Queues of visitors still stretch along the Kremlin's walls, waiting to enter Lenin's Mausoleum to view the 'Father of the Great October Revolution.'

Jutting out like arteries from the heart of the city are long thoroughfares that take one through various stages of Moscow's history. These roads, and ringroads, offer an abundance of sights, including the Bolshoi Theater, Novodevichy Monastery, Tretyakov Art Gallery and the Exhibition Park of Economic Achievements. The city has a wealth of breathtaking and poetic creations, as the famous Russian writer Anna Akhmatova remarked: 'As you stroll through the city, you'll find...all of Moscow is truly soaked with verses, saturated with meter, time after time.'

The Arbat district, which celebrated its 500th anniversary in 1993, embodies both Russia's history and the changes currently sweeping the country. Here, b*abushki*, grandmothers, amble along carrying net bags filled with cabbages and potatoes, while long-haired musicians jam on guitars and saxophones. Moscow continues to bask in the light of past splendors, but is now passionately embracing liberty for the first time in decades.

With the dawn of Gorbachev's 'second revolution' came a virtual explosion in communications, culture and national awareness. In what was termed 'the new Russian Renaissance,' the people experienced greater freedoms than were ever permitted throughout the entire history of socialism. Mikhail Gorbachev's p*erestroika* and *glasnost*, and Boris Yeltsin's heroic stance became the symbols of the new generation.

When Boris Yeltsin and his followers triumphed over the abortive coups of August 1991 and October 1993, democratic reforms lit up the country. A new constitution and Federal Assembly were created, and a market economy stumbled into action for the first time in the country's existence. New freedoms and opportunities have flowered from the ruins of 70 years of Marxist-Leninist rule. There has never been a more exciting time to visit Russia.

The towns and villages surrounding the city's outskirts, known collectively as the Golden Ring, reveal a quieter and quainter lifestyle. This area is considered the cradle of Russian culture. The small towns, like Sergiyev Posad (the center of Russian Orthodoxy), Rostov, Vladimir and Suzdal (the most ancient Russian town), were built between the 10th and 17th centuries and are magnificently preserved. Antiquated villages, onion-domed churches, frescoes and icons by the 15th-century artist Andrei Rublev, colorful wooden *dacha* (country homes) and endless groves of *beryoza* (birch trees) provide a delightful contrast to the bigger cities. The serene sites are reminiscent of a 19th-century Tolstoyan novel, a time-frozen portrait of Russia's past.

Compared to even a few years ago, Russian cities and towns now boast many more entertainment opportunities, places to eat and items to buy; and it is a lot easier to get things done. In the old Soviet Union, most enterprises, and people for that matter, were strictly isolated and controlled. After years of suppression, a taste of democracy and individualization has led to an 'anything goes' atmosphere. Because of the whirlwind creation of new businesses and the current free-for-all feeling, Moscow has been nicknamed *Deeky Zapad*, the Wild West. But as capitalism takes hold, so, unfortunately, does poverty, crime and corruption. Today's visitors must be more guarded with their money and valuables.

Many travelers enter the country through one of the Russian Tour Agencies, such as Intourist, which provides hotels, meals and sightseeing, but there are other ways. Visitors can also enter on individual or business visas, stay in Russian homes or hostels instead of hotels, or even camp. For the more adventurous, biking, climbing, hiking and rafting trips are available.

Despite its technological, cultural and sporting achievements, Russia has yet to produce a food surplus or an adequate supply of clothing. Rarely do Russian citizens enjoy a choice of fruits and vegetables, and sometimes even the basics, such as toilet paper and soap, are not readily available. The ordinary Russian still stands in long queues to buy most things, and occasionally some items, such as sausage, sugar and tea, are rationed. Many complain that living standards are worse now than under Communism. Consequently, visitors should not expect all the tourist amenities found in the West. Remember that travelers receive what the country can most readily provide, and that is usually much more than is available to the average citizen. A sure remedy for the lack of certain supplies is to take anything you cannot do without, from prescription drugs to peanut butter. However, many new Western-style stores have opened that stock most things.

If you do not read Cyrillic or speak the Russian language, take a Russian phrase book; a smile, some patience and the knowledge of a few Russian words will be great-

Historical Chart

700–882: The Vikings begin to leave Scandinavia and establish trading settlements with the Slavs in northwestern Russia. Kievan state in the south is formed and named after the Slavic Prince Kii. In 862, the Norseman Rurik defeats the important Slavic town of Novgorod and becomes one of the first Vikings to rule in Russia. In 880, Rurik's successor, Oleg, conquers the Slavic-ruled Kiev, unites the two states and makes Kiev his capital. The ruling class is known as 'Rus', (thought to be derived from the Viking word *ruotsi*, meaning rower or oarsman). This term is later applied to the people of Eastern Europe; eventually the areas are united into the Russian states.

977: Novgorod gains its independence from Kiev.

978–1015: Rule of Prince Vladimir, who introduces Byzantine Christianity into Russia.

1015–1054: Rule of Yaroslav the Wise. Kiev becomes the first center of the Orthodox Church.

1113–1125: Rule of Vladimir Monomakh. The two principalities of Novgorod and Kiev are united again under his rule. The crown of Monomakh is worn by the later rulers of Russia. The decline of Kievan Rus begins after his death.

1147: Prince Yuri Dolgoruky 'Long Arms' founds Moscow. He builds a kremlin and defensive walls around the city.

1169: Prince Andrei Bogoliubsky transfers the capital from Kiev to Vladimir.

1223: First Mongol invasion of Russia.

1237: Batu Khan, grandson of Genghis Khan, invades Moscow and goes on to conquer many of Russia's other regions. The Mongol Tatars dominate Russia for the next 250 years.

1240: The Prince of Novgorod, Alexander Nevsky, defeats the Swedes in an important battle along the Neva River. Nevsky rules as Grand Prince in Vladimir from 1252–1263.

1299: The Church Metropolitan flees Kiev and takes up residence with the Grand Prince in Vladimir.

1325–1340: Reign of Ivan I, nicknamed Kalita 'Moneybags' because of his strong economic hold over the other principalities. Ivan is named Grand Prince in 1328, and chooses Moscow as his residence. The seat of the Orthodox Church is moved from Vladimir to Moscow. In 1337, St Sergius founds the Monastery of the Holy Trinity in Sergiyev Posad.

1353–1359: Reign of Ivan II.

1362–1389: Reign of Dmitri Donskoi. In 1380, the Grand Prince defeats the Tatars in the Battle of Kulikovo on the Don, becoming the first Russian prince to win a decisive battle over the Mongol army. Two years later the Mongols burn Moscow to the ground.

1453: The Ottoman Turks conquer Constantinople, which releases the Russian Orthodox Church from Byzantine domination. Less than a decade later, the head of the Orthodox Church takes on the title of Metropolitan of Moscow and All Russia and receives his orders from the Grand Prince.

1460–1505: Reign of Ivan III (Ivan the Great). He marries Sophia, the niece of the last Byzantine Emperor, in 1472 and adopts the crest of the double-headed eagle. Moscow is declared the Third Rome. During his rule, Ivan the Great rebuilds the Kremlin and annexes the city of Novgorod. He refuses to pay any further tribute to the Mongols and defeats their armies. Two centuries of Tatar oppression in Russia come to an end.

1533–1584: Reign of Ivan IV (Ivan the Terrible) who is crowned in 1547 in the Moscow Kremlin with the title of Czar (derived from Caesar) of All Russia. He organizes the *Oprichniki*, a special bodyguard to prosecute the *Boyars* (landowners). He defeats the Tatars in the far eastern territories. Russia loses the Livonian War and access to the Baltic. St Basil's cathedral built.

1584–1598: Reign of Fyodor I, son of Ivan IV. Establishment of Moscow Church Patriarch.

1598–1613: The Time of Troubles. Boris Godunov rules as Czar from

1598 to 1605. Claim to the throne by two false Dmitris. Second false Dmitri seizes the throne with Polish support. Battles with Polish armies.

1613–1645: Mikhail Romanov is elected Czar. The Romanov Dynasty continues to rule Russia until 1762.

1645–1676: Reign of Alexei I.

1676–1682: Reign of Fyodor III. When he dies, his feeble-minded brother, Ivan V, and half-brother, Peter (Peter the Great), are proclaimed joint czars. The *Streltsy* (marksmen) briefly gain control over the government. Sophia, Peter's half-sister, acts as Regent.

1689–1725: Reign of Peter the Great. During his enlightened rule, Peter adopts the Julian calendar, transfers the capital from Moscow to St Petersburg, introduces Western culture and customs to his country and builds the first Russian fleet along the Baltic. In 1721, he assumes the title of Emperor of All Russia.

1725–1727: Reign of Catherine I, the widow of Peter the Great, who becomes Czarina with the help of her guard Menshikov.

1727–1730: Reign of Peter II, Peter the Great's grandson.

1730–1740: Reign of Anna Ivanova, daughter of Ivan V and niece of Peter the Great.

1740–41: Reign of Ivan VI.

1741–1761: Reign of Elizabeth, daughter of Peter the Great and Catherine I. In 1755, the first university is founded in Moscow.

1761–1762: Reign of Peter III, grandson of Peter the Great.

1762–1796: Reign of Catherine II (Catherine the Great), German-born wife of Peter III. The first foreign woman to rule as Czarina. Russia becomes a major power.

1796–1801: Reign of Paul I, son of Catherine the Great.

1801–1825: Reign of Alexander I, son of Paul I. In 1812, Napoleon's armies flee Moscow. Rise of the Decembrist movement.

1825–1855: Reign of Nicholas I, son of Paul I. On December 14, 1825 the Decembrists attempt to overthrow the Czarist autocracy and gain freedom for the serfs. Bolshoi Theater opens in 1825. In 1851, the first railway opens between St Petersburg and Moscow.

1855–1881: Reign of Alexander II, son of Nicholas I. In 1861, Alexander signs a decree to emancipate the serfs.

1867: Sale of Alaska to the United States; Karl Marx's *Das Kapital* is translated into Russian.

1881: Alexander II is assassinated by members of the Peoples' Will group.

1881–1894: Reign of Alexander III. The brother of Lenin, Alexander Ulyanov, along with four others, attempt to assassinate the Czar.

1894–1917: Reign of Nicholas II. Nicholas marries the granddaughter of Queen Victoria. In 1895, workers hold public rallies to celebrate May Day, day of worker Solidarity. In 1903, the Social Democratic Party splits into two factions: Bolsheviks and Mensheviks. The first revolution takes place in 1905 (known as Bloody Sunday) in St Petersburg. World War I breaks out in 1914. In 1916, Rasputin murdered by Count Yusupov. Second revolution begins in February, 1917. Czar Nicholas abdicates and a Provisional Government is formed under Kerensky's leadership. In October 1917, Lenin and the Bolsheviks overthrow the Provisional Government and establish the Socialist Soviet State. In 1918, Nicholas and his family are executed in the Ural town of Sverdlovsk.

1918–1924: In 1918, Lenin moves capital from Petrograd to Moscow. First Soviet constitution is adopted. Switch to Gregorian calendar. The Communist Government nationalizes industry, introduces censorship of the press and forms the Cheka police force. Lenin introduces the New Economic Policy (NEP). When Lenin dies in 1924, St Petersburg (Petrograd) is renamed Leningrad.

1924–1953: Joseph Stalin. In 1927, Trotsky is expelled from the Party. In 1928, Stalin introduces the First Five Year Plan and Collectivization. A widespread famine sweeps the nation, eventually killing ten million people.

1934–1941: Stalin's assassination of Leningrad Party Chief Sergei Kirov signals the beginning of the Great Terror. Half the delegates of the 17th Party Congress are purged, along with 90 per cent of the country's generals. Of approximately 20 million people arrested, seven million are shot immediately while the rest are sent to gulag camps for rehabilitation.

1941–1945: World War II. Hitler invades the USSR in 1941, and the siege of Leningrad lasts for 900 days until 1944. The Soviet Union suffers 20 million casualties.

1945–1953: Occupation of Eastern Europe.

1953–1964: Stalin dies and is succeeded by Nikita Khruschev, who founds the KGB, the committee for state security, in 1954. In 1956, at the 20th Party Congress, he denounces Stalin in a secret speech. Two-thirds of the Orthodox churches and monasteries are closed down. In 1961, the Soviets send the first man, Yuri Gagarin, into space, and the Congress votes to remove Stalin's body from its place of honor alongside Lenin in the Kremlin Mausoleum.

1964–1982: Khruschev's forced resignation is engineered by Leonid Brezhnev, who immediately rescinds Khruschev's Rule 25 restricting Party officials to 15 years in office. The discovery of large gas and oil reserves boosts the economy, but these benefits are undermined by poor planning and lack of incentives. Alcohol consumption quadruples in 20 years. Further repressions stimulate the dissident and Samizdat movements.

1968: Invasion of Czechoslovakia.

1979: Invasion of Afghanistan.

1982–1984: Brezhnev dies and is succeeded by Yuri Andropov, former head of the KGB.

1984–1985: Andropov dies and is succeeded by Konstantin Chernenko, Brezhenev's 72-year old protégé who dies one year later.

1985–1991: Mikhail Gorbachev.

December 21, 1991: the Soviet Union ceases to exist.

1992–: Boris Yeltsin, President of the Russian Republic, formed the 11-member Commonwealth of Independent States.

ly appreciated. So much so, that you may even find yourself invited to someone's home for dinner, where you will quickly discover that Russians are among the warmest and most hospitable people you will ever meet.

Dos vidanya!

Perestroika

On March 11, 1985, 54-year-old Mikhail Sergeyevich Gorbachev was elected the new General Secretary of the Communist Party. Following in the footsteps of such past rulers as Ivan the Terrible, Peter the Great, Stalin and Brezhnev, Gorbachev inherited a stagnating economy, an entrenched bureaucracy and a population living in fear and mistrust of its leaders.

Gorbachev's first actions were to shut down the production and sale of vodka and ardently pursue the anti-corruption campaign instituted by a former president, Yuri Vladimirovich Andropov. In 1986, Gorbachev introduced the radical reform policies of *perestroika* (restructuring), *demokratizatsiya* (democratization) and *glasnost* (openness), now household words. He emphasized that past reforms had not worked because they did not directly involve Soviet citizens. *Perestroika* introduced the profit motive, quality control, private ownership in agriculture, decentralization and multi-candidate elections. Industry concentrated on measures promoting quality over quantity; private businesses and cooperatives were encouraged; farmers and individuals could lease land and housing from the government, and keep the profits made from produce grown on private plots; hundreds of ministries and bureaucratic centers were disbanded. A law was passed that allowed individuals to own small businesses and hire workers so long as there was 'no exploitation of man by man.'

In a powerful symbolic gesture, Andrei Sakharov and other political prisoners were released from internal exile. (After winning the 1975 Nobel Peace Prize, Sakharov, the physicist and human rights activist, was banished for nearly seven years to the city of Gorky. He died in Moscow on November 14, 1989.) One hundred Soviet dissidents from 20 cities were allowed to form the Democratic Club, an open political discussion group. Glasnost swept through all facets of Soviet life.

For the 40 million followers of the Russian Orthodox religion, and people of other religious beliefs, Gorbachev stated that 'believers have the full right to express their convictions with dignity.' On December 1, 1989, Gorbachev became the first Soviet leader to set foot in the Vatican, where he declared: 'We need spiritual values; we need a revolution of the mind... No one should interfere in matters of the individual's conscience. Christians, Moslems, Jews, Buddhists and others live in the Soviet

Union. All of them have a right to satisfy their spiritual needs—this is the only way toward a new culture and new politics that can meet the challenge of our time.' As Peter the Great understood, modernization meant Westernization, and Gorbachev reopened the window to the West. With the fostering of private business, about 5 million people were employed by over 150,000 cooperatives. After April 1, 1989, all enterprises were allowed to carry on trade relations with foreign partners, triggering the development of joint ventures. Multi-million-dollar deals were struck with Western companies, such as Chevron, Pepsi, Eastman-Kodak, McDonald's, Time-Warner and Occidental.

At the 1986 Iceland Summit, Gorbachev proposed a sharp reduction in ballistic missiles, and in December 1987, he signed a treaty with US President Ronald Reagan to eliminate intermediate-range nuclear missiles. In January 1988, the Soviet Union announced its withdrawal from Afghanistan. Nine months later Andrei Gromyko retired and Gorbachev was elected President of the Supreme Soviet.

During a visit to Finland in October 1989, Gorbachev declared: 'The Soviet Union has no moral or political right to interfere in the affairs of its Eastern European neighbors. They have the right to decide their own fate.' And that is what they did. By the end of 1989, every country throughout Eastern Europe saw its people protesting openly for mass reforms. The Iron Curtain crumbled, symbolized most poignantly by the demolition of the wall between East and West Berlin.

In December 1989, Gorbachev met with US President George Bush at the Malta Summit, where the two agreed that 'the arms race, mistrust, psychological and ideological struggle should all be things of the past.'

Elections and Economy

On March 26, 1989, there was a general election for the new Congress of People's Deputies—the first time since 1917 that Soviet citizens had had the chance to vote in a national election. One thousand five hundred delegates were elected together with an additional 750, who were voted in by other public organizations. The 2,250-delegate body then elected 542 members to form a new Supreme Soviet.

Ousted a year earlier from his Politburo post for criticizing the reforms, the Congress candidate Boris Yeltsin won 89 per cent of the Moscow district vote. As Moscow crowds chanted 'Yeltsin is a Man of the People' and 'Down with Bureaucrats,' a surprising number of bureaucrats had, in fact, lost to members of such groups as the Church Metropolitan of Leningrad. Andrei Sakharov was also elected. An interesting aspect of the election rules was that even candidates who ran unopposed could lose, if over half the votes pulled a lever of no confidence, a privilege not enjoyed by voters in most Western countries.

At the beginning of l990, Soviet citizens once again headed to the polls to elect their own regional and district officials, this time with the additional opportunity of choosing candidates from other independent and pro-democracy movements. Scores of Communist Party candidates were defeated by former political prisoners, adamant reformers, environmentalists and strike leaders. Yeltsin was voted in as President of the Russian Federation, the Soviet Union's largest republic with more than half the country's population and Moscow as its capital. In June 1990, Yeltsin resigned from the Communist Party, declaring that 'in view of my...great responsibility toward the people of Russia and in connection with moves toward a multi-party State, I cannot fulfill only the instructions of the Party.'

Yeltsin's ascent underscored the fact that for all Gorbachev's unprecedented reforms and innovative policies, he had failed to bring the country's economy out of stagnation; because of this he lost his popularity at home. An extensive poll conducted throughout the Soviet Union revealed that more than 90 per cent considered the economic situation critical. Some of the disheartened commented that 'glasnost has produced more copies of Solzhenitsyn than salami.' Food and fuel were in critically low supplies, and the population anticipated the worst food shortages since World War II. Ration coupons were issued for meat, sugar, tea and soap. After the launch of a probe to Mars, graffiti in Moscow appeared exclaiming: 'To Mars for Soap!'

Modernization still did not approach Western standards: there were few computers and most areas continued to use the abacus. It was estimated that 40 per cent of the crops had been wasted because of poor storage, packing and distribution methods. Many Soviets felt that their living conditions had worsened: 'We live like dogs. The leash has become longer but the meat is a bit smaller, and the plate is two meters further away. But at least we can now bark as much as we want.'

Gorbachev was also faced with a budget deficit of over 100 billion rubles. The severe shortages boosted the black market, which provided goods for up to 85 per cent of the population. On November 1, l989, the government drastically cut the bank ruble exchange rate by 90 per cent to curb black-market exchanges (up to 20 times the official rate) and bring the ruble closer to an open exchange on the world market. The Prime Minister stated that 43 million people (15 per cent of the population) were living below the poverty level. There was also an estimated 23 million unemployed, the new paradox of this modern Soviet society.

Compounding failing measures and political contradictions, the nation was rocked by a series of disasters: Chernobyl, the earthquake in Armenia, ethnic unrest and extensive strikes in mines and factories across the country (a 1989 law legalized strikes). But Gorbachev remained confident and pressed on with *perestroika*: 'This is a turbulent time, a turbulent sea in which it is not easy to sail the ship. But we have a compass and we have a crew to guide that ship, and the ship itself is strong.'

In one of the most important changes in the country's political and economic system since the 1917 Bolshevik Revolution, Mikhail Gorbachev was elected by Congress as the Soviet Union's first executive President. This new post, replacing the former honorary chairmanship of the Supreme Soviet, had broader constitutional powers. The President now had the right to propose legislation, veto bills passed by Congress, appoint and fire the Prime Minister and other senior government officials, and declare states of emergency (with the approval of the republics).

Gorbachev himself summarized the results of all his policies: 'Having embarked upon the road of radical reform, we have crossed the line beyond which there is no return to the past... Things will never be the same again in the Soviet Union'—or in the whole communist world. Gorbachev's second revolution became one of the most momentous events in the second half of the 20th century.

The Communist Party

The Bolshevik Party, formed by Lenin, began as a unified band of revolutionaries whose 8,000 members organized the mass strike of the l905 St Petersburg revolt. By October 1917, the Bolshevik Party (soon renamed the Communist Party) had over 300,000 members, many of whom became the leaders and planners of the newly formed Soviet State.

Before the fall of Communism, there were more than 20 million Party members, a third of them women. Membership was open to any citizens who 'did not exploit the labor of others,' abided by the Party's philosophy and gave three per cent of their monthly pay as dues to the Party. Members were also required to attend several meetings and lectures each month, provide volunteer work a few times a year and help with election campaigns. Approximately 200,000 of these members were full-time officials, *apparatchiks*, paid by the Party. The Komsomol, or Communist Youth Organization, had 40 million additional members, while 25 million school children belonged to the Young Pioneers. Eligibility for party membership began at age 18.

On February 7, l990, after 72 years of Communist rule, the Soviet Communist Party's Central Committee voted overwhelmingly to surrender its monopoly on power. On March 15, l990, the Soviet Congress of People's Deputies amended Article Six, which had guaranteed the Communist Party its position as the only 'leading authority' in government. In its revised form, Article Six stated that the Communists, together with other political parties and social organizations, have the right to shape

State policy. During the 28th Party Congress, the Party voted to reorganize its ruling body, the Politburo, to include Communist Party leaders from each of the 15 republics, in addition to the top 12 Moscow officials. Instead of being selected by the Central Committee, the Party in each republic chose its own leaders, guaranteeing, at the time, a voice in the Party to even the smallest republic.

Other amendments revised the Marxist view that private property was incompatible with Socialism. Individuals could own land and factories as long as they did not 'exploit' other Soviet citizens. New economic policies replaced direct central planning, instituted price reforms, created a stock exchange and allowed farmers to sell their produce on the open market. Additional new laws decreed that 'the press and other mass media are now free; censorship of the mass media is forbidden,' and that 'all political movements had access to the airwaves with the right to establish their own television and radio stations.' The monopoly enjoyed by the Communist Party on State-run radio and television ended. Even advertising, long denounced 'as a means of swindling the people' and a 'social weapon of the exploiter's class,' became acceptable. These momentous changes paved the way toward a multi-party democracy and a free-market economy.

By the end of August 1991, Boris Yeltsin stood in the Russian Parliament building, the White House, and declared: 'I am now signing a decree suspending the activities of the Russian Communist Party!' All Communist newspapers such as *Pravda* were temporarily shut down. Gorbachev followed by issuing decrees to end Soviet Communist rule. These decrees dissolved the party's structure of committees and policy-making, which included the Central Committee. Archives of the Party and the KGB were seized, and the government confiscated all of the Party's assets throughout the country. It would take two years before the Communist Party regained some of its powers.

Attempted Coup of August 1991

Gorbachev's vision of a second revolution never included an attempted coup. During his last year in office, many of his actions contradicted all that he had worked toward. After strongly supporting accelerated reforms, Gorbachev suddenly rejected the '500-Day Plan,' which proposed converting the sluggish centralized economy into a market-oriented one. Then, in December 1990, he appointed the conservative Boris Pugo as his Minister of the Interior. On January 11, 1991, Lithuania announced its independence; two days later Pugo sent in troops. Soviet troops were also sent into Latvia to quell demonstrations. This prompted Eduard Shevardnadze, the Foreign Minister, to resign, stating: 'We are returning to the terrible past...reformers have slumped into the bushes. A dictatorship is coming.'

During the Gulf War, the Chairman of the KGB, Vladimir Kryuchkov, charged that foreign governments were trying to destabilize Soviet society; the Russian military had become much more sensitive to the reactionary elements gathering force.

Gorbachev banned Yeltsin's rally of support in March 1991 and renewed censorship of the print and television media. The people in Moscow demonstrated anyway and troops were sent in. One of Gorbachev's aides said: 'March 28 was the turning point for Mikhail Sergeyevich. He went to the abyss, looked over the edge, was horrified at what he saw and backed away.' Gorbachev had to move closer to an alliance with Yeltsin to survive.

Those in the government became uneasy with the upcoming republics' treaty; much of Moscow's power would be usurped if it was signed. Leading bureaucrats realized they could lose their jobs and began planning ways to undermine Gorbachev's power. Even though he had created an unprecedented wave of changes, Gorbachev's popularity at home had now fallen to practically zero. After five years of promises, reforms had only made the living standards of average citizens worse. When prices had risen by over 50 per cent, the population became increasingly reluctant to trade their goods for worthless banknotes —inflation rose to over 1,000 per cent and the ruble collapsed. Despite a grossly dissatisfied population, disjointed government and repeated warnings of a plot against him, Gorbachev left for a vacation in the Crimea to work on the Union Treaty.

On the Sunday afternoon of August 18, 1991, Gorbachev was told that Yuri Plekhanov, a top KGB official, had arrived to see him. Gorbachev sensed something was wrong and tried to use the telephones; all five lines were dead. Then Valery Boldin, the Chief of Staff, entered the room, saying that Gorbachev had to sign a referendum declaring a state of emergency within the country. If he did not sign, the vice president would take over leadership duties. Since Gorbachev refused to go along with the conspiracy, thousands of troops were sent into Moscow. Ironically, the coup members failed to arrest Boris Yeltsin who, that morning, had rushed off to his office in the Parliament building 45 minutes earlier than usual.

The next morning, the coup leaders announced that Gorbachev, 'with serious health problems,' could no longer govern. But it became obvious from the outset that the coup was ill-planned. None of the opposition leaders was arrested. Yeltsin, holed up in the White House, was receiving calls from around the world and ordering food from Pizza Hut. At one point, Yeltsin went outside and climbed on top of a tank in front of 20,000 protesters. He appealed for mass resistance and named himself the 'Guardian of Democracy.' The crowd swelled to well over 100,000. By the end

of the day, troops were
switching to Yeltsin's side,
and many of the élite commando divisions were now
protecting the White House.

By August 20, the coup
attempt was weakening; many
of the planners stayed at home.
Crowds of people raised
the old white, blue and red Russian flag.
The famous cellist, composer and
conductor Mstislav Leopoldovich
Rostropovich, a survivor of the Siege
of Leningrad, even flew in from Paris
and played music within the Parliament
building. Tank divisions descended upon
the White House later in the day.
Swarms of people

blocked their way; after three were killed, the tanks retreated, refusing to fire on their own people.

Three days after the attempted coup, Yeltsin announced its failure. He sent officials to the Crimea to bring Gorbachev safely back to Moscow. The shaken presi-

dent and his family returned by airplane early the next morning. Seven members of the State Emergency Committee, also called the 'Gang of Eight,' were arrested; the eighth, Boris Pugo, shot himself in the head.

The crowds stood cheering, not so much for Gorbachev's return, but for their savior, Boris Yeltsin. Communism had disintegrated with the attempted putsch. Thousands celebrated as the statue of 'Iron Felix' Dzerzhinsky, the founder of the secret police after the 1917 Revolution, was toppled from its pedestal in front of the KGB building. A Russian flag and crucifix were put in its place—a monument to the millions who had died in prison camps at the hands of the KGB. Unbelievably, a new era had begun.

The End of the Soviet Union

The Soviet Union ceased to exist on December 21, 1991. The great ideological experiment begun by Lenin's Bolshevik Revolution, constituted on December 30, 1922, ended nine days short of its 70th year. 'One State has died,' announced Russian television, 'but in its place a great dream is being born.' The birth was of the Commonwealth of Independent States. Four days later, Gorbachev, the eighth and final leader of the Soviet Union, submitted his resignation. He no longer had a Soviet Union to govern. Boris Yeltsin claimed his office in the Kremlin.

Boris Yeltsin

Boris Nikolayevich Yeltsin was born into a poor family in Sverdlovsk in 1931. He went on to dismantle the entire Soviet empire. In an historic meeting in Alma Alta, the capital of Kazakhstan, Yeltsin convinced the leaders of the former Soviet republics to sign a new treaty forming the 11-member Commonwealth. In February 1992, Yeltsin officially put the Cold War to rest in a meeting with US President George Bush. He proclaimed a 'new era,' in which the two nations would join as allies to seek 'an enduring peace that rests on lasting common values.'

By the time Yeltsin took control, the economy was in disarray. Without GOSPLAN (the former central planning commission) and GOSNAB (the former central supply organization), factories everywhere had no idea what to produce or where to ship their goods. With the help of economic advisor Yegor Gaidar, Yeltsin announced the lifting of price controls. Gradually, over 600 commodities exchanges were formed and the Moscow Stock Exchange building returned to its original function. Russians received government vouchers redeemable for cash, or shares in businesses that were previously State-owned. People in private enterprises began to flourish, from street vendors to entrepreneurs. Newly rich businessmen operated with the latest technology and bought expensive cars. (Today, Russia is the largest market in the world for luxury cars.) It was possible for some young people to make more money in one day than their parents had in months, or even years. But, for many, especially the elderly, the new order meant standing in longer queues and spending hours in the cold trying to sell pitiful possessions to make ends meet.

Newspapers were also freed of censorship. Advertisements interrupted television programs. Soap operas were watched avidly—over 60 per cent of the population tuned in to the Mexican series The Rich Also Cry. Western imports, including MTV, Santa Barbara and Beverly Hills, 90210, deluged Russian television. And foreigners could now travel legally to once-restricted cities.

Yeltsin's biggest crisis since the attempted coup of 1991 arose after he dissolved the obstructionist Russian legislature at the end of September 1993, and moved to replace it with a new elective body. Yeltsin said he was acting to stem a 'senseless struggle that was threatening to lead Russia into a political abyss...the body is an outmoded Soviet-era institution sustained in office by a useless constitution.'

A growing animosity had been brewing between Yeltsin and his opposition, which had tried and failed to impeach him six months earlier in March 1993. Yeltsin had conducted a referendum in April in which Russian voters had expressed their preference for him and his policies. However, the Supreme Soviet instantly claimed Yeltsin's order to dissolve the legislature as null and void. Vice President Alexander Rutskoi, now a Yeltsin rival, was immediately elected acting president and Yeltsin was impeached on a 144-6 vote. The Parliament chairman, Ruslan Khasbulatov, called on Russian trade unions to go on strike to protest Yeltsin's order. Communist and nationalist leaders appeared on the White House balcony and urged their supporters to stay on. Many were taken with the irony of the gathering, on the very site where Yeltsin, next to Rutskoi, had faced down the right-wing coup plotters in August 1991. But this time Yeltsin was the coup plotter. While both sides waged all-out political warfare, many Muscovites could not care less if there was a coup. One citizen stated: 'We are tired of the political battles and want to live a normal life and earn some decent money.'

About a week after this crisis began, parliament supporters smashed through police lines, stormed the mayor's office and attacked the headquarters of the State television company, which exploded into the worst political violence since the 1917 Bolshevik Revolution. 'There can be no forgiveness for attacking innocent people,' announced Yeltsin. 'The armed revolt is doomed.' Yeltsin then countered by creating a state of emergency and sending in armored personnel carriers, tanks and élite commando units, which fired upon the White House. A new military tactic was also employed—blasting pop group Dire Straits and Russian Rap from loudspeakers near the White House. Thirteen days later, the opposition leaders surrendered after a massive barrage by tanks and paratroopers. The battle left 187 people dead and the White House a blackened shell with nearly every window blown out. Half a year later, the arrested White House hardliners, who had tried to topple the government in 1991 and 1993, were pardoned by the new Parliamentary Duma.

Yeltsin continued to promise that his struggling nation would not retreat from economic reform. To aid the reform process, many countries pledged financial support to Russia. In January 1994, US President Bill Clinton journeyed to Moscow for a summit with Yeltsin. In an historic meeting, the Ukraine also participated and signed an agreement to disarm all of the 1,800 nuclear warheads that had fallen to it after the collapse of the Soviet Union. Clinton told Yeltsin: 'You are in the process of transforming your entire economy while you develop a new constitution and democracy as well. It boggles the mind and you have my respect.'

After two decades of exile in the United States, the Russian writer Alexander Solzhenitsyn returned to live in Moscow in 1994. Solzhenitsyn, the winner of the Nobel Prize for Literature in 1970, was banished by the former Soviet government in 1974 for writing The *Gulag Archipelago*, which preserved the memory of the Soviet holocaust. It was not until late 1989 that Gorbachev gave permission for Solzhenitsyn's works to be published again in Russia. Before Solzhenitsyn decided to, and was allowed to, return to Russia, he wanted to finish writing his four-volume *The Red Wheel*, an epic history leading up to the October Revolution of 1917; the work totals over 5,000 pages: 'Our history has been so hidden. I had to dig so deep, I had to uncover what was buried and sealed. This took up all my years.'

Many years before his return to Russia, Solzhenitsyn had said: 'All of us in prison in the 1940s were certain that Communism would fall. The only question was when...In a strange way, I was inwardly convinced that I would go back.' In 1993, a political poll in St Petersburg showed that 48 per cent of the respondents wanted Solzhenitsyn as their Russian President; Yeltsin received only 17 per cent. In *The First Circle*, Solzhenitsyn described that in a tyranny a real writer is like a second government. If all goes well in Russia, the authoritarian voice will vanish. Alexander Solzhenitsyn has gone home, but he knows that there is a long road ahead: 'If it took Russia 75 years to fall so far, then it is obvious that it will take it more than 75 years to rise back up. I know we are still faced with incredible hardships for years to come.'

Russia Today

In 1992, Yeltsin addressed the US Congress, saying: 'The world can sigh in relief, the idol of Communism has collapsed. I am here to assure you, we shall not let it rise again in our land.'

Two years after Yeltsin had banned Communist activity on Russian soil, the constitutional court lifted Yeltsin's order, ruling that it violated the constitution. Thus, the Communist Party participated in the country's first true multi-party election on December 12, 1993. In the election, a new Russian constitution was also voted in, which gave the president more power and Parliament less. The constitution granted Russia's 149 million citizens many economic freedoms and civil liberties that had been stifled since the Bolshevik takeover. These included the right to own land, the right not to be wiretapped and the right to travel freely at home and abroad. It also provided for a new Parliament, known as the Federal Assembly, with the Federation Council as its upper chamber and the Duma as its lower. A month after the ballot, those elected assembled in Moscow to launch the new parliamentary democracy. Yeltsin stated: 'We must preserve this for the sake of national peace and to make sure dictatorship never returns to Russia.'

Today, the Communists are again one of the largest organized political forces in the land. But they are no longer the only party. Taking part in the election were other hardline groups, among them the Liberal Democratic Party, the Agrarian Party, the Centrist Democratic Party and the Women of Russia Party. The pro-reform parties included Russia's Choice, the Yavlinsky Bloc and the Russian Unity and Accord Party. The Beer-Lovers Party was one of the many parties on the fringe.

Even though Yeltsin opponents appeared to win the majority of the 450 seats in the lower chamber, the Duma, they have been forced to compromise with Yeltsin backers. One of the Duma members elected was the leader of the ultra-nationalist Liberal Democratic Party, Vladimir Zhirinovsky. He advocated party dictatorship, Russian military expansion, the expelling of millions of non-Russians and ending payments on foreign debt. He also wanted only blonde native Russian-speaking newscasters and promised cheap vodka for all. His party shocked the world by winning nearly a quarter of the Russian vote in the election, which many saw as a protest by a population feeling the pain of reform. Zhirinovsky, Yeltsin's strongest opponent, plans to run in the 1996 presidential elections. Other men elected were reactionary journalist Alexander Nevzorov, weightlifting champion Yuri Vlasov and psychic healer Anatoly Kashpirovsky.

The upper chamber, the 178-seat Federation Council, roughly equivalent to the

US Senate, met under the new State symbol, the two-headed eagle. First Deputy Prime Minister Vladimir Shumeiko, a close ally of Yeltsin, was elected as the first Speaker. In addition to the sweeping changes, criminals were now allowed to choose a trial by jury, and those juries could also challenge the power of the State.

A few weeks after Parliament convened, Yegor Gaidar, the architect of Russia's free-market reforms and leader of the Russia's Choice party, unexpectedly quit his post as Economic Minister. As a result, the ruble plummeted. (The Russian Central Bank had already pumped more than one billion dollars into the economy—more than a quarter of its hard currency reserves—to stabilize the monetary system.) Launched in January 1992, Gaidar's reforms freed most prices from State control, privatized a third of State-owned enterprises and created a new class of entrepreneurs. But since their introduction no more than 10 per cent of the population seemed better off, while over 50 per cent complained of being worse off. The continuing credit squeeze (Russia only developed a true currency market in 1993) created more unemployment, delayed paychecks and wiped out the savings accounts of average citizens. Some commented wryly that the system was recreating the old aristocratic and peasant classes.

The Russian comedian, Mikhail Zhvanetsky, joked about the economy: 'Much has changed but nothing has happened. Or is that much has happened and nothing has changed.' Many believe that nearly a century of suppressed initiative combined with a government-controlled lifestyle will take at least a generation to alter.

The country's weak economic state has also fueled an increase in the crime rate. Up to 80 per cent of private enterprises in Russia are said to pay tribute to the Mafia. Moscow has the atmosphere of a frontier town, doing full credit to its Wild West nickname. The contrasts are bewildering: new millionaires in chauffeur-driven limousines glide past dilapidated tenements in which pensioners have barely enough money to buy a loaf of bread. Small-time black-marketeers earn more than the intellectual élite; young and enterprising businessmen amass fortunes, while professionals struggle to make ends meet. The dichotomy of extraordinary monetary achievement and oppressive backwardness continues to mar the road ahead. Life expectancy has fallen in the last few years; infant mortality, suicides, accidents, and murders are on the rise.

Ordinary Russians can be forgiven for wondering if this transition to a Western-style democracy and economy is merely another short-lived phase in their country's history. So many promises in the past have proven hollow, from czars' reforms to the Bolsheviks' conviction that they would lead the way to a better world. Gorbachev warned: 'If reforms continue pushing people into a dead end, discontent could spring loose and extremism move in. And then, to halt the lawlessness, the military would step in.' But despite its chaos, the Russian spirit remains strong. Few other nations have endured so much turmoil. And, most likely, Russia can survive yet another difficult period. If Yeltsin and the new Federal Assembly are able to create a stable economy and curb crime, foreign capital will flow in. Reforms would then take hold more effectively and Russia's vast natural wealth could be harnessed. After nearly a century of isolation and stagnation, this cannot be achieved overnight.

Since the days of Gorbachev's *perestroika,* too many new processes have been started and too many private industries created to turn back. Also, for the first time since the beginning of Communist rule, the people themselves are able to fulfill their own potentials and voice their concerns. Without border restrictions, freedom now comes before ideology. Liberated by the policies of Gorbachev and Yeltsin, the population will not stand for a return to totalitarianism. Russians will no longer be dictated to by the State, they want a say in their society. The Russian government has no choice but to move optimistically forward on the path of reform.

Facts for the Traveler

Planning Your Trip

Traveling to and around Russia requires careful, advanced planning. Read some literature on the cities you plan to visit and talk to people who have been there. Locate travel agents or other specialist organizations that deal with travel to Russia.

INTOURIST

Many travelers organize their stay through Intourist, one of the largest Russian travel agencies for foreigners. An Intourist branch is located in most cities that are officially open to tourists. When visitors stay in Russian Intourist hotels, which have an Intourist Service desk, hotel reservations must usually be prepaid before entering the country. Tourist visas are not generally issued by a Russian embassy or consulate without a confirmed hotel reservation or proof of Russian sponsorship. It often takes up to one month for reservations and itineraries to be confirmed. Once you have confirmed and paid for your Intourist itineraries, the travel agency will issue Intourist vouchers—a booklet containing coupons for hotels, transfers and tours.

GROUP TOURS OR INDEPENDENT TRAVEL

There are a multitude of package and special-interest group tours from which to choose. The advantage of a group tour—especially if it is your first trip and you do not speak the language—is that everything is set up for you. Travel agencies handling Russian excursions have a list of the package tours available. Most group tours have preset departure dates and fixed lengths of stay, and usually include visits to Moscow and St Petersburg. The group rate includes the round-trip airfare, visa-processing fees, first-class accommodation, up to three meals a day, transportation within Russia, sightseeing excursions and a bilingual guide. Any last-minute changes to your itinerary can delay the process for weeks. Special-interest groups offer trips that include some sightseeing, but otherwise focus on more specific areas, such as sports, ecology, the arts, citizen diplomacy, religion or world peace.

Adventure tourism has also opened up a whole new array of opportunities, among them rafting, hiking, climbing, biking, kayaking, horse-back riding and even transarctic expeditions (see Useful Addresses in the Practical Information section for more information, page 249).

Compared to most other countries, independent travel to Russia is difficult. You cannot simply go to a Russian embassy or consulate, pay a visa-processing fee and take off. Before issuing a visa, the embassy will first check that you have proof of a

Women cleaning in preparation for a service, Church of the Holy Trinity, Moscow

hotel reservation or official sponsorship. The visa will then only cover the dates of your booked accommodation. However, you can extend your visa while in the country. The official reason for this visa restriction is that hotel space in Russia is limited. Hotels are pre-booked far in advance, and the government does not want visitors to arrive with nowhere to stay. Recently motels, hostels, bed-and-breakfasts and even campsites have sprung up, but these should also be booked in advance—cheap accommodation is in big demand. The easiest way to book a place to stay is through a travel agency, which can also organize visas and internal travel arrangements. Other options for the independent traveler are homestays or hostel accommodation, whose only drawbacks are that they may not be centrally located and the hosts may not speak English well (see the Practical Information Hotel section for these listings, beginning on page 240).

VISAS

All travelers to Russia must have visas. There are three types: Tourist, Business and Visitor. Travel agencies can supply you with a Tourist visa application form or you can collect one at a Russian embassy or consulate. Three passport-size photographs and a photocopy of the information page of your passport are also required. Depending on how quickly you need the visa returned to you, from two hours to two weeks or more, a corresponding processing fee is charged, which you must send in with your application form. Once confirmation of your hotel reservation or sponsored stay is received, the visa is issued. For visa information, you can call your local Russian embassy or consulate.

Independent travelers are advised to book accommodation at least six to eight weeks in advance to guarantee space and the best rates in hotels. Each city you plan to visit must be written on the visa. Once in Russia, you can lengthen your stay or visit additional cities by making arrangements with the Service desk at your hotel.

If you are sponsored by a Russian organization, you can receive a Business visa. Ask the organization to fax you an invitation showing the dates of your stay. Give this to the Russian embassy or consulate, which will usually issue Business visas without proof of hotel reservations. (Multi-entry visas are also issued with the proper papers.)

If hosted by a relative or friend, you can enter on a Visitor visa. You must send your host a duplicate of your filled out visa application form, not a photocopy. The host must then take it to his own travelers' organization, OVIR, which will issue a visitor's invitation to you after several months. The visitor is only allowed to travel to the cities and stay with the persons designated on the visa. You must make these arrangements far in advance. Don't panic if your visa has not arrived as your departure date nears, Russian embassies and consulates are notorious for issuing visas at the last minute. Try to apply as far in advance as possible.

You may need visas before you can cross the Russian border into other Commonwealth states or the three Baltic countries. Check before you go.

When to Go

The season of travel affects hotel prices and the itineraries of many tour programmes. The peak season lasts from May until September. In the spring (April 1–May 15) and fall (September 1–October 31) seasons, prices are lower and the cities less crowded. Summer in Moscow can be humid and dusty; at the same time, the White Nights in St Petersburg are spectacular. Indian summer in fall is quite pleasant. If you do not mind the cold and snow, the winter season is cheapest and accommodation is most readily available. The rainiest months for both cities are July and August.

International Flights and Connecting Trains

Most major airlines fly to Moscow (Airport Sheremetyevo II) and St Petersburg (Pulkovo II). Moscow is connected to over 120 cities in Europe and 70 countries around the world. Inquire at travel agencies and telephone the different airlines to discover the best rates. The advance-purchase (14 to 21-day APEX) fares usually give the most value for money. **Delta**'s flight to Moscow or St Petersburg from New York (either non-stop or with a stop in Frankfurt) costs approximately $800 return; Los Angeles to Moscow is about $1,000 return. **British Airways** offers flights to Moscow and St Petersburg from London for about $600/£400 return. British Airways also offers daily flights between New York and Moscow ($800 return), and Los Angeles and Moscow (about $1,000 return). **KLM** flies from Amsterdam to Moscow, **Lufthansa** from Frankfurt, and **SAS** from Stockholm and Copenhagen. **Aeroflot** also flies from most major cities to Moscow and St Petersburg—San Francisco to Moscow tickets are about $1,000 return. Flights to Khabarovsk in eastern Siberia (where you can pick up the Trans-Siberian in Vladivostok) are also available from San Francisco. From the East Coast of the United States, flights to Moscow start at about $800 return. The fares quoted above are for low season, APEX with restrictions. In peak season, rates go up.

Aeroflot is the largest airline in the world, carrying 100 million passengers per year. You can fly from and to a multitude of destinations in Asia and Europe on Aeroflot with stopovers in Moscow (a Transit visa and hotel confirmation are required). Even though Aeroflot does not have an enviable reputation for passenger service and comfort, its in-flight conditions have improved, although they may still not equal the standards of other overseas carriers. Since flying from points outside Europe can involve large time differences, consider a stay in a European city for a day or two to recover from jet lag. Stopovers are sometimes included or provided for a minimal extra charge. (See Useful Addresses in the Practical Information section for airline locations and telephone numbers, beginning on page 249.)

Another pleasant way to travel is to take a train from a European city to Moscow or St Petersburg. **Finnair** flies daily from New York to Helsinki from about $700 return. After a few relaxing days in Helsinki, you can take a train to St Petersburg or Moscow. (Finnair also flies daily from Helsinki to Moscow or St Petersburg.) There are two trains that leave Helsinki for St Petersburg every day, one Russian and one Finnish. The Russian one leaves at 15:06 and arrives at 23:15. The Finnish train departs at 06:25 and arrives in St Petersburg at 13:45; both arrive on the day of their departure with a one hour time change. Soft berth one-way costs approximately $130/265FM (first class, $245/491FM). The Moscow train leaves each day at 17.08 and arrives the next morning at 09:10; it costs about $250/506FM ($375/760FM first class) each way. If the train has hard berths, these are usually cheaper. Instead of dealing with reservations at the last minute in Helsinki, you can book and pay for the train through your travel agency (this is strongly recommended since the trains fill in advance). You can also book space directly. The address is: Finish State Railways, Ticket Office, Railwaystation, SF-00100 Helsinki, Finland. Fax (358-0) 7074240, tlx 12-301124. A handling fee is also charged. Return trains leave Moscow at 18:17 and arrive in Helsinki at 09:02 the next day. Trains from St Petersburg (Russian) depart at 06:25. and arrive in Helsinki at 12:07 the same day. The Finnish train leaves at 15.55 and arrives in Helsinki at 21:26.

TIME ZONES

Russia has 11 time zones. Moscow and St Petersburg are in the same time zone. Many train and plane schedules are listed throughout the country as Moscow time. Always check to see what time is actually meant by the listing. The time difference between Moscow and the US West Coast is 11 hours, the East Coast eight hours, and London three hours. Helsinki is one hour behind.

PACKING

For your own convenience, travel as light as possible. Most airlines allow up to two pieces of luggage and one piece of cabin baggage. Luggage allowance is very strict when exiting Russia. Often, all bags are weighed, including your cabin baggage. You may be charged per additional kilo for luggage weighing over 20 kilos in coach class and 30 kilos in first or business class. This is usually the procedure for internal flights as well.

DOCUMENTS

Keep your passport, visa, important papers, tickets, vouchers and money in your hand luggage at all times. Also carry a photocopy of your passport and visa. Bear in mind that you will need to show identification to get into certain places. Serious photographers with a lot of film should have it inspected separately—Russian X-rays are not always guaranteed to be film-safe.

CLOTHES

The season of the year is a major factor in deciding what to bring. Summers are warm, humid and dusty, with frequent thunderstorms, especially in Moscow. Bring a raincoat or an umbrella. The White Nights of St Petersburg are delightful in the summer, but you will occasionally need a pullover or light jacket. Winters are cold and damp, with temperatures well below freezing. It can snow between November and April, when the cold Arctic winds sharpen the chill. Be prepared with your warmest clothes—waterproof boots, gloves and long underwear. Interiors are usually well-heated, so dress in layers. It is best to bring everything with you, since Western-style clothing is very expensive, and Russian clothing is mostly of poor quality—except for *shapki*, the Russian fur hats. Bring slightly smarter attire for ballets and banquets. A must is a good pair of walking shoes that can get dirty. Wearing shorts or sleeveless shirts may prevent you from entering a church during services.

MEDICINE

Take a good supply of medicine, prescription drugs, and remedies for flu and minor illnesses. Recommended: aspirin or Tylenol, throat lozenges, cold formulas, a course of antibiotics against a very bad cold or infection, vitamins (especially C), laxatives, lip salve, travel sickness pills, water-purifying tablets, contact-lens cleaners. For an upset stomach: indigestion tablets, Alka-Selzer, Pepto Bismal. If diarrhea strikes, cut out heavy foods, drink plenty of fluids and ask for rice in restaurants. Take Lomotil if necessary. Each hotel has a resident nurse or doctor and a small apothecary stand with a few medications for sale. See the Practical Information section for a listing of medical facilities and pharmacies, page 297.

PERSONAL ARTICLES

Remember that Russia lacks many supplies that you take for granted. Some things to consider taking with you are: cosmetics, lotions, shampoo, conditioner, razors, shaving cream, toothpaste, lavatory paper, tissues, sanitary towels or tampons, a water bottle for long trips, soap, washing powder, an all-purpose plug, pantyhose, a sewing kit, adhesive and strong wrapping tape, pens, an extra pair of glasses or contact lenses, contact lens solutions.

FILM

Film is expensive and hard to find. Bring whatever you plan to use. Since using a flash is prohibited in many museums and churches, have some high-speed film on hand. If you can wait, it is advised to have your film,

Four bronze horses pulling the chariot of Apollo,
Bolshoi Ballet theatre

especially slides, processed at home. See the Practical Information section for film center locations, page 298.

GADGETS

Voltage varies from 220 to 127. Some hotels have plugs for 220/110V. Pack an adapter/transformer. New hair dryers, travel irons and electrical shavers are now made with safety ends that do not fit into many adapters—check before you go. Duel voltage coils are useful for boiling water and brewing tea and coffee in your hotel room, but you should use them with extreme caution. A portable cassette or CD player may be welcome. Bring plenty of batteries for your camera, alarm clock and watch. Also handy is a Swiss army knife or penknife that has a bottle opener and corkscrew.

SIGHTSEEING

A Russian phrase book and dictionary are necessary. Try to master the Cyrillic alphabet before you leave. It will be especially helpful in places like the Metro. Bring reading material and travel literature—the Russian government is the largest book publisher in the world, though most books are in Russian. Gift-giving is part of Russian *gostyepriimstvo*, hospitality. Buy a small supply of gifts for your guides and new friends: paperbacks, travel picture books, fashion magazines, T-shirts, music cassettes, cosmetics, colognes.

CUSTOMS

Visitors arriving by air pass through a passport checkpoint in the airport terminal. Those arriving by train do this at the border. Uniformed border guards check passports and stamp visas. Passports are never stamped. One page of the visa is removed upon arrival, the rest of it is turned in upon leaving the country. Russian custom declaration forms are issued during your flight or train journey, or you can pick them up from stands located near the baggage claim area in the airport. Fill in exactly how much foreign currency you are bringing into the country; there is no limit unless it is extremely high. Declare your valuables (gold, silver, jewelry, etc.). Your valuables could be confiscated when departing with no proof that you brought them into the country. An inspector will inspect your luggage and stamp your declaration form. Do not misplace it—you need it to exchange money and leave the country. On departure, another declaration form (same format) must be filled out, which is compared to your original. Make sure you are not leaving the country with more foreign currency than you declared upon arrival. Even though Russian customs have become considerably easier and faster than in past years, your bags may be thoroughly searched when you leave. Do not overwrap items; they may be selected for inspection.

It is forbidden to bring in what is considered anti-Russian material and pornography. You may be asked to show all your printed matter. Drugs, other than medicinal, are highly illegal. Any video or small-film camera, VCR, personal computer or typewriter should also be noted on the customs form. You must depart with these items (unless you have official permission to leave them behind), or you will be subject to a duty of up to the full worth of the goods in question. You cannot leave with antiques, icons or expensive works of art unless you have permission from the Ministry of Culture. Caviar, other than officially bought can also be confiscated. Beware, metal cans shine like beacons under X-ray. Check if you need a visa before continuing to locations outside of Russia, such as the Baltic or other Commonwealth states.

CURRENCY EXCHANGE

In 1994, all purchases were to be officially made in rubles, unless an establishment had an official license to accept foreign currency. But since the ruble is worth less each day, places often prefer payment in foreign cash if you don't have rubles (check their exchange rates). Bear all this in mind when eating out or shopping. Have some rubles, foreign cash and a credit card on hand. (Traveler's checks are not as widely accepted.) You can convert hard currency to rubles at the airport or, the easiest way, in your hotel. Take some cash with you—often, traveler's checks and credit cards are not accepted. Some banks and street kiosks also exchange foreign currency. However, some kiosks do not have an official exchange, which means they will not stamp your declaration form. The customs declaration form should be presented when money is legally exchanged. The date and amount converted is noted on the form. You can reexchange your unused rubles at the end of your trip, not before, at the airport or border. Remember when you exit that you cannot convert more rubles than you officially exchanged. It is still considered illegal to change foreign currency on the black market, if the opportunity presents itself, be discreet (see the section on Hazards, page 54).

The ruble was worth about $1.60 before November 1, 1989. On this date the former Soviet government devalued it by 90 per cent; it is now worth less than a cent. The intention of devaluation was to bring the ruble closer to its actual value and discourage huge black-market activities. In 1992, the ruble was floated on the world market. Since 1995, the ruble has sometimes been selling in excess of 3,000 to $1. Given Russia's unstable economy, future exchange values are impossible to predict. Check the currency section in your newspaper to find out the current exchange rate.

You may occasionally come across different ruble exchange rates. For foreigners, banks and hotels deal with the official daily exchange rate. Always check first to see what rates are used; they could be different from the ones you are using.

Maybe Yes, Maybe No

December 24. A few words about my room. Every piece of furniture in it bears a tin tag with the words **Moscow Hotels** *and then the inventory number. The hotels are collectively administered by the state (or the city?). The double windows of my room have been sealed shut for the winter. Only a small flap toward the top can be opened. The small washtable is made of tin, lacquered below and with a very polished top and a mirror in addition. The bottom of the basin has three drain holes that cannot be plugged. A thin stream of water flows from a faucet. The room is heated from the exterior, but given its particular location, the floor is also warm and even when the weather is moderately cold, the heat becomes oppressive as soon as you close the little window. Every morning before nine, when the heat is turned on, an employee knocks at the door to check if the trap window has been shut. This is the only thing that one can rely on here. The hotel has no kitchen, so one can't even get a cup of tea. Once, the evening before we drove out to see Daga, we asked to be awakened the following morning, and a Shakespearian conversation on the theme of "waking" ensued between Reich and the Swiss (which is the Russian name for hotel porter). The man's reply to our request to be awakened: "If we think of it, we'll wake you. But if we don't think of it, we won't. Actually, we usually think of it, in which case we do wake people. But to be sure, we also occasionally forget to when we don't think of it. In which case we don't. We're of course under no obligation, but if we remember in time, then natuarally we do. When do you want to be awakened?—At seven. We'll make a note of that. See, I'm putting the message here, let's hope he finds it. Of course if he doesn't, he won't wake you. But usually we in fact do." In the end we were of course not wakened and they explained: "You were already up, what was the point of waking you?"*

Walter Benjamin, Moscow Diary

TRAVELER'S CHECKS AND CREDIT CARDS

Traveler's checks and credit cards are now accepted at some banks, restaurants, and shops. It is advisable to bring cash, especially small notes and change. Very often the shops will not have your currency and will give change in a mixture of other foreign currencies. Bear in mind that many shops, bars and restaurants only accept rubles.

If you need to cash traveler's checks or get money from your credit card, and your hotel cannot do this, there are now a number of places that can. At the **American Express Office**, located at 21a Sadovo-Kudrinskaya Street, tel 254-0671/4495/ 2111 (another office is in the Mezhdunarody Hotel), you can cash traveler's checks or get cash from your AMEX card. (You also need a personal check to get money with the credit card.) American Express charges a commission of five per cent on each exchange. The office is open Monday to Friday, 09:00 to 17:30, and Saturday, 12:30 to 13:30. Get there early because they often run out of foreign currency. Also note that sometimes this office will only exchange into rubles. If you have trouble getting what you need here, the following location is often more predictable in its transactions.

The **Dialog Bank** is in the Slavyanskaya Hotel at 2 Berezhkovskaya Embankment, across from the Kievskaya Metro station. The bank is in the lobby to the left upon entering. The bank is run by foreigners and not connected with the Russian banks; it does not usually run out of dollars or pounds. They cash traveler's checks and may issue foreign cash on a credit card with a personal check, but check first. Dialog Bank also charges five per cent commission. It is open Monday to Friday, 10:00 to 17:00 and is closed from 13:15 to 14:00.

VALUABLES

Hotels usually have safety deposit boxes by the front desk. It is advisable to lock up your valuables, money, passport and airline tickets, even if it is only a lock on your suitcase—thefts have been reported from hotel rooms. In case of loss or theft, notify the Service Bureau at your hotel. Always carry your money in a safe place. Buy a moneybelt, so you can carry your money and valuables with you. Unfortunately, over the last few years crimes against tourists have risen—pockets are being picked and bags stolen. Take extra care when in large crowds and markets.

HEALTH

Immunizations are not required, unless you are coming from an infected area. Other than the cold, food and pollution, Russia does not have many health risks. Some people may have trouble adjusting to Russian cuisine, which includes heavy breads, thick greasy soups, smoked fish and sour cream. Vegetables and fruit are often in low supply. Bring indigestion or stomach-disorder remedies. If you are a vegetarian or require a special diet, bring along what you need, even if it is instant, freeze-dried mixes or nutritional supplements. In winter, be prepared for a possible cold. Drink only bottled or boiled water, never tap. Russian bottled water does have an enormously high salt content; you may prefer soda or tea. Local juices or flavored sugar waters cannot always be trusted, and be wary of iced drinks. Foreign food products, bottled waters and medicinal items are now available. In case of any illness, medical care in Russia is free of charge. Recently, a few Western-style medical and dental clinics have opened with foreign doctors and medications, but they will usually be for hard currency. Each hotel usually has its own resident physician. In the event of serious illness, contact your embassy or consulate and consider leaving the country for proper care. If you have a health ailment, it is advisable to purchase travel medical insurance before the trip.

Do note that even though some areas of Russia are experiencing unrest, it is considered safe to walk around Moscow at any time during the day or evening. As in any big city, use your common sense and take care of your valuables. (See the Practical Information Section for medical listings, page 297.)

Getting Around

When arriving in Moscow, group travelers are automatically taken by bus to their hotel. Individual travelers staying in Russian Intourist hotels should hold a transportation voucher issued at home before departure. Report to the Intourist desk at the train station or air terminal upon arrival. The airports are about 45 minutes from the city center; the train stations are centrally located. For those without transportation, inquire at the Intourist desk, or bargain with drivers of taxis or individual cars for a ride into town. Find out what an average ride costs beforehand, so you do not pay an exorbitant amount. If you arrive at a train station and do not have a lot of luggage, try taking the Metro to your destination.

Remember to reconfirm your departure flight. This can be done through the Service desk at your hotel or by telephoning the airlines directly. Reconfirm internal flights as well, as they tend to be overbooked.

Travel Between Cities

If on a group tour, or with Intourist, most of your bookings will have been taken care of before your arrival. Report any changes in plans to Intourist. If you would like to extend your visa, visit another city that is not on your itinerary, make other hotel, train or plane reservations, or simply book a sightseeing excursion, check at the hotel's Service desk. Always do this as soon as you can.

■ BY AIR

The airports used for internal flights are much more crowded and chaotic than the international airports. Special preference is usually given to foreign groups at check-in, and Intourist waiting areas are provided. Passports and visas are required at check-in. Boarding passes are issued, either with open seating or with seat numbers, and rows written in Cyrillic. Groups are usually seated first on the plane. Remember that Russians are quite assertive and will push vigorously to get on the plane, especially with open seating. On internal flights, there is one class and no non-smoking sections. Sometimes the only meal consists of seltzer water, bread and cucumbers. Take some snacks. There is no airport departure tax. Airline tickets may be sold to foreigners in hard currency, but remember rubles are the only legal tender. You can reserve and buy Aeroflot tickets at most major hotels, which is a lot easier than going to the overcrowded Aeroflot offices.

You can also reserve and buy airline tickets on foreign airlines at their representative offices (see Useful Addresses in the Practical Information section, page 253).

■ BY TRAIN

Trains are much more fun than flying. The Red Arrow trains between Moscow and St Petersburg are a splendid way to travel. Board the sleeper at night and arrive the next morning for a full day of sightseeing. Since there are several train stations in each city, make sure you know which one you are departing from. In Moscow, trains for St Petersburg leave from the *Leningradski Vokzal*, the Leningrad station. In St Petersburg, they leave from the *Moskovski Vokzal*, the Moscow station. (*Vokzal* stems from Vauxhall station in London.)

The trains always leave on time with a single five-minute warning broadcast before departure—so pay attention. First class has two berths to a compartment and second class has four. This is an excellent way to meet Russians. A personal car attendant will bring tea, brewed in the car's *samovar*, and biscuits, and wake you up in the morning. Remember to turn off the radio at night or the National Anthem will blast you awake at 06:00.

The compartments are not segregated. If there is a problem, the attendant can usually arrange a swap. It is difficult for foreigners to buy train or air tickets at local stations or ticket counters. Tickets are usually bought through Intourist or at a hotel Service desk. Each city visited must be listed on your visa.

If you would like to buy train tickets, go to 15 Petrovka Street, the main booking office. Get there early, about 08:30, and when the doors open at 09:00, rush up to the second floor to counters 13, 14 or 15. The train attendant may charge you a minor fee for sheets and towels once you have settled into your compartment.

■ BY BUS AND COACH

Group tourists are shown around Moscow and St Petersburg by coach. Often the buses are not air-conditioned, but all are heated during winter. If you are an individual traveler, you can sign up through Intourist or your hotel's Service desk for city sightseeing excursions; check at these locations for tour listings. Comfortable coach excursions are also offered to areas in the Golden Ring. Always remember the number of your bus; parking lots tend to fill up quickly.

■ LOCAL BUSES, TRAMS AND TROLLEYS

Local transportation operates from 06:00 to 01:00 and is charged by distance. Rides tend to run by the honor system. Either you put the cost into a machine and roll out a ticket by hand or you must pre-purchase tickets at a special kiosk. These get stamped with a device on the wall. Sometimes there are control checks—fines are minimal. You may find someone in a crowded bus muttering 'peredaitye pazhalsta,' 'please pass this on,' and thrusting a few rubles into your hand. This is meant to be passed back to the ticket machine where a ticket, in turn, will find its way back to the donor. Even if you do not speak Russian, people will help to direct you to the proper bus or stop. Never be afraid to ask, even if in sign language. Many Russians understand a little English, German or French.

■ METRO

The Metro is the fastest and cheapest way to get around Moscow and St Petersburg. More than eight million people ride the Moscow Metro daily. Trains run every 90 seconds during rush hour. Central stations are beautifully decorated with chandeliers and mosaics. Metro stations are easy to spot: entrances on the street are marked with a large M. Even the long escalator rides are great entertainment. Metro maps can be purchased in hotels and are posted inside each station, or use the one in this book. To ride a Metro, purchase a token at the ticket counter or through the machines. Other automatic machines also give change. Deposit the token into the turnstile and wait for the green light. All station and transfer areas are clearly marked in Russian. If you do not read Cyrillic, have someone write down the name of your destination in Russian. People are always helpful and will point you in the right direction.

■ TAXIS

You can order a taxi from the Taxi Service desks located in the lobbies of most hotels, but the taxi may take a while to arrive. A service fee is charged. If the desk says nyet, no taxis available, simply walk to the front of the hotel. Often a taxi or private car can be found. Unlike most other countries, a taxi ride is not as simple as it seems. First, Russian taxi drivers usually stop and ask you where you want to go. Then, the driver decides if he wants to take you. If so, then the negotiating begins. If you look foreign, he will start the bidding high and in foreign currency, even though, legally, payment should be made in rubles and each taxi should have a meter. (Note that inflation is increasing faster than meters can be changed or reprogrammed; your ruble fee may be calculated as a few times more than the actual amount on the meter.) Taxi fees are also higher in the evening. It is also wise to find out the average cost of where you are going before you start bargaining. Hailing taxis on the street can also be a problem. You can negotiate any form of payment, if not all for rubles, try part rubles and part dollars or even a few Marlboro cigarettes (try to carry a few packs at all times). Officially, it is illegal to pay in foreign currency, but many travelers do in order to get a ride. Hitching is quite common—taxis are not always available and drivers of private cars are often eager to earn some extra cash by picking up paying passengers.

■ CAR HIRE
Many hotels offer chauffeur-driven cars. A guide can also be hired for the day. These services must be paid for in foreign currency. Outside the hotel, you will usually find many car owners and off-duty taxi drivers open to suggestions. Some can be hired for the day to take you around town. Make your own payment agreement beforehand. Moscow and St Petersburg have some rent-a-car companies, although driving in Russia is chaotic. In addition, all signs are written in Russian and gas stations, which are hard to find, often have huge queues. It is best to hire a car with a driver or use public transportation. It is also possible to drive your own car in from Europe. This requires advance planning and permits, since a few borders are crossed and special insurance is necessary. Some automobile rental companies in Moscow are: **Hertz**, tel 448-8035; **InNis**, tel 927-1187; **Autosan**, tel. 280-3600; **Business Car**, tel 233-1796/231-8225; **Mosrent**, tel. 248-0251; **Rozec**; tel. 241-5393; and **Intourservice**, tel 203-0096.

Being There

HOTELS
Most group tours are provided with first-class hotel accommodation. Russian hotels usually offer deluxe, first-class or tourist accommodation. For individual travelers, hotels are often the most expensive part of the stay. To visit Russia, you must pay the fixed rate for Russian or Western-style hotels, which can be expensive, costing from $75 to $200 per person per night. (Note that in many instances it costs only a little extra for a double room.) Recently, more of a selection of cheaper hotels, hostels and

bed-and-breakfasts have become available (see hotel listings in the Practical Information section, page 240). You can camp at designated camping sites, but this must be set up before entering the country and arranged far in advance. Upon arrival at your hotel, hand in your passport and visa. The hotel registers you within the country and returns everything within a few days. Notice that the hotel dates of your stay are stamped on the back of your visa. If you exit the country and have not been stamped, you may be pulled aside for questioning. Make sure a hotel stamp appears on the back of your visa.. You may also be issued with a *propusk*, hotel card. Keep this with you at all times. You need to show it to the doorman, who might block your entrance until the card is shown. This is because Russians are frequently not allowed to enter the major hotels, unless they are registered guests. The name of the hotel is written in Russian on the hotel card, which you can show to taxi drivers.

Many Russian hotels still have a *dezhurnaya*, a hall attendant, on each floor. When you show her your hotel card, she will give you the key. The 'Westernized' hotels issue your key at the front desk. The *dezhurnaya* is also positioned to notice everything that happens in your hallway. She is very helpful and friendly; if you have a question, she is the one to ask. Most rooms are quite adequate, but may not match your idea of a first-class hotel, particularly those outside Moscow and St Petersburg. They have a bathroom, television and telephone, but many lack room service. A laundry bag is provided in each room; dry-cleaning services are not often available. Give your laundry to the maid or *dezhurnaya*. It is usually a same-day or two-day service. Generally, Western-style hotels provide better services.

A word of warning: Housekeepers in some Russian hotels lack a respect for privacy and will enter your room without knocking or return your laundry at midnight. Use the chain lock. Also, most Russian hotels do not have a central switchboard, which means someone calling the main number of the hotel will not be able to contact you. Each room has a telephone with a corresponding seven-digit number. Only if the caller knows this number can he or she call you directly, either from another room in the hotel or from outside. Each spring/summer many hydroelectric plants shut down for a few weeks for cleaning, and large sections of the city may be without hot water, including your hotel.

Russian hotels have a restaurant, a few cafés located on different floors, foreign currency bars and a post office. A brochure is usually provided in each room listing the facilities and telephone numbers. Most Intourist hotels are accustomed to catering to groups. Sometimes it is impossible for an individual to get a table in a restaurant for lunch or dinner without a reservation. This can be frustrating. Make a reservation in the morning at the Service desk. Many hotels now offer a 'Swedish table,' a cafeteria-style restaurant. Check to see if your hotel has one. Here you will find inex-

The Church of St George, Pskov Hill

pensive smorgasbords for breakfast, lunch or dinner. Western-style hotels have restaurants and cafés, which are easier to get into, but usually charge accordingly.

COMMUNICATIONS

Communication has become relatively easier. In the past, making calls to other countries could literally take days. There are now a number of ways to make an international call. You can book a call abroad for a specific time, which rings through to your room, at the Service Bureau in your hotel. But be warned, these do not often come in at your exact booking time. Try to reserve a call for the evening. This way, if the call is late, you will be in your room and will not have to miss a tour. There is also a central number in each city that you can dial directly to place a telephone order yourself. The operator usually speaks English. In Moscow, dial 8-194, and in St Petersburg, 314-4747. Most Western-style hotels now have satellite dishes hooked up to telephone lines in their business centers. They allow you to make calls, but are expensive. Always check, some charge for a three-minute minimum. Most hotels are also equipped with fax and telex services.

Direct long-distance dialing is now possible in Moscow and St Petersburg. First dial 8 and wait for the tone. Dial 10 (international), then the country code, area code and telephone number. During peak hours, it can be difficult to get calls through. Also, many hotels do not have direct dialing facilities. If not, try calling from a friend's home for rubles; it will be much cheaper.

If you have an AT&T calling card and wish to call the United States, you can try calling a USA Direct number. In Moscow, this number is 155-5042. If this does not connect, try calling Helsinki USA direct on (10-358)-9800-100-10. Another quick, but expensive, way to call direct is from a Comstar telephone booth. They can be found at more than 25 locations in Moscow, including Room 301, 10 Petrovka, in the Passage Department Store. International payphones, faxes, telexes and electronic mail are available here. The main numbers for Comstar are 979-1692 and 210-0962.

It may be easier to get somebody to call you from abroad. They should dial 7, the country code for Russia, 095 for Moscow and then the telephone number. Many Russian hotels still do not have switchboards. Tell the person who will call you the seven-digit number for the telephone in your room.

Be prepared for international calls to be expensive. Local calls can be made from the hotel room, in many establishments, free of charge. Long-distance calls within the CIS can also be made from your room if you know the area code. For example, Moscow is 095 and St Petersburg 812. To call Moscow from St Petersburg dial 8, to get a long-distance tone, then 095 and the seven-digit number.

Special 'long-distance' telephones can also be used for calling other cities within the CIS. These Mezhdugorodny, inter-city telephone booths, line the streets. You can also go to the city's long-distance telephone center, *peregovorny punkt*. A local call from a payphone costs, at the time of writing, 150 rubles for three minutes, up from the original 2 kopeks. When you hear a beeping tone, deposit another token. You can buy telephone tokens at kiosks and stores throughout the city—most local telephone booths take only tokens (if you do not have a token one-ruble coins still sometimes work). Do not lose your telephone numbers; Russia has never compiled a telephone directory. However, business directories are now available. (Two excellent editions are The *Traveller's Yellow Pages for Moscow* and The *Traveller's Yellow Pages for St Petersburg*, which are available in both cities, see Recommended Reading on page 299.) Tracking down an individual's telephone number can take hours. An information operator sometimes needs to know the name (and patronymic), address and date of birth of the person you wish to call. For information in Moscow, dial 00 for personal numbers, 09 for business and 07 for local long-distance.

Post offices send telegrams and packages, but do not wrap your packages. Their contents are usually inspected before shipping. (Most hotels have post offices.) Mail is slow and erratic—many travelers arrive home before their postcards. Any mail sent to Russia takes several weeks to a month. If you are staying for a long time, mail can be addressed to either Poste Restante or care of Intourist. The Moscow address is Hotel Intourist (Poste Restante), 3/5 Tverskaya Street, K-600 Moscow, Russia, 103009; in St Petersburg: Poste Restante, C-400/ 6 Nevsky Prospekt, St Petersburg. If you know what hotel you will be staying in, have mail addressed to you care of that hotel. Mail in Russian hotels will not be delivered to your room, nor will you be contacted when it arrives. You must check at the lobby Service counter, where you will have to sift through the whole stack of guests' mail. To get mail out quickly, try Federal Express or DHL (see the Practical Information section for locations, page 298).

RUSSIAN CURRENCY

Russian currency is the *ruble*. It comes in note denominations of one, three, five, ten, 25, 50, 100, 200, 500, 5,000, 10,000, 20,000, 50,000 and 100,000. The ruble is divided into 100 *kopeks*. There are one, two, three, five, ten, 15, 20, 50 kopek coins, not widely used; one ruble, 150 and 200 ruble coins also exist. Because of inflation, some establishments have begun weighing the bricks of money.

SHOPPING HOURS

Most local stores open between 08:00 and 10:00, and close between 17:00 and 20:00. They also close for an hour between 12:00 and 15:00 for lunch. Similarly, restaurants and cafés close for a few hours during the day. If you are on a tight schedule, check their operating hours first. *Beriozkas* are open from 09:00 to 20:00–23:00. Some also close for a one-hour lunch break. Check the Practical Information section at the back of the book for shop listings, and holiday and festival dates, when stores are usually closed.

PHOTOGRAPHY RESTRICTIONS

In the former Soviet Union, you could photograph anything you wished except for the following: military installations, border areas, airports, railway stations, bridges, tunnels, power and radar stations, telephone and telegraph centers, industrial enterprises, and from airplanes while flying over the country. The new government is less strict, but laws and attitudes are still in a state of flux and old habits die hard. If you are not sure, inquire before you shoot. Ask permission at factories, State institutions and farms, and of individuals, who may not want their pictures taken. Understand that the people are sometimes sensitive about foreigners photographing what they perceive as backward or in poor condition. Always remain courteous.

TRAVEL RESTRICTIONS

You cannot officially venture more than 35 kilometers outside of the city. (You can go for day trips to towns in the Golden Ring area. If you stay overnight, you may need the towns added to your visa.) Only the cities specified on the visa can be visited. Unless the visa is extended, you must exit the country on the date shown on the visa.

HAZARDS

Especially in the big cities, you are likely to be approached by people asking 'Do you speak English?' and the trying to sell you anything from lacquer boxes and caviar to army watches. Some may even want to buy your clothes. The government is trying to discourage speculation, since most want to sell their wares for foreign currency; dealing directly in hard currency is still illegal. Work out your own bargain, but be discreet. Many will ask to change money; it is best to stay away—or beware and pay attention for sometimes the exchanger will present false or out-of-circulation bills (in 1991, 50 and 100 ruble notes were removed from circulation and new ones introduced), or will roll lower notes inside higher notes; robberies are on the increase. In marketplaces, it has been known for a small group to surround a person, and while pretending to sell souvenirs, others go through the tourist's shoulderbag. Also, do not carry money in pockets or inside jackets; wear a moneybelt. (Often the bank, hotel or kiosk exchange rates are about the same as the black market's; it does not merit the energy searching for back-alley exchanges. The black-market rate is published in the *Commersant* newspaper, which is also sold in English at newsstands.)

As in any big city, always be on guard. Nowadays in Russia, mafia activities are on the rise, as are crimes against tourists. One added note: males may be approached by an attractive lady in a hotel bar or even in the elevator. Prostitution is becoming a large problem in Moscow and St Petersburg. Paying for more than a drink can lead to arrest. Plainclothes policemen often patrol hotels.

ETIQUETTE

Often Russians appear very restrained, formal or even glum. But there is a dichotomy between public (where for so many generations they dared not show their true feelings) and private appearances. In private and informal situations or after friendship is established, the Russian character is charged with emotional warmth, care and humor. They are intensely loyal and willing to help. Arriving in or leaving the country will merit great displays of affection, usually with flowers, bear hugs, kisses and tears. If invited to someone's home for dinner, expect large preparations. Russians are some of the most hospitable people in the world. If you do not like too much alcohol, watch out for the endless number of toasts.

The formal use of the patronymic (where the father's first name becomes the children's middle name) has been used for centuries. For example, if Ivan names his son Alexander, Alexander's patronymic is Ivanovich. Especially in formal or business dealings, try to remember the person's patronymic: Alexander Ivanovich or Mariya Pavlova (whose father's name is Pavel, or Paul). As in the West, where Robert is shortened to Bob, Russian first names are also shortened once a friendship is established. Call your friend Alexander 'Sasha,' Mikhail 'Misha,' and Mariya 'Masha,' or use the diminutive form, 'Mashenka.'

COMPLAINTS

Many restaurants and cafés have a *kniga zhalov*, service

Old style wooden church, Vladimir

book, where you can register complaints. Hotel complaints can be reported at the Service desk. Remember that rules, regulations and bureaucracy still play a large role in Russian life, with many uniformed people enforcing them. People here are not always presumed innocent until proven guilty. When dealing with police or other officials, it is best to be courteous while explaining a situation. For example, police in the streets will randomly pull over vehicles to spot-check the car and registration. If you are pulled over, it does not mean you have done anything wrong. If you are kept waiting, as in restaurants for service, remember that everyone else is waiting too. Be patient and remember that you are in a foreign country. Do not lose your temper (humor often works better), mock or laugh when not appropriate.

A few commonly used words are *nyet* and *nelzya*, which mean 'no' and 'it's forbidden.' The Russian language uses many negations. If people tell you something is forbidden, it may mean that they simply do not know or do not want to take responsibility. Ask elsewhere.

Food

Russian cooking is both tasty and filling. In addition to the expected borsch and beef stroganov, it includes many delectable regional dishes from the other states, such as Uzbekistan, Georgia or the Ukraine.

The traditions of Russian cooking date back to the simple recipes of the peasantry, who filled their hungry stomachs with the abundant supply of potatoes, cabbages, cucumbers, onions and bread. For the cold northern winters, they would pickle the few available vegetables and preserve fruits to make jam. This rather bland diet was pepped up with sour cream, parsley, dill and other dried herbs. In an old Russian saying, peasants described their diet as *Shchi da kasha, Pishcha nasha*, 'Cabbage soup and porridge are our food.' The writer, Nikolai Gogol, gave this description of the Russian peasant's kitchen: 'In the room was the old familiar friend found in every kitchen, namely a *samovar* and a three-cornered cupboard with cups and teapots, painted eggs hanging on red and blue ribbons in front of the icons, with flat cakes, horseradish and sour cream on the table along with bunches of dried fragrant herbs and a jug of *kvas* [a dark beer made from fermented black bread].' Russians remain proud of these basic foods, which are still their staples today. They will boast that there is no better *khleb*, bread, in the world than a freshly baked loaf of Russian black bread. And Raisa Gorbachev even presented Nancy Reagan with a cookbook containing hundreds of potato recipes.

Peter the Great introduced French cooking to his empire in the 18th century.

While the peasantry had access only to the land's crops, the nobility hired its own French chefs, who introduced eating as an art form, often preparing up to ten elaborate courses of delicacies. Eventually, Russian writers ridiculed the monotonous and gluttonous life of the aristocrats, many of whom planned their days around meals. In his novel *Oblomov*, Ivan Goncharov coined the term 'Oblomovism' to characterize the sluggish and decadent life of the Russian gentry. In *Dead Souls*, Nikolai Gogol described a typical meal enjoyed by his main character in the home of an aristocrat:

> On the table there appeared a white sturgeon, ordinary sturgeon, salmon, pressed caviar, fresh caviar, herrings, smoked tongues and dried sturgeon. Then there was a baked 300-pound sturgeon, a pie stuffed with mushrooms, fried pastries, dumplings cooked in melted butter, and fruit stewed in honey... After drinking glasses of vodka of a dark olive color, the guests had dessert... After the champagne, they uncorked some bottles of cognac, which put still more spirit into them and made the whole party merrier than ever!

Vodka has always been the indispensable drink of any class on any occasion. Whether rich or poor, no Russian is abstemious. Anton Chekhov wrote of a group of peasants who, 'on the Feast of the Intercession, seized the chance to drink for three days. They drank their way through fifty rubles of communal funds...one peasant beat his wife and then continued to drink the cap off his head and boots off his feet!'

Most travelers on a group tour in a Russian hotel will be provided with up to three meals a day. *Zavtrak*, breakfast, consists of coffee or tea, juice, eggs, kasha, cheese, cold meats or sausage and a plentiful supply of bread and butter. Some hotels now offer a Swedish table, providing a better selection. If you do not normally start the day with a heavy breakfast, take along a bottle of instant coffee and cream, packaged oatmeal, or other cereal, and an electric coil to boil water in your room. *Obyed*, lunch consists of soup, bread, salad and, usually, a choice of meat, chicken or fish with potatoes, a pickled vegetable and a sweet dessert of cakes or *morozhnoye*, ice cream. Over 170 tons of ice cream are consumed in Moscow and St Petersburg each day. Salads or vegetables include cucumbers, tomatoes, cabbage, beets, potatoes and onions, but fresh vegetables and fruit are not abundant. *Smetana*, sour cream, is a popular condiment—Russians like it on everything—some even drink a glass for breakfast. *Oozhiin*, dinner is similar to lunch, except vodka, wine, champagne or cognac will usually be served.

Most Russian hotel restaurants do not offer a wide selection; on a group tour you will be served a fixed menu each day with few alternatives. Western-style hotels and restaurants usually have a larger and more varied selection of food, and faster service. Tipping is accepted (5–10 per cent), but use your own judgment. Russian waiters are notorious for disappearing at the moment you have a question. If you are discour-

Vegetable vendors, Suzdal

aged with the service, the meal or the language barrier (although many menus are written in English, German and Russian), remember to be diplomatic and patient. Find the manager or the Service desk to express a complaint, or ask for the restaurant's *kniga zhalov*, complaints book.

DINING AND DRINKING

The first point to remember when dining out is that most Russians consider eating out an expensive luxury and enjoy turning dinner into a leisurely, evening-long experience. Many restaurants provide entertainment, so do not expect a fast meal. In the European fashion, different parties are often seated together at the same table, an excellent way to meet the locals.

If you are short of time, try to eat in your hotel. If the hotel does not have a *Shvetski Stol*, Swedish table buffet, you can make a dining room reservation earlier in the day at the Service desk. To speed up a meal you can even preorder your appetizers, so that they are on the table when you arrive. Check to see how long a dish takes to prepare—a meat dish may take ten to 15 minutes, while chicken can take up to an hour. Many Russian hotels are set up to accommodate group tours, so individual travelers can sometimes find it difficult to get a meal.

If you are going out to a Russian restaurant, it is advisable to make a reservation. If you see the sign *Mect Het*, No Space Available, put your head around the door; often, if the proprietor notices a foreigner, he will miraculously find an empty table.

Most restaurants (in Cyrillic *pectopah*, pronounced 'restoran') are open from 11:00 to 23:00, and close for a few hours in the afternoon. Restaurants with music and dancing can be expensive. Sometimes no liquor is served, but you can often take your own. Many of the newly opened co-op restaurants specialize in regional cuisines, such as *shashlik*, shish kebab, or other spicy dishes. Others may provide one

(opposite) Pushkin

choice as the plat du jour. Even though there may not be a wide selection, the food is usually tasty and the meal served quickly in pleasant surroundings.

Bars are found in all the major hotels. These are usually open to 02:00. Often, hotels have a small bar or café on your floor. Drink only bottled water since Russian water is salty; there are many types of bottled sodas. Beware of iced drinks, chilled fruit juices and *kompot*, fruit in sugared water, which are often made from the local water.

If invited to a Russian home, expect a large welcome. Russians love hospitality and usually prepare a spread. If you can, take along a bottle of champagne or vodka, which is harder for Russians to buy. A toast is usually followed by knocking back an entire shot of vodka—before the next toast. Since toasts can continue throughout the evening, you may want to consider sipping a few, to the chagrin of your host. Some popular toasts are: *Za Mir I Druzhbu* (To Peace and Friendship), *Do Dnya,* (Bottoms Up) and, the most popular, *Na Zdorovi-ye* (To Your Health).

ON THE MENU

The Russian menu is divided into four sections: *zakuski* (appetizers), *pervoye* (first course), *vtoroye* (second course) and *sladkoe* (dessert). The order is usually taken all together, from appetizer to dessert. *Zakuski* are Russian-style hors d'oeuvres that include fish, cold meats, salads and marinated vegetables.

Ikra is caviar: *krasnaya* (red from salmon) and *chornaya* (black from

sturgeon). The sturgeon is one of the oldest fish species known, dating back over 30 million years. Its lifespan is also one of the longest. No sturgeon is worth catching until it is at least seven years old, and *beluga* are not considered adult until after 20 years. The best caviar is *zernistaya*, the fresh unpressed variety. The most expensive is the black *Beluga*; another is *Sevruga*. Caviar is usually available at Russian restaurants and can be bought in the *Beriozkas*. Caviar, in Russia, has long been considered a health food. Czar Nicholas II made his children eat the pressed *payushnaya* caviar every morning. Since they all hated the salty taste, their cook solved the problem by spreading it on black bread and adding banana slices. The caviar-banana sandwich became the breakfast rage for many aristocratic families. Russia is still the largest producer of caviar in the world, processing over 1,000 tons per year; 20 per cent of the catch is exported. The largest roe comes from the *beluga*, a dark grey caviar appreciated for its large grain and fineness of skin. Caviar from the *sevruga* is the smallest and has the most delicate taste.

Many varieties of Russian soup are served, more often at lunch than dinner. *Borsch* is the traditional red beet soup made with beef and served with a spoonful of sour cream. *Solyanka* is a tomato-based soup with chunks of fish or meat and topped with diced olives and lemon. *Shchi* is a tasty cabbage soup. A soup made from pickled vegetables is *rasolnik*. *Okroshka* is a cold soup made from a *kvas* base.

Russian meals consist of *mya'so* (meat), *kur'iitsa* (chicken) or *rii'ba* (fish). *Bifshtek* is a small fried steak with onions and potatoes. Beef stroganov is cooked in sour cream and served with fried potatoes. *Kutlyeta po Kiyevski* is Chicken Kiev, stuffed with melted butter; *Kutlyeta po Pajarski* is a chicken cutlet; *Tabak* is a slightly seasoned fried or grilled chicken. The fish served is usually salmon, sturgeon, herring or halibut. Other dishes include *blini*, small pancakes with different fillings; *pelmeni*, boiled dumplings filled with meat and served with sour cream; and *pirozhki*, fried rolls with a meat filling. Desserts include *vareniki* (sweet fruit dumplings topped with sugar), *tort* (cake), *ponchiki* (sugared donuts) and *morozhnoye* (ice cream).

Chai, tea, comes with every meal. It is always sweet; ask for *biz sak'hera*, for unsweetened tea. Many Russians stir in a spoonful of jam instead of sugar. Coffee is not served as often. Alcoholic drinks consist of *pivo*, beer; *kvas*, like near-beer; *shampanskoye*, champagne; *vino*, wine; and vodka. Alcoholic drinks are ordered in grams; a small glass is 100 grams and a normal bottle consists of 750 grams or three quarters of a liter. The best wine comes from Georgia and the Crimea: there are both *krasnoye* (red) and *beloye* (white). The champagne is generally sweet. The best brandy comes from Armenia—*Armyanski konyak*. *Nalivka* is a fruit liqueur. Vodka is by far the favorite drink and comes in a number of varieties other than Stolichnaya, Moskovskaya or Russkaya. There is *limonnaya* (lemon vodka), *persovka* (with hot peppers), *zubrovka* (flavored with a special grass), *ryabinovka* (made from ash berries), *tminaya* (caraway flavor), *starka* (a smooth dark vodka), *ahotnichaya vodka* (hunter's vodka), and *zveroboy* (animal killer!). One of the strongest and most expensive is *Zolotoye Koltso*, the Golden Ring. Vodka can be most easily found in the *Beriozkas*, along with beer, champagne, wine and Western alcohols. For a listing of restaurants and cafés, see the Practical Information Section, page 256.

Shopping

Most group travelers to Russia do not have much time between excursions to shop. But then, Russia is not a shopper's paradise. Stores have never overflowed with specialty goods and many items are in short supply. However, since the fall of Communism, more and more stocked stores, private shops and Western-style establishments are opening.

THE BERIOZKAS

Beriozkas offer value for money and a wider choice of goods than in any other Russian shops. For the traveler, Beriozkas are well worth visiting for they are stocked with a large variety of Russian-made goods and the merchandise is genuine. It makes it much easier when souvenir shopping can be done in one spot.

The most popular Russian souvenir is probably the *matryoshka*, the painted set of nested dolls. *Khokhloma* lacquerware comes in the form of trays, cups, spoons, bowls and vases. There are also miniature painted lacquer boxes and brooches from the Golden Ring villages of Palekh and Fedoskino.

Other good buys are handicrafts, wood carvings, amber, fur hats, embroidered shawls and linens, lace, filigree jewelry, ceramics, samovars, balalaikas, painted eggs, caviar, tea and tea sets, vodka, books, records and *znachki* (small pins used for trading). These stores also have a small supply of food, snacks, sodas, liquor and cigarettes.

Most *Beriozkas* are open from 09:00 to 20:00 daily and close for a one-hour lunch break between 12:00 and 15:00. Your hotel also has small kiosks and post offices that sell foreign newspapers, magazines, books, postcards, stamps and pins. Recently, more Russian and Western-style food and souvenir stores have opened throughout the city.

LOCAL STORES

If you have time, try to visit a few local stores. They will give you a much better idea of how ordinary Russians shop. These stores will not accept traveler's checks or

The co-operative market, Moscow

credit cards. Some of the store designations are: *univermag*, large department store; *kommissioniye*, commission or second-hand store; *co-op*, cooperative; *rinoks*, the farmers' market; and *kiosks*. Most stores are open daily (except Sundays) from about 10:00 to 20:00, and close for an hour for lunch.

Shopping Tips
The procedure for purchasing an item in a local store involves several steps. First, locate the desired item and find out its price. Second, go to the *kassa*, cashier's booth, and pay. Third, take the receipt to the salesgirl, who will wrap and hand over your purchase. Prices are usually posted, especially in food stores. If you find it difficult to work out how much you owe, for example one kilo of chocolate is 4,250 rubles and one kilo of candy is 893 rubles and you want a quarter kilo of each, gesture to the salesgirl to write down the total for you. Many stores still use abacuses to tally. Know your exact bill; if you are even a few rubles out, you may have to return to the cashier to pay the discrepancy. Sometimes you will have to force your way to the counter. If you have to stand in a long line (a way of life for most of the population), take the opportunity to practice your Russian. If you have any questions, don't be afraid to ask; many Russians know a few words of English and will be happy to help. If you see something you like, buy it—it will probably have gone when you go back. Always take along a small string or shopping bag; many stores and markets do not provide them.

For a more complete listing of *Beriozkas* and local stores, see the Practical Information Shopping Section, page 274.

Cows of Moscow

The proceedings of these cows in the early morning in the heart of the city, wandering alone, was a mystery. On inquiring I was told that throughout Moscow various families possess, among their worldly goods, a cow. Vast numbers of the larger houses have considerable spaces enclosed in the rear of their dwellings—gardens, courts, grassy places. Likewise the innumerable cottages in the by-streets have within their gates green plots and outhouses. In very many of these there is a cow. During the summer time, when there is a pasture, the first duty to be observed in all these dwellings is to open the gates and let out the cow. If there is a delay in this performance a loud warning from the outhouse or court awakes the servant to it. The cow let out, he may go to bed again. She knows her way by certain streets towards a certain barrier of the city. As she goes other cows join her from other cottages or houses, and by the time they all arrive near the barrier they are a considerable body. Here they find a man blowing a horn, whose business it is to conduct them to some pasture outside the town, to take care of them during the day, to collect them by his horn in the afternoon, and to bring them back to the barrier at a given time. When he has done this his business is over. Each cow knows her way home, and finds it unmolested up to the very heart of the city, the Kremlin. What a simple and convenient method for insuring good and pure and fresh milk to the family! Each materfamilias can water it according to her wants or tastes, and she can omit the chalk—a blessed privilege!

GTLowth, Across The Kremlin, 1868

Moscow

Introduction

For centuries Moscow has been an inseparable part of the life of all Russia. Moscow's history dates back more than 800 years to 1147, when Prince Yuri Dolgoruky established a small outpost on the banks of the Moscow River. The settlement grew into a large and prosperous town, which eventually became the capital of the principality of Moscovy. By the 15th century, Moscow was Russia's political, cultural and trade center, and during the reign of Ivan the Great, it became the capital of the Russian Empire. Ivan summoned the greatest Russian and European architects to create a capital so wondrous that 'reality embodied fantasy on an unearthly scale,' and soon the city was hailed as the 'New Constantinople.' In the next century, Ivan the Terrible was crowned the first czar of all Russia in the magnificent Uspensky Cathedral inside the Kremlin. The words of an old Russian proverb suggested the power within the Kremlin: 'There is only God and the center of government, the Kremlin.' People from all over the world flocked to witness the splendors in the capital of the largest empire on earth. By the 18th century, a foreign traveler wrote that Moscow, 'so irregular, so uncommon, so extraordinary, and so contrasted, had never before claimed such astonishment.'

In 1712, after Peter the Great transferred the capital to St Petersburg, Moscow remained a symbol of national pride. Many eminent writers, scientists, artists and musicians, such as Pushkin, Tolstoy, Lomonosov, Repin and Tchaikovsky, lived and worked in Moscow, which never relinquished its political significance, artistic merit and nostalgic charm. Even when Napoleon invaded in 1812, he wrote: 'I had no real conception of the grandeur of the city. It possessed fifty palaces of equal beauty to the Palais d'Elysée furnished in French style with incredible luxuries.' After a terrible fire destroyed Moscow during Napoleon's hasty retreat, Tolstoy wrote that:

> 'It would be difficult to explain what caused the Russians, after the departure of the French in October 1812, to throng to the place that had been known as Moscow; there was left no government, no churches, shrines, riches or houses—yet, it was still the same Moscow it had been in August. All was destroyed, except something intangible, yet powerful and indestructable... Within a year the population of Moscow exceeded what it had been in 1812.'

Moscow symbolized the soul of the empire, and Tolstoy later observed that Moscow remains eternal because 'Russians look at Moscow as if she is their own mother.' *Moskva* is said to derive from the Finnish word *maska ava*, meaning mother bear.

Moscow has also played an important role in the country's political movements:

The revolutionary writers Herzen and Belinksy began their activities at Moscow University; student organizations supported many revolutionary ideas, from Chernyshevsky's to Marx's; and Moscow workers backed the Bolsheviks during the October 1917 Revolution and went on to capture the Kremlin. In 1918, after more than two centuries, Moscow once again became Russia's capital. But this time, the city would govern the world's first socialist State—the Soviet Union. Trotsky, Lenin's main supporter, wrote:

> ...finally all the opposition was overcome, the capital was transferred back to Moscow on March 12, 1918... Driving past Nicholas's palace on the wooden paving, I would occasionally glance over at the Emperor Bell and Emperor Cannon. All the barbarism of Moscow glared at me from the hole in the bell and the mouth of the cannon... The carillon in the Saviour's Tower was now altered. Instead of playing 'God Save the Czar,' the bells played the 'Internationale,' slowly and deliberately, at every quarter hour.

After eight centuries of history, modern Moscow is the largest city in the country with a population of over nine million. It is not only the center of the new Commonwealth, but also the capital of the Russian Federative State. The Kremlin remains the seat of government. With the formation of the Commonwealth of Independent States and the collapse of Communist Russia, Moscow is now the hub of an enterprising new metropolis. New businesses, co-ops and joint ventures are initiated daily. Democracy and capitalism, along with an ever more influential mafia, have already made a big impression; everybody is trying to find his or her own place in the new society. However, the opportunities and changes have created new extremes: from the unemployed to multi-millionaires, the homeless to real-estate moguls, poor borrowers to rich bankers and destitute pensioners to enterprising youth.

Whether the visitor has a few days or several weeks, there is always plenty to do and see. Moscow has over 2,500 monuments, 50 theaters and concert halls, 4,500 libraries, 125 cinemas and 70 museums, visited annually by over 20 million people from 150 countries. Moscow is also rich in history, art and architecture. One of the most memorable experiences of your trip to Russia will be to stand in **Red Square** and look out on the golden magnificence of the cathedrals and towers of the **Kremlin** and **St Basil's Cathedral.**

Other attractions include the **Novodevichy Convent**, which dates from 1514, and the **Andronikov Monastery**, which houses the **Andrei Rublev Museum of Old Russian Art**, including the famed iconist's masterpieces. Moscow's museums and galleries contain collections of Russian and foreign masters. There are also the fascinating side streets to explore, little changed since the time of Ivan the Terrible. The nighttime reflections of the Kremlin's ancient clock tower and golden onion domes on the Moskva River bring to mind the lyrics of one of Russia's most popular songs: 'Lazily

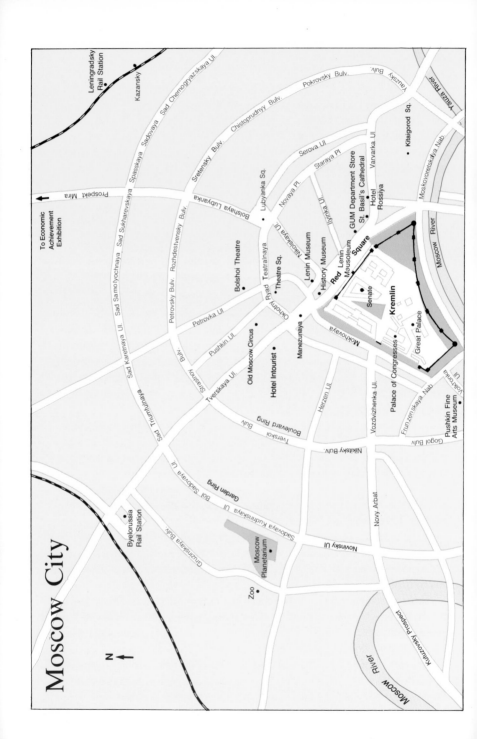

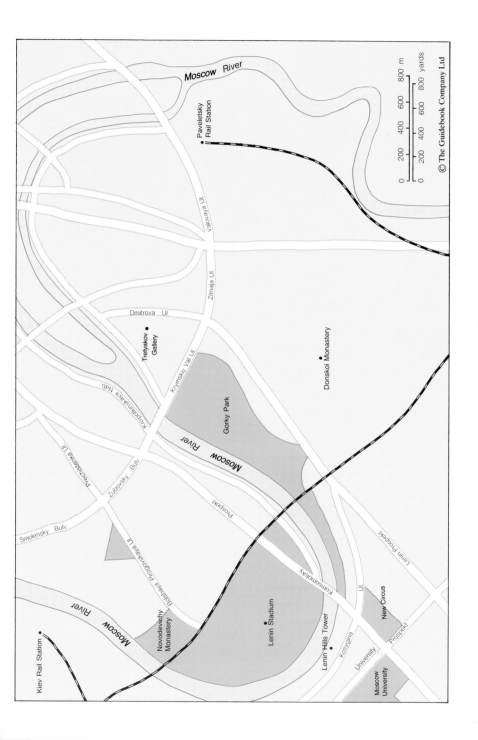

Moscow River

Paveletsky
Rail Station

Valovaya Ul.

Zitnaja Ul.

Dmitrova Ul.

Tretyakov
Gallery

Donskoi Monastery

Krymsky Val Ul.

Kropotkinskaya Nab.

Gorky Park

Moscow River

Prechistenka Ul.

Zubovsky Bulv

Prospekt

Smolensky Bulv

Bolshaya Progovskaya Ul.

Komsomolsky

Lenin Prospekt

New Circus

Moscow River

Kiev Rail Station

Novodevichy
Monastery

Lenin Stadium

Lenin Hills Tower

Kosygina
Ul.

University

Prospekt

Moscow
University

0   200   400   600   800 m
0   200   400   600   800 yards

© The Guidebook Company Ltd

the river like a silvery stream, ripples gently in the moonlight; and a song fades as in a dream, in the spell of this Moscow night.' Moscow has an eternal enchantment that can be felt in the early light of dawn, in the deepening twilight, on a warm summer's day or in the swirling snows of winter.

ARRIVAL

The route from the *Sheremetyevo* International Airport into the city center winds along the Leningradsky Highway, linking Moscow with St Petersburg. About 14 miles (23 kilometers) from the airport are large anti-tank obstacles, **The Memorial to the Heroes** who defended the city against the Nazi invasion in 1941; notice how close the Germans came to entering the city. The highway turns into Leningradsky Prospekt at a place that used to mark the outer border of the city. Here the street was lined with summer cottages. The **Church of All Saints** (1683) stands at the beginning of the prospekt. Other sights along the route are Peter the Great's Moorish Gothic-style **Petrovsky Palace**, built in 1775, and the 60,000-seat Dynamo Stadium. At number 33 is the **Palace of Newlyweds**, where marriage ceremonies are performed. As you approach the center of Moscow, the Byelorussky Railway Station is on your right. Trains run from here to destinations in Western and Eastern Europe. This station marks the beginning of one of Moscow's main thoroughfares, Ulitsa Gorgovo (Gorky and Tverskaya streets). A map of Moscow is made up of a system of rings. The Kremlin and Red Square lie at the center. Five concentric rings circle Red Square, each marking an old boundary of the city, showing its age like a cross-section of a tree.

Centuries ago, each ring was fortified by stone, wooden or earthen ramparts, which could only be entered through a special gate. The area around the Kremlin, once known as *Kitai-gorod*, formed the original border of the city in the 15th and 16th centuries. Many of the streets and squares in this area carry their original names: Petrovskaya Vorota (Peter's Gate), Kitaisky Proyezd (Kitai Passage), Ulitsa Varvarka (St Barbara Street) and Valovaya Ulitsa (Rampart Street).

The second ring is known as Bulvarnoye Koltso, Boulevard Ring. The city's sub-urbs were placed beyond this ring in the 17th century. The Sadovoye Koltso, Garden Ring, is the third ring that runs for ten miles (16 kilometers) around the city. This is also connected by the Koltso Metro line that stops at various points around the ring. The fourth ring, which stretches for 25 miles (40 kilometers) around the city, was known as the Kamer-Kollezhsky Rampart; it served as a customs boundary in the 18th and 19th centuries. The fifth ring is the Moscow Circular Road, marking the present boundary of Moscow. The area past this ring is known as the Green Belt, a protected forested area where many Muscovites have country and summer houses, known as *dacha*.

METRO

One of the quickest and easiest ways of getting around Moscow is by Metro. It is also the most popular method of transportation—over 10 million people use the Metro daily. Construction began in 1931, under Stalin. Many Soviet and foreign architects and engineers spent four years building the deep stations, which served as bomb shelters during World War II. The first line was opened on May 15, 1935. Today, ten lines and nearly 150 stations connect all points of the city. The Metro (with over 125 miles/200 kilometers of track) operates daily from 06:00 to 01:00; the trains are frequent, arriving every 90 seconds during rush hour.

Many of the older stations are beautifully decorated with mosaics, marble, stained glass, statues and chandeliers, and are kept immaculate. Some of the more interesting ones are: Okhotny Ryad, Mayakovskaya, Byelorusskaya, Novoslobodskaya, Komsomolskaya, Kievskaya and Teatralnaya.

The Metro is easy to use by looking at a map. All the color-coded lines branch out from a central point, and are intersected by the brown Koltso (Circle) line. Entrances above ground are marked by a large M. Take the sometimes long and fast escalator down to the station. Maps are located before the turnstiles. From 1935 to 1991, the Metro cost only five kopeks; now the price keeps pace with inflation. You must purchase a token, using Russian currency only, at the automatic machines in the Metro stations—the machines will give change if you do not have the exact fare (change for large ruble notes or ten-day and monthly passes can be purchased at the cashier window). Place the token in the turnstile and wait for the green light; pass through quickly—the stall can close suddenly.

Since station names are written only in Russian, ask somebody to write down the name of your destination. If you have trouble finding your way, show it to the attendant, who usually stands at the entrance, or ask: people are very helpful to strangers and many understand some English. The trains can be crowded and commuters push to get to where they are going. Stand near a door as your stop approaches. The names of stops are announced in each car. Maps of the route are also posted inside each train car (in Russian); you can also use the Metro map at the back of this book. Metro tours can be booked through Intourist.

Even since the fall of Communism, Muscovites still display a proprietary pride in their Metro; it is clean and graffiti-free, with reserved seats at the front of each carriage for the elderly and disabled. But nowadays, you may come across hawkers, beggars and musicians in the stations.

Red Square

Most visitors begin their acquaintance with Moscow in *Krasnaya Ploshchad*, **Red Square**, the heart of the city. It was first mentioned in 15th-century chronicles as the *Veliky Torg*, the Great Marketplace and main trading center of the town. From the time of Ivan the Great, the square was used as a huge gathering place for public events, markets, fairs and festivals. Many religious processions came through the square led by the czar and Patriarch of the Orthodox Church. It was also the scene of political demonstrations and revolts, and the site of public executions. The square received its present name in the 17th-century from the old Russian word *krasny*, meaning both red and beautiful. From the Middle Ages, it was a popular open-air market, and it remained so until GUM, the shopping arcade, was completed in 1893 and the traders moved under cover.

This magnificent square encompasses an area of over 70,000 square meters and is bounded by the **Kremlin** walls, **St Basil's Cathedral**, the **Lenin Mausoleum**, the **Historical Museum** and the **GUM Department Store**.

Today, national celebrations are held here, especially on May Day when it is filled with huge parades and festivities. The closest Metro stop is Okhotny Ryad.

St Basil's Cathedral

Red Square's most famous and eye-catching structure is **St Basil's Cathedral**. This extraordinary creation was erected by Ivan IV (the Terrible) from 1555 to 1561, to commemorate the annexation to Russia of the Mongol states of Kazan and Astrakhan. Since this occurred on the festival of the Intercession of the Virgin, Ivan the Terrible named it the Cathedral of the Intercession. The names of the architects were unknown until 1896, when old manuscripts mentioning its construction were found. According to legend, Ivan the Terrible had the two architects, Posnik and Barma, blinded so they could never again create such a beautiful church. However, records from 1588, a quarter of a century after the cathedral's completion, indicate that Posnik and Barma built the chapel at the northeast corner of the cathedral, where the holy prophet Basil (Vasily) was buried. Canonized after his death, Basil the Blessed died the same year (1552) that many of the Mongol Khannates were captured. Basil had opposed the cruelties of Ivan the Terrible; since most of the population also despised the czar, the cathedral took on the name of St Basil's after Ivan's death.

The cathedral is built of brick in traditional Russian style with colorful, asymmetrical, tent-shaped, helmet and onion domes situated over nine chapels, each dedicated to a saint on whose feast day the Russian army won a victory. The interior is filled with 16th- and 17th-century icons and frescoes, and the gallery contains bright wall

The Church of the Resurrection on-the-Debre, Kostroma

and ceiling paintings of red, turquoise and yellow flower patterns. Locals often refer to the cathedral as the 'stone flower in Red Square.' The French stabled their horses here in 1812 and Napoleon wanted to blow it up. Luckily, his order was never carried out.

The interior, now open to the public, has undergone much restoration. Inside is a branch of the Historical Museum that traces the history of the cathedral and Ivan IV's campaigns. Under the bell tower (added in the 17th century) is an exhibition room where old sketches and plans trace the architectural history of St Basil's.

The museum is open daily from 09:30 to 17:30 except Tuesdays and the first Monday of each month. In 1991, the cathedral was given back to the Russian Orthodox Church to celebrate Russian New Year and Easter services; Yeltsin attended the first Easter service.

In front of the cathedral stands the bronze **Monument to Minin and Pozharsky**, the first patriotic monument in Moscow built from public funding; it originally stood in the middle of the square. Sculpted by Ivan Martos in 1818, the monument depicts Kozma Minin and Prince Dmitri Pozharsky, whose leadership drove the Polish invaders out of Moscow in 1612. The pedestal inscription reads 'To Citizen Minin and Prince Pozharsky from a grateful Russia 1818.'

Near the monument is **Lobnoye Mesto**, the Place of Skulls. A platform of white stone stood here for more than four centuries, on which public executions were carried out. Church clergymen blessed the crowds and the czar's orders and edicts were also announced from here.

THE LENIN MAUSOLEUM

By the Kremlin wall on the southwest side of Red Square stands the **Lenin Mausoleum**. Inside, in a glass sarcophagus, lies Vladimir Ilyich Lenin, who died on January 21, 1924. Three days after his death, a wooden structure was erected on this spot. Four months later, it was rebuilt and then replaced in 1930 by the granite, marble and black labradorite mausoleum, designed by Alexei Shchusev. 'Lenin' is inscribed in red porphyry. For more than 70 years, Russians and foreigners have stood in the line that stretches from the end of Red Square to the mausoleum to view the idolized revolutionary leader and 'Father of the Soviet Union.' Two guards man the entrance, and at every hour on the hour, as the Kremlin clock chimes, the ceremonial changing of the guard takes place. Exactly two minutes and 45 seconds before the hour, two armed sentries march toward the entrance of the Mausoleum to relieve the stationed guards. (Since 1993, the guard changing has occasionally been banned by the new government.) On January 21, 1994, many die-hard Communists and Lenin loyalists once again gathered at the mausoleum to commemorate the 70th anniversary of Lenin's death. Photography is prohibited and cameras should be placed out of sight in a bag. Even the slightest impolite gesture, such as placing hands in pockets, will draw a reprimand from the security guards. Once inside, visitors are not allowed to pause and hold up the line. If you are with a group, the tour will usually be brought to the front of the line. If you are not with a tour group, foreign tourists can wait at the corner of the Historical Museum (facing Manezhnaya Square), where officers organize a separate, much shorter line and take you straight in on Tuesdays, Wednesdays, Thursdays and Saturdays from noon to 13:00, and on Sundays from 13:00 to 14:00. The mausoleum is open on the same days in summer from 09:00 to 13:00, and on Sundays from 09:00 to 14:00; in winter, it is open from 11:00 to 14:00, and on Sundays from 11:00 to 16:00. But also check, the times often change. After the attemped coup of 1991, the lines to Lenin's Tomb diminished dramatically. And there is a new phenomenon, unthinkable until recently: there are times when nobody is queuing to see the former leader. Ironically though, with the new wave of capitalism, Lenin souvenirs are now more popular than ever. And Lenin's formaldehyde experts are offering their eternal Lenin Delux preservation techniques to anyone around the world for a price of just over a quarter of a million dollars.

Marble reviewing stands on both sides of the mausoleum hold up to 10,000 spectators on national holidays. Atop the mausoleum is a tribune, where the heads of the former Soviet government and Communist Party once gathered on May and Revolution days. Below the mausoleum was a laboratory that constantly monitored the temperature and deterioration of Lenin. And below this, there was a gymnasium where the Kremlin guards worked out.

Behind the mausoleum, separated by a row of silver fir trees, are the remains of many of the country's most honored figures in politics, culture and science, whose ashes lie in urns within the Kremlin walls. They include Lenin's sister, his wife, Sergei Kirov, Maxim Gorky, AK Lunacharsky, the physicist Sergei Korolyov and the cosmonaut Yuri Gagarin. Foreigners include John Reed and William Hayword (USA), Arthur McManus (England), Clara Zetkin and Fritz Heckert (Germany), and Sen Katayama (Japan). There are also the tombstones of previous leaders of the Communist Party: Sverdlov, Dzerzhinsky, Frunze, Kalinin, Voroshilov, Suslov and Stalin, who was once buried next to Lenin in the mausoleum. Nearby are the granite-framed common graves of 500 people who died during the October 1917 Revolution.

THE HISTORICAL MUSEUM

At the opposite end of the square from St Basil's is a red-brick building, decorated with numerous spires and *kokoshnik* gables. This houses the **Historical Museum**. It was constructed by Vladimir Sherwood between 1878 and 1883 on the site where Moscow University was founded in 1755 by the Russian scientist Mikhail Lomonosov. When opened in 1883, the museum had over 300,000 objects and was supported by private donations. Today, the government museum contains over four million

(following pages) Red Square looking towards St Basil's Cathedral

items in 48 halls that house the country's largest archaeological collection, along with manuscripts, books, coins, ornaments and works of art from the Stone Age to the present day. These include birch-bark letters, clothing of Ivan the Terrible, Peter the Great's sleigh, Napoleon's sabre and the Decree on Peace written by Lenin. The museum is open daily from 10:00 to 18:00 except Tuesdays and the last day of each month.

GUM

Next to the Historical Museum, stretching across the entire northeastern side of Red Square, is the three-story State Universal Store, known as **GUM**. It is the largest shopping center in Russia, with a total length of 1.5 miles (2.5 kilometers), selling half a million items to almost a quarter of a million Russians and 100,000 foreigners every day. GUM's 100th anniversary was celebrated in 1993. The initials G.U.M. stood for *Gosudarstvenny Universalny Magazine*, the Government Department Store, until 1990, when the Moscow city government turned it into a joint stock company owned mainly by the employees. The initials now stand for *Glavny Universalny Magazine*, the Main Department Store.

It was designed in 1893 by Alexander Pomerantsev to replace a market destroyed by one of Napoleon's fires in 1812, as his troops were attempting to occupy Moscow. When it was built it was known as the Upper Trading Stalls. It was a showcase for goods and one of the world's most modern commercial areas with 200 shops, built of steel and concrete with ornate glass roofing and even electrical and heating systems. But today, with no major repairs since 1953, its walls are crumbling and its beauty fading. The store is trying to raise money for renovations and so recapture its prerevolutionary splendor. The grand ceremonial entrance on Red Square, closed since the Bolshevik Revolution, was reopened in 1992. It is worth visiting to see the interiors of old Russian shops, its ornate bridges, ornamental stucco designs and the large glass roof. Souvenir shops are on the ground floor. It is open daily from 08:00 to 21:00 and closed on Sundays.

THE ALEXANDROV GARDENS

The entrance to these charming gardens is opposite the Historical Museum at the Kremlin's wrought-iron Corner Arsenal Gate. The gardens were laid out on the banks of the Neglinnaya River by Osip Bovet from 1819 to 1822 for Alexander I. The river was later diverted by a system of pipes to flow beneath the park. An eternal flame burns before the **Tomb of the Unknown Soldier**, who died for his country during World War II. It was unveiled on May 8, 1967, on the eve of Victory Day.

It is a tradition for newlyweds on their wedding day to lay flowers on the tombstone, on which is inscribed: 'Your name is unknown, your feat immortal. To the fallen 1941–45.' Along the alley, in front of the tomb, are blocks of red porphyry that hold earth from 'Hero Cities,' including Moscow and St Petersburg, designated after World War II. Also in the gardens are a memorial to the War of 1812 and a granite obelisk with the names of the world's great revolutionaries and thinkers. The latter was originally erected in 1913 to commemorate the 300th anniversary of the Romanov Dynasty. On Lenin's orders in 1918, the double-headed eagle was replaced by the obelisk.

The central alley of the Alexandrov Gardens leads to the Troitsky Bridge that approaches the entrance of the Kremlin.

The Kremlin

'The earth, as we all know, begins at the Kremlin. It is the central point.' (Poet Mayakovsky).

The Moscow **Kremlin**, an outstanding monument of Russian history, winds around a steep slope high above the Moskva River, enclosing an area of over 70 acres next to Red Square. The Russian word *kreml* was once used to describe a fortified stronghold that encased a small town. A Russian town was usually built on a high embankment, surrounded by a river and moat, to protect against invasions. The word *kreml* may originate from the Greek *kremnos* meaning steep escarpment. The medieval *kremlin* acted as a fortress around a town filled with palaces, churches, monasteries, wooden peasant houses and markets. The Moscow Kremlin was built between the Moskva River and Neglinnaya River, which now flows underground. It is about half a mile (one kilometer) long, up to 62 feet (19 meters) high and 21 feet (6.5 meters) thick. Twenty towers and gates, and over ten churches and palaces lie inside its walls. The Moscow Kremlin has a fascinating eight-century history. The closest Metro stops are Okhotny Ryad and Biblioteka Imena Lenina.

History

The Kremlin is the oldest historical and architectural feature of Moscow. The first written account of Moscow comes to us from a chronicle of 1147, which describes Prince Yuri Dolgoruky of Suzdal receiving Prince Svyatoslav on Borovitsky (now Kremlin) Hill. Nine years later, Dolgoruky ordered a fort built on this same hill, which later became his residence. In 1238, the invading Mongols burned the fortress to the ground. By 1326, the Kremlin had been surrounded with thick oak walls and Grand-Prince Ivan I had built two stone churches in addition to the existing wooden

(following pages) The roofs of Moscow, the Kremlin is in the foreground

ones. During this time, the Metropolitan of Kiev moved the seat of the Orthodox Church from Vladimir to Moscow. In 1367, Prince Dmitri Donskoi replaced the wooden walls with limestone to fortify them against cannon attack; Moscow was then referred to as *Beli Gorod*, the White Town. The Mongols invaded again in 1382; they razed everything and killed half the population. Within 15 years, the Kremlin walls were rebuilt and the iconists Theophanes the Greek and Andrei Rublev painted the interior frescoes of the new Cathedral of the Annunciation.

Ivan III (1460–1505) and his son, Vasily III, were responsible for shaping the Kremlin into its present appearance. When the Mongols no longer posed a threat to the city, the leaders concentrated more on aesthetic than defensive designs. Ivan the Great commissioned well-known Russian and Italian architects to create a magnificent city to reflect the beauty of the 'Third Rome' and the power of the Grand Prince and Metropolitan. The white stone of the Kremlin was replaced by red-brick walls and towers, and the Assumption and Annunciation cathedrals were rebuilt on a grander scale. During the reign of Ivan IV, the architecture took on more fanciful elements and asymmetrical designs with colorful onion domes and tall pyramidal tent roofs, as embodied in St Basil's—a style now termed Old Russian. The Patriarch Nikon barred all tent roofs and ornamental decorations from churches when he took office in 1652, terming the external frills sacrilegious. By 1660, though, the reforms of Nikon had created such schisms in the church that he was forced to step down. Immediately, the old decorative details were again applied to architecture.

Catherine the Great drew up plans to redesign the Kremlin in the new neo-classical style, but they were never carried out. During the War of 1812, Napoleon quartered his troops inside the Kremlin for 35 days. Retreating, he tried to blow it up, but townspeople extinguished the burning fuses, though three towers were destroyed. In the mid-1800s, the Kremlin Palace and Armory were built. In 1918, the Soviet government moved the capital back to Moscow from St Petersburg and made the Kremlin its permanent seat. Lenin signed a decree to protect the works of art and historical monuments and ordered the buildings restored and turned into museums. The Kremlin remains the center of Russian government.

VIEW FROM RED SQUARE

Red-ruby stars were mounted on the five tallest towers of the Kremlin in 1937, replacing the double-headed eagle. The towers of the Kremlin were named after the icons that used to hang above their gates. The most recognizable tower is the 201-foot- (67-meter-) high **Spasskaya (Saviour) Clock Tower**, which stands to the right of St Basil's. It used to serve as the official entrance of the czars, who had to cross a moat over an arched stone bridge to reach the gate. It is now the main entrance of government officials, who pull up in black limousines. The Saviour Icon once hung

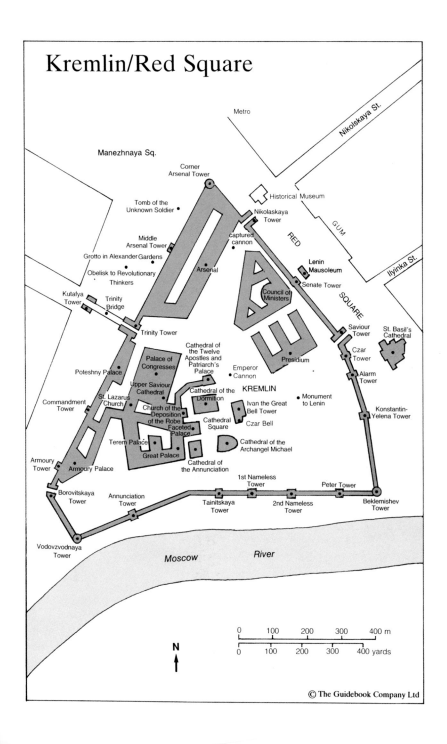

Kremlin/Red Square

Metro

Nikolskaya St.

Manezhnaya Sq.

Corner
Arsenal Tower

Historical Museum

Tomb of the
Unknown Soldier

Nikolaskaya
Tower

GUM

Middle
Arsenal Tower

captured
cannon

RED

Grotto in Alexander Gardens

Ilyinka St.

Arsenal

Lenin
Mausoleum

Obelisk to Revolutionary
Thinkers

Senate Tower

Kutafya
Tower

Trinity
Bridge

Council of
Ministers

SQUARE

Trinity Tower

Saviour
Tower

St. Basil's
Cathedral

Cathedral of
the Twelve
Apostles and
Patriarch's
Palace

Palace of
Congresses

Presidium

Czar
Tower

Poteshny Palace

Emperor
Cannon

Alarm
Tower

Upper Saviour
Cathedral

Cathedral of the
Dormition

KREMLIN

Commandment
Tower

St. Lazarus
Church

Church of the
Deposition
of the Robe

Ivan the Great
Bell Tower

Monument
to Lenin

Konstantin-
Yelena Tower

Faceted
Palace

Cathedral
Square

Czar Bell

Terem Palace

Cathedral of the
Archangel Michael

Armoury
Tower

Great Palace

Armoury Palace

Cathedral of
the Annunciation

1st Nameless
Tower

Peter Tower

Borovitskaya
Tower

Annunciation
Tower

Tainitskaya
Tower

2nd Nameless
Tower

Beklemishev
Tower

Vodovzvodnaya
Tower

Moscow   River

| 0 | 100 | 200 | 300 | 400 m |

| 0 | 100 | 200 | 300 | 400 yards |

N

© The Guidebook Company Ltd

above the Spasskaya gate. Inscriptions in Latin and Old Russian name the Italian Solario as the tower's builder in 1491. In the middle of the 17th century, the Scottish architect Christopher Galloway mounted a clock on its face; this clock was replaced in 1918. Like Big Ben in London, the chimes of the Spasskaya Tower are broadcast over the radio to mark the hour.

The tower behind Lenin's Mausoleum is known as the **Senate Tower**; it stands in front of the Senate building. To the right of the mausoleum stands the **Nikolskaya Tower**, where the Icon of St Nicholas was kept. In 1492, Solario built a corner tower next to a courtyard used by Sobakin Boyars. The **Sobakin Tower** is now called the **Corner Arsenal Tower**, where munitions were stored.

ENTERING THE KREMLIN

The two main entrances to the Kremlin are through the Kutafya and Borovitskaya towers. Most group tours are taken through the latter gate on the west side, which is closest to the Kremlin Armory. If you are near the Alexandrov Gardens, go through the **Kutafya Tower** and across the Trinity Bridge (which runs through the middle of the gardens). The Kutafya watchtower, built in the early 16th century, was approached by a drawbridge that spanned a moat. The tower was connected by a stone bridge, under which the Neglinnaya River once ran, to the **Troitskaya** (Trinity) **Tower**. Built in 1495, it was named after the Trinity-Sergius Monastery in Sergiyev Posad. Clergy and military officers entered through the Trinity, the tallest tower at 240 feet (80meters).

PALACE OF CONGRESSES

As you enter the Kremlin through the Kutafya and Trinity Towers, the modern **Palace of Congresses** is on your right. Khrushchev approved the plans for this large steel, glass and marble structure. Built by Mikhail Posokhin, it was completed in 1961 for the 22nd Congress of the Communist Party. When no congresses or international meetings are in session, the palace is used for ballet and opera performances. Sunk 45 feet (15 meters) into the ground so as not to tower over the Kremlin, the Palace contains 800 rooms, and the auditorium seats 6,000.

THE ARSENAL

The yellow two-story building to the left of the entrance tower was once used as the **Arsenal**. Peter the Great ordered its construction in 1702 (completed in 1736), but later turned it into a Trophy Museum. Along the front of the arsenal are 875 cannons and other trophies captured from Napoleon's armies in 1812. Plaques on the wall list the names of men killed defending the arsenal during the Revolution and World War II.

View of the Kremlin from the Moskva River

Senate Building

As you walk through the square, the three-story triangular building of the former Council of Ministers is directly ahead. Catherine the Great had it built in the classical style by Matvei Kazakov in 1787. After Lenin moved the capital from Petrograd (St Petersburg) to Moscow in 1918, the Soviet government and the Bolshevik Party took up residence in the building. It is now used by the Senate; its large green dome is topped by the national flag. The front wall plaque is marked by Lenin's portrait and the inscription: 'Lenin lived and worked in this building from March 1918 to May 1923.' The Central Committee of the Communist Party once met in **Sverdlov Hall**. The hall's 18 Corinthian columns are decorated with copies (the originals are in the Armory) of bas-reliefs portraying czars and princes. Lenin's study and flat are in the east wing. Special objects stand on his desk, such as the Monkey Statue presented to him by Armand Hammer in 1921. The study leads to a small four-room apartment that Lenin shared with his wife and younger sister. Across from the Senate, near the Spasskaya Tower, is the **Presidium** and the **Kremlin Theater**, which was built between 1932 and 1934. The building has also served as a military school and the former residence of the President of the USSR. The theater seats 1,200. These buildings can only be visited with special permission.

Patriarch's Palace

Opposite the former Senate is the four-story **Patriarch's Palace** and his private chapel, the **Church of the Twelve Apostles**, which now house the **Museum of 17th-Century Life and Applied Art** with over 1,000 exhibits. Patriarch Nikon commissioned the palace for himself in 1635. After Nikon banned elaborate decorations on church buildings, he had the architects Konstantinov and Okhlebinin design the structure in simple white Byzantine fashion. The palace was placed near the main cathedral and the Trinity Gate, where clergy formally entered the Kremlin. The vaulted **Krestovskaya Chamber**, the Hall of the Cross, built without a single support beam, was used as a formal reception hall. Every three years, the chamber was used for making consecrated oil for the Russian churches. In 1721, Peter the Great gave the palace to the Church Council of the Holy Synod. The museum has an interesting collection of rare manuscripts, coins, jewelry, furniture, fabrics, embroidery and table games. The books include an ABC primer written for the son of Peter the Great. Two of the halls are decorated to look like a 17th-century house. Some of the displays in the Church of the Twelve Apostles are wine coffers and ladles, on which Bacchus is carved. These objects belonged to the society of the Highest and Most Jolly and Drunken Council, founded by Peter the Great to make fun of (non-progressive) church rituals. The museum is closed on Thursdays.

Emperor Cannon

Next to the Palace is the 40-ton **Emperor Cannon**. Its 890mm bore makes it the largest cannon in the world. It was cast in 1586 by Andrei Shchokhov and never fired. A likeness of Fedor I is on the barrel. The decorative iron cannon balls (weighing one ton each) were cast in the 19th century.

Across from the cannon in the southeastern corner of the Kremlin lie the **Tainitsky** (Secret) **Gardens**. Winter fairs are held here for children during New Year celebrations. A statue of Lenin rests on the highest spot, known as **Kremlin Hill**. To the left of the statue is the **Cosmos Oak**, which cosmonaut Yuri Gagarin planted on April 14, 1961. This vantage point affords a good view of the Kremlin and Spasskaya Tower. The **Czar's Tower** stands to the right of it and is decorated with white-stone designs and a weathervane. A wooden deck used to stand on top of the tower, from which Ivan the Terrible supposedly watched executions in Red Square. The tower directly behind Lenin is the **Nabatnaya** (Alarm) **Tower**; the bell that used to hang here is on display in the Armory Museum. Farther to the right is the **Konstantino-Yeleninskaya Tower**, which honors St Constantine and St Helen. In earlier days, it was also referred to as the Torture Tower, since it housed a torture chamber. The corner tower is called **Moskvoretskaya**, built in 1487 by Marco Ruffo. It was known as Beklemischevskaya, named after Ivan Beklemisch, whose home stood next to it in the 16th century; his spirit is said to have haunted it. The Mongols broke through this tower to enter the Kremlin in the 17th century.

Emperor Bell

The largest bell in the world stands on a stone pedestal by the Secret Gardens. The bell, 18 feet (six meters) high, weighs 210 tons. The surface bears portraits of czars and icons. It was designed in 1733 by Ivan Matorin and his son Mikhail, and took two years to cast. An 11.5-ton fragment broke off during the fire of 1737, when water was thrown on it. After the fire, the bell was returned to its casting pit, where it lay for a century. The architect Montferrand raised the bell in 1836.

The square between the Spasskaya Tower and the bell was known as **Ivan's Square**, along which government offices were located. Here, criminals were flogged and officials read the czar's new decrees.

Bell Tower

Behind the Emperor Bell stands the three-tiered **Bell Tower of Ivan the Great**. Built between 1505 and 1508, the tower contains 21 bells that hang in the arches of each section, the largest of which is the Uspensky (Assumption) Bell, weighing 70 tons. The Old Slavonic inscription around the gilded dome notes that it was added to the

(following pages) The Palace of the Congresses under the Soviet system

The Brotherhood Grave

Late in the night we went through the empty streets and under the Iberian Gate to the great Red Square in front of the Kremlin. The church of Vasili Blazhenny loomed fantastic, its bright coloured, convoluted and blazoned cupolas vague in the darkness. There was no sign of any damage...Along one side of the square the dark towers and walls of the Kremlin stood up. On the high walls flickered redly the light of hidden flames; voices reached us across the immense place, and the sound of picks and shovels. We crossed over.

Mountains of dirt and rock piled high near the base of the wall. Climbing these we looked down into two massive pits, ten or fifteen feet deep and fifty yards long, where hundreds of soldiers and workers were digging in the light of huge fires.

A young soldier spoke to us in German. 'The Brotherhood Grave,' he explained. 'Tomorrow we shall bury here five hundred proletarians who died for the Revolution.'

He took us down into the pit. In frantic haste they swung the picks and shovels, and the earth-mountains grew. No one spoke. Overhead the night was thick with stars, and the ancient Imperial Kremlin wall towered up immeasurably.

'Here in this holy place,' said the student, 'holiest of all Russia, we shall bury our most holy. Here where are the tombs of the Tsars, our Tsar—the People—shall sleep...' His arm was in a sling from the bullet wound gained in the fighting. He looked at it. 'You foreigners look down on us Russians because for so long we tolerated a medieval monarchy,' he said. 'But we saw that the Tsar was not the only tyrant in the world; capitalism was worse, and in all the countries of the world capitalism was Emperor...Russian revolutionary tactics are best...'

As we left, the workers in the pit, exhausted and running with sweat in spite of the cold, began to climb wearily out. Across the Red Square a dark knot of men came hurrying. They swarmed into the pits, picked up the tools and began digging, digging, without a word.

So, all the long night volunteers of the People relieved each other, never halting in their driving speed, and the cold light of the dawn laid bare the great square, white with snow, and the yawning brown pits of the Brotherhood Grave, quite finished.

We rose before sunrise, and hurried through the dark streets to Skobeliev Square. In all the great city not a human being could be seen; but there was a faint sound of stirring, far and near, like a deep wind coming. In the pale half-light a little group of men and women were gathered before the Soviet headquarters, with a sheaf of gold-lettered red banners, and the dull red—like blood—of the coffins they carried. These were rude boxes, made of unplaned wood and daubed with crimson, borne high on the shoulders of rough men who marched with tears streaming down their faces, and followed by women who sobbed and screamed, or walked stiffly, with white, dead faces. Some of the coffins were open, the lid carried behind them; others were covered with gilded or silvered cloth, or had a soldier's hat nailed on the top. There were many wreaths of hideous artificial flowers.

All the long day the funeral procession passed, coming in by the Iberian Gate and leaving the square by way of the Nikolskaya, a river of red banners, bearing words of hope and brotherhood and stupendous prophecies, against a background of fifty thousand people—under the eyes of the world's workers and their descendants for ever...

John Reed, Ten Days That Shook the World

belfry in 1600 by Boris Godunov. This was once the tallest structure (243 feet, 81 meters) in Moscow and was used as a belfry, church and watchtower. When the enemy was sighted, the bells signaled a warning. A small exhibition hall is on the ground floor of the belfry.

CATHEDRAL OF THE ASSUMPTION

In front of the bell tower stands the Kremlin's main church, the **Assumption Cathedral** or **Uspensky Sobor**. It faces the center of Cathedral Square, the oldest square in Moscow, built in the early 14th century. In 1475, Ivan the Great chose the Italian architect Aristotile Fioravante to design the church. He modeled it on the Cathedral of the Assumption in Vladimir.

This church, also known as the Cathedral of the Dormition of the Virgin, was built on the site of a stone church by the same name, first constructed by Ivan I. For two centuries, this national shrine stood as a model for all Russian church architecture. Within its walls, czars were coronated and patriarchs crowned. It also served as the burial place for Moscow metropolitans and patriarchs.

Combining Italian Renaissance and Byzantine traditions, the cathedral is built from white limestone and brick with *zakomara* rounded arches, narrow-windowed drums and five gilded onion domes. The ornamental doorways are covered with frescoes painted on sheet copper; the southern entrance is especially interesting, decorated with 20 biblical scenes in gold and black lacquer.

The spacious interior, lit by 12 chandeliers, is covered with exquisite frescoes and icons that date back to 1481. The artists, Dionysius, Timofei, Yarets and Kon, wove together the themes of heaven and the unity of Russia's principalities, symbolizing the 'Third Rome.' Some of these can still be seen over the altar screen. The northern and southern walls depict the life of the Blessed Virgin. In 1642, more than 100 masters spent a year repainting the church, following the designs of the older wall paintings. These 17th-century frescoes were restored after the Revolution. The elaborate **iconostasis** (altar screen) dates from 1652. Its upper rows were painted by monks from the Trinity-Sergius Monastery in Sergiyev Posad in the late 1600s. The silver frames were added in 1881. To the right of the royal gates are two 12th-century icons from Novgorod: St George and the Saviour Enthroned. A 15th-century copy of the country's protectress, the Virgin of Vladimir, also lies to the left. The original (in the Tretyakov Gallery) was brought to Moscow from Vladimir in 1395 by Vasily I. The icons, Saviour of the Fiery Eye, the Trinity and the Dormition of the Virgin, were specially commissioned for the cathedral in the 14th and 15th centuries. Napoleon's armies used some of the icons as firewood and tried to carry off tons of gold and silver. Most of it was recovered—the central chandelier, Harvest, was cast from silver recaptured from the retreating troops.

Two Persian War masks from the 16th century (above); a pair of decorative breastplates (below)

The Metropolitan Peter (co-founder of the cathedral) and his successor are buried in the southern chapel. The 15th-century fresco *Forty Martyrs of Sebaste* separates the chapel from the main altar. Other metropolitans and patriarchs are buried along the northern and southern walls and in underground crypts. Metropolitan Iov is buried in a special mausoleum, above which hangs the icon of Metropolitan Peter, the first Moscow metropolitan. The gilded sarcophagus of Patriarch Hermogenes (1606–12) stands in the southwest corner covered by a small canopy. During the Polish invasion, Hermogenes was imprisoned and starved to death. After Patriarch Adrian, Peter the Great abolished the position and established the Holy Synod. The Patriarch seat remained vacant until 1917. In 1991, Patriarch Alexei was voted in by church elections. Only after 1991 was the Russian Orthodox Church, headed by the Patriarch, allowed to govern itself again.

Ivan the Terrible's carved wooden throne stands to the left of the southern entrance. Made in 1551, it is known as the Throne of the Monomakhs. It is elaborately decorated with carvings representing the transfer of imperial power from the Byzantine Emperor Monomakus to the Grand-Prince Vladimir Monomakh (1113–25), who married the emperor's sister. The Patriarch's throne can be found by the southeast pier; the clergy sat upon the elevated stone that is decorated with carved flowers. The *Last Judgment* is painted over the western portal. Traditionally, the congregation exited through the church's western door. The final theme portrayed was the Last Judgment as a reminder to people to work on salvation in the outside world. The cathedral is closed on Thursdays.

CHURCH OF THE DEPOSITION OF THE ROBE

Next to the Assumption Cathedral is the smaller single-domed **Church of the Deposition of the Virgin's Robe**, built by Pskov craftsmen from 1484 to 1485. It once served as the private chapel of the patriarch and was linked by a small bridge to his palace. It later became a court chapel in 1653. The iconostasis was executed by Nazari Istomin in 1627. The interior wall paintings are devoted to the Blessed Virgin. The northern gallery displays an exhibition of wooden handicrafts. It is closed on Thursdays.

TEREM PALACE

In the small courtyard next to the church are the **Terem Palace** and the **Golden Palace of the Czarina**, which served as the reception site for czarinas in the 16th century. The Terem Palace resembles a fairy-tale creation with its checkerboard roof and 11 golden turrets. It housed the children and female relatives of noblewomen, and was built for Czar Mikhail Romanov, whose private chambers on the fourth floor were later occupied by his son Alexei. Many State functions took place here and in the Hall of the Cross. The czar received petitions from the population in the Golden Throne Room. Only the czar's wife, personal confessor and blind storytellers were allowed into the private chapel and Royal Bedchamber, which is whimsically decorated. All the chapels of the Terem were united under one roof in 1681, including the churches of the Resurrection, Crucification, Saviour and St Catherine. The adjoining Golden Palace of the Czarina was built in 1526 by Boris Godunov for his sister Irina, who was married to Czar Fedor I. This was her own private reception hall. When Fedor died, Irina refused the throne (the last son of Ivan the Terrible had died earlier in an epileptic attack); her brother, Boris Godunov, became the first elected czar. Admission to the Terem is by special permission only.

PALACE OF FACETS

Facing the bell tower is the two-story Renaissance-style **Palace of Facets**, one of Moscow's oldest civic buildings, constructed by Ruffo and Solario between 1487 and 1491. It took its name from the elaborate stone facets decorating its exterior. State assemblies and receptions were held here—Ivan the Terrible celebrated his victory over Kazan in 1532 in this palace, and Peter the Great celebrated here after defeating the Swedes at Poltava in 1709. After Ivan III, all wives, including the crowned czarinas, were barred from attending State ceremonies and receptions in the Hall of Facets; a small look-out room was built above the western wall, from which the women could secretly watch the proceedings. Today the Hall is used for State occasions. Entrance to the Palace of Facets is by special permission only.

CATHEDRAL OF THE ANNUNCIATION

This white-stone cathedral, with its nine gilded domes, stands next to the palace. It was built from 1485 to 1489 by Pskov craftsmen as the private chapel of the czars. After a fire in 1547, Ivan the Terrible rebuilt the cathedral with four additional chapels. Inside, frescoes that date back to 1508 were painted by Theodosius; many were restored in the 1960s. The iconostasis contains icons by Andrei Rublev, Theophanes the Greek and Prokhor of Gorodets, painted in 1405. Portraits of princes, Greek philosophers and poets, such as Plato, Aristotle and Virgil, can be found on the pillars and in the galleries. It is closed on Thursdays.

ARCHANGEL CATHEDRAL

The third main cathedral of the Kremlin is the five-domed **Cathedral of the Archangel** (1505–08), which served as the burial place of the czars. It stands directly across from the Annunciation Cathedral. Ivan the Great commissioned the Italian architect Alevisio Novi to rebuild the church that stood here. Novi combined the styles of Old Russian and Italian Renaissance; notice the traits of a Venetian palazzo. The surviving

(following pages) The Assumption Cathedral

frescoes date from 1652 and depict aspects of Russian life. A large iconostasis (1680) is filled with 15th- to 17th-century icons, including the *Archangel Michael*, by Rublev. Nearly 50 sarcophagi line the walls of the cathedral, containing grand-princes and czars and some of their sons. White tombstones give their names in Old Slavonic. The first grand-prince to be buried here was Ivan I in 1341, who built the original church. After Peter the Great moved the capital to St Petersburg, the czars were buried in the Peter and Paul Fortress, except for Peter II, who died in Moscow. It is closed on Thursdays.

Behind the cathedral stands **Peter's Tower**, named after the first Moscow Metropolitan. The fourth unadorned tower from the corner is the **Tainitskaya** (Secret) Tower, which had an underground passage to the Moskva River. The next one over is the **Annunciation Tower**, which contained the Annunciation Icon. The round corner tower is called the **Vodovzvodnaya**, the Water-Drawing Tower (1633), in which water was raised from the river to an aqueduct that led inside. This is Russia's first pressurized system; it was used for pumping water to the Royal palaces and gardens.

GRAND KREMLIN PALACE

Built from 1838 to 1849, the **Grand Palace**, behind the Archangel Cathedral, was the Moscow residence of the Imperial family. Nicholas I commissioned Konstantin Thon to erect it on the site of the former Grand-Prince Palace. There are 700 rooms and five elaborate reception halls; two of these, along the southern wall overlooking the river, were combined to form the Meeting Hall of the Russian Federation. The long gold and white St George Hall has 18 columns decorated with statues of victory. The walls are lined with marble plaques bearing the names of heroes awarded the Order of St George (introduced by Catherine the Great) for service and courage. The six bronze chandeliers hold over 3,000 light bulbs.

This hall is now used for special State receptions and ceremonies; cosmonaut Yuri Gagarin received the Golden Star Hero Award here in 1961. The Hall of St Catherine served as the Empress' Throne Room. The Hall of Vladimir connected the Palace of Facets, the Golden Palace of the Czarina and the Terem Palace. The ground-floor rooms used to contain the Imperial family's bedchambers. Entrance is by special permission only.

AMUSEMENT PALACE

The **Poteshny** (Amusement) **Palace**, situated behind the Grand Palace and the Cammandent's Tower, was built in 1652 by Czar Alexis as the residence of his father-in-law. After he died, Alexis turned the palace into a theater.

ARMORY PALACE

The **Oruzheinaya Palata** (Armory Palace) is the oldest museum in the country. In 1485, Grand-Prince Vasily III, son of Ivan the Great, constructed a special stone building on the edge of the Kremlin grounds to house the royal family's growing collection of valuables. It also contained the czar's workshops and a place to store armor and weapons. In the late 1600s, Peter the Great converted it into a museum to house the art treasures of the Kremlin. The present building, designed in 1651 by Konstantin Thon, has nine exhibition halls that trace the history of the Kremlin and the Russian State. It also houses a magnificent collection of Western European decorative and applied art from the 12th to 19th centuries.

Hall I (Halls I–IV are on the first floor) exhibits armor and weaponry from the 13th to 18th centuries. Hall II has displays of gold and silver from the 12th to 17th centuries, including jewelry, chalices (one belonging to Yuri Dolgoruky), bowls and watches. Hall III contains gold and silver jewelry from the 18th to 20th centuries, including snuff boxes and the fabulous Fabergé eggs. Hall IV has a collection of vestments, including a robe of the first Metropolitan Peter, Peter the Great, and a coronation robe of Catherine the Great. One robe presented to the Metropolitan by Catherine contains over 150,000 semi-precious stones.

Hall V (Halls V–IX are on the ground floor) exhibits many of the foreign gifts of silver and gold from the 13th to 19th centuries from England, France, Sweden, Holland and Poland. Hall VI is known as the Throne and Crown Room. The oldest throne belonged to Ivan the Terrible. A Persian Shah presented Boris Godunov with a throne encrusted with 2,000 precious stones in 1604, and the throne of Czar Alexei Romanov contains over 1,000 diamonds. The most interesting is the Double Throne used by Peter the Great and his half-brother Ivan, when they were proclaimed joint czars. Peter's older half-sister, Sophia, acted as Regent and used to sit in a secret compartment in the throne behind Peter to advise him. The Crown of Monomakh (first worn by Grand Prince Vladimir Monomakh in 1113) was used by all grand-princes and czars until Peter the Great. The room also contains gowns and jewelry. Halls VII and VIII contain saddles, bridles and sleigh covers. Hall IX is the Carriage Room, containing the world's largest collection of carriages dating back to Boris Godunov. The most elaborate is the coronation coach made for the Empress Elizabeth. The Diamond Fund Exhibit is a collection of the crown jewels and precious gems. These include the Orlov Diamond (189 carats) that Count Orlov bought for his mistress, Catherine the Great. Catherine the Great's coronation crown is covered with pearls and 4,936 diamonds. (This section is opened with special permission.) A new section of the Armory displays gifts to the former USSR from foreign countries.

(above) Terem Palace interior, (opposite) Tomb cover dating from 1630

The Armory is one of the most interesting museums in Moscow and should definitely be visited. The Intourist Service Desk can book a tour. Only group tours are permitted. These are usually conducted daily, except Thursdays and Fridays, at 09:00, 11:00, 14:30 and 16:30 in English. Check, for these times often change.

The Armory Tower is behind the Armory Palace. One can exit through the Borovitskaya Tower (1490). (Kremlin Hill was originally called Borovitskaya. *Bor* in Old Russian means a thick forest.) This gate used to be the service entrance to the Kremlin.

Old Moscow

The area to the east of the Kremlin is known as **Kitai-gorod**. *Kitai* is derived from either the Mongolian word for central or the Old Russian *kiti* meaning bundle of stakes. These protective palisades surrounded the area. (One small fragment remaining from the original 16th-century wall is near the northern entrance of the Rossiya Hotel.) *Gorod* is the Russian word for town. (In modern Russian, *Kitai* means China. Foreign settlements were later established in this area.) In the 14th century, the central town was surrounded by a protective earthen rampart and served as the central *posad*, market and trade area, where merchants and townspeople lived. Beyond the rampart lay the forest. Later, Ivan the Terrible constructed a larger fortified stone wall. The original area of Kitai-gorod (which formed Moscow's second ring) stretched in the form of a horseshoe from the History Museum on Red Square, along the back of GUM Department Store, and east down to what is now the Hotel Rossiya and the banks of the Moskva River. On each side of GUM are the small streets of Nikolskaya and Ilyinka. The Rossiya Hotel (behind St Basil's) is bordered by Varvarka Street and Kitaisky Prospekt.

The *Iversky Vorota*, Iversky Gates, used to serve as the main entrance to Red Square. The Chapel of the Iverian Mother of God stood above the gates. The chapel held the Virgin of Iver icon, said to possess mystical powers. The gates were also the access route from *Kitai-gorod*, China Town, to the *Byeli-gorod*, White Town. Upon setting out on long journies, Muscovites also stopped to pray here. Both the chapel and the gates were pulled down after the Revolution to allow larger masses of people and machinery to enter Red Square. At one point, the square was almost renamed the Square of Proletarian Parades.

NIKOLSKAYA STREET

This street begins at the northeastern corner of Red Square and runs along the left side of GUM. After the Revolution until 1991, its name was 25th of October Street, commemorating the first day of the 1917 Revolution. In the l7th century, the area was nicknamed the Street of Enlightenment; Moscow's first learning academy, printing yard and bookshops lined the passage. The street was originally named after the nearby Nikolsky Monastery.

The first corner building, as you leave the square, was the **Governor's Office**, where the writer Alexander Radishchev was held before his exile to Siberia (by Catherine the Great) in 1790. His book, *A Journey from St Petersburg to Moscow*, described the terrible conditions of serfdom. The **Old Royal Mint** stands inside the small courtyard. An inscription on the gates shows that Peter the Great built the mint in 1697. When he later moved it to St Petersburg, the vice-governor had his office here.

Kazansky Cathedral once stood on the corner opposite GUM. To celebrate the expulsion of Polish forces in Moscow, Prince Pozharsky paid for the cathedral to be built in 1612; a statue of him stands in front of St Basil's. Pozharsky had walked back to Moscow from Poland carrying his icon, Our Lady of Kazan. In 1932, Stalin had the cathedral torn down and replaced the site with kiosks and public toilets. Today, the cathedral is being reconstructed and a donation box stands in front.

Across the street from the Royal Mint are several buildings that remain from the **Zaikonospassky Monastery**, founded by Boris Godunov in the early 1600s. The name means 'Icon of our Saviour;' the monastery used to make and sell icons. The red and white **Saviour's Church** was built in 1661. The church and adjoining buildings housed the **Slavic-Greek-Latin Academy**, Moscow's first and largest academy for higher education, which operated from 1687 to 1814. Among the first students were the poet Kantemir, the architect Bazhenov and Mikhail Lomonsov (1711–65), who became a renowned poet, historian and educator. Known as the 'Father of Russian Science,' Lomonsov established Moscow University under Empress Elizabeth in l755.

At number 15 was the **first Printing Yard**, now the History and Archives Institute. Ivan the Terrible brought the first printing press to Russia in 1553. Still hanging on the green building are the emblems of the old printing yard, a lion and unicorn, together with a sundial, mounted in 1814. The thick black gates lead to the colorfully tiled **Building of the Old Proofreader**, where Ivan Fedorov spent a year printing Russia's first book. Ivan the Terrible visited Fedorov daily until *The Acts of the Apostles* (now in the State Public Library) was completed on March 1, l564. The first Russian newspaper,*Vedomosti*, was printed here in 1703. The present building was constructed in 1814 and was used as the printing center for the Holy Synod, the council established by Peter the Great that regulated church affairs.

At number 19 is the **Slavyansky Bazaar**, one of Moscow's oldest and most popular restaurants. When it opened in the 1870s, it became a popular meeting place for Moscow merchants who negotiated deals over the delicious *blini* pancakes. It was

FABERGÉ

In 1842, during the reign of Nicholas I, Gustav Fabergé founded the first Fabergé workshop in St Petersburg. His son, Peter Carl, later extended the French family business to the cities of Moscow, Kiev, Odessa and London. These workshops produced a wealth of exquisite jewelry, clocks, cut glass, and other decorative objects made from gold, silver and semi-precious stones.

For over a century, Fabergé crafted unique art objects for the Imperial Court. Master craftsmen like Mikhail Perkhin, Erik Kollin, Henrik Wigström and Julius Rappoport had their own Fabergé workshops and sometimes spent years designing and crafting a single piece of art.

The fabulous Fabergé eggs were a favorite gift presented by the Romanov family and other members of the aristocracy. The first Fabergé Easter egg was commissioned in 1885 by Alexander III. When Carl Fabergé proposed creating an Easter gift for the Empress Maria Feodorovna, the Czar ordered an egg containing a special surprise. On Easter morning, the Empress broke open what appeared to be an ordinary egg, but inside, a gold yolk contained a solid gold chicken with a replica of the Imperial Crown. The Empress was so delighted by the egg that the Czar ordered one to be delivered to the Court each Easter. Alexander's son, Nicholas II, continued the Fabergé tradition and ordered two eggs each Easter, one each for his wife and mother.

On Easter morning 1895, Nicholas gave his mother a Fabergé egg decorated with diamonds, emeralds and a star sapphire. Hand painted miniatures depicting Danish scenes, known by the Dowager Empress (the former Princess Dagmar of Denmark), were hidden inside what became known as the Danish Egg. In 1900 Fabergé presented the Imperial Family with an egg that contained a golden replica of the Trans-Siberian railroad; the train actually moved and could be wound up with a tiny golden key. The 1908 Easter egg had a portrait of Nicholas II on its surface with a model of Alexander I's palace inside. Other eggs contained flowers (that bloomed by pressing a tiny button) and a model boat.

By the time of the Revolution, Fabergé had created over 50 eggs. When the Russian Exhibition was held in Moscow in 1882, Carl Fabergé received the Gold Medal; later in 1900 at the Exposition Universelle in Paris, he won the Grand Prix award along with the Legion of Honor. Today one of the most extensive Fabergé collections in the world can be seen at the Armory Museum in the Moscow Kremlin.

A jeweled enameled egg, a gift from Czar Nicholas II to his wife Alexandra, 1913 here on June 21, 1877, that the stage directors Konstantin Stanislavsky and Vladimir Nemirovich-Danchencko worked out the details for the formation of the Moscow Art Theater over an 18-hour lunch.

Opposite the Printing House is the former **Chizhov Coach Exchange**. The Chizhov family hired out horse-drawn carriages and carts as taxis. The Coach Exchange was popular year-round, when Moscow streets were either muddy or frozen. In winter, Muscovites could hire a Chizhov *troika*, sled. Next door is the one-domed **Church of the Dormition**.

The small passage known as **Tretyakov Proezd** links **Nikolskaya Street** with **Okhotny Ryad**. The wealthy merchant Sergei Tretyakov knocked a passage through the Kitai-gorod wall in 1871 to gain quick access to the banks along Okhotny Ryad.

Nikolskaya Street leads to Lubyanka Square where it turns into Myasnitskaya Street, which runs east to the Leningradsky (St Petersburg) and Yaroslavky train stations and Sokolniki Park.

Halfway down Nikolskaya Street, take a right on **Ilyinka Proyezd**. Near the corner stands the red baroque 17th-century **Cathedral of Bogoyavlensky** (Epiphany), once part of a monastery established in the 13th century by Prince Daniil. The cathedral stands on the site of Moscow's first stone church, built by Ivan I. Many of the sculptures that were in the church are now on display in the Donskoi Monastery. The wealthy Boyar Golitsyn family had their burial vaults here until the mid-18th century; they were switched to the Donskoi Monastery outside of the city when a cholera epidemic prohibited burial in the city center.

The Pharmacy Shop at number 21 is over a century old. The first pharmacy was set up in the Kremlin by Ivan the Terrible in 1581. Beginning in the 1600s, pharmacies sold medicinal herbs in Moscow. Many of the herbs were grown in the area of what is now the Alexandrov Gardens near the Kremlin.

In the small park stands the **Monument to Ivan Fedorov** (1510–83), the first Russian printer. The passage is still lined with small bookshops; a popular one is Knizhnaya Nakhodka.

ILYINKA STREET

Ilyinka Passage leads into this street, which begins on Red Square and continues past the right side of GUM. It was once the main thoroughfare of Kitai-gorod. In 1497, Ivan the Great gave a parcel of land on this street to 500 Novgorod merchant families to establish the Moscow-Novgorod Trade Exchange, at a time when Novgorod was still independent of Moscovy. The wealthy merchants erected **St Ilyia Church**, recognizable by its single dome and *zakomara* gabled arches. From 1935 to 1991 this street was named after the popular revolutionary figure Kuibyshev. The passage was once the busy thoroughfare of Moscow's bank and financial district. The classical building of the **Moscow Stock Exchange** (1875), with its large Ionic columns, once again bustles with commercial activity.

The wealthy merchant Pavel Riabushinsky commissioned Fedor Shekhtel to build the Riabushinsky Bank in 1904. Shekhtel also designed the nearby Moscow Merchants Building in 1909. Riabushinsky was a highly respected spokesman for the merchant class and chairman of the Moscow Stock Exchange.

As Ilyinka Passage continues past the street of the same name, it turns into Ribny Pereulok, Fish Lane, where many food stalls were once set up. From 1795 to 1805, the Italian architect Quarenghi built the **Old Merchant Arcade**, *Gostiny Dvor*, which occupied an entire block. This Corinthian-columned white structure was once filled with boutiques; it is now an office building.

Varvarka Street

Ribny Pereulok leads into **Ulitsa Varvarka**, which starts near St Basil's and continues past the Rossiya Hotel. Near the hotel are the remains of the 16th-century brick rampart walls that surrounded Kitai-gorod; this wall was over 2,500 meters long and six meters high. After the Revolution until 1991, the street was known as Razin, named after Stenka Razin, a popular Cossack rebel who was executed in Red Square in 1671.

The immense structure behind St Basil's is the **Rossiya Hotel**, completed in 1967 by the architect Chechulin. The hotel is the largest in the world, with rooms for 6,000 people and a superb view of the Kremlin and the district on the other side of the Moskva River. One of Moscow's largest *Beriozkas* is located at the back of the hotel. It also has many cafés and restaurants, the large Central Concert Hall and the Zariadi Cinema. In old Russian, *zariadi* meant beyond the trading stalls. This area used to lie beyond the old marketplace on the outer fringes of Red Square.

The salmon and white **Church of St Varvara** (Barbara) stands at the beginning of the street, which is named after this saint. The 16th-century church was rebuilt in the 18th-century by the architect Matvei Kazakov. It now houses a branch of the All Russia Society for the Protection of Monuments. This passage once stretched from the Kremlin, along the old trade route, to the towns of Vladimir and Kolomna. Prince Dmitri Donskoi used this route to return home after his victorious battle with the Mongols in the Battle of Kulikovo in 1380.

The small cube-shaped and five-domed **Church of St Maximus** stands nearby. Built in 1698 by Novgorod merchants, it held the remains of St Maximus, an ascetic prophet who died in 1433. It now houses a branch of the Society for Environmental Protection.

Between these two churches, at number 4 Varvarka, is the **Old English Inn**, a white-washed house with tiny irregularly placed windows and a steep wooden roof. It originally belonged to a wealthy Russian merchant until, in 1556, Ivan the Terrible presented it to Sir Richard Chancellor, an English merchant who began trade relationships with Russia. Ivan even proposed marriage to Queen Elizabeth I, but she declined and instead offered Ivan asylum in England whenever he might need it. Later the inn was used by English merchants for their stores and living quarters, and English diplomats also stayed here. It has recently been restored and houses findings from local archaeological digs.

Next to the Inn is the **House of Boyars Romanov**, now a branch of the State History Museum that has displays of life from 17th-century Boyardom. The rich Boyar, Nikita Romanov, had his home in the center of Kitai-gorod. Nikita's sister, Anatasia, was married to Ivan the Terrible. Nikita's grandson, Mikhail, who was born in the house, was later elected to the throne in 1613 and began the reign of the Romanov Dynasty. The house was restored in the l9th century and is furnished to look like an early noble household. It is open from 10:00 to 18:00, and is closed on Tuesdays and the first Monday of each month.

At the back of the Rossiya Hotel is the **Church of St George on Pskov Hill**. The colorful church, with red walls and a blue belfry (1818), was erected by Pskov merchants in 1657. At number 8 is the former Cathedral of the Znamensky Monastery, now a concert hall with 250 seats.

On the other side of the Rossiya Hotel, on Kitaisky Proezd by the Moskva River, is the **Church of the Conception of St Anne in the Corner**. The church stood at the corner of the Kitai-gorod wall and was named after the Virgin's mother, St Anne. The barren wife of Prince Vasily III, Solomonia (whom he later divorced), often prayed here.

KITAI-GOROD SQUARE

Varvarka Street leads north into **Kitai-gorod Square** (which has a Metro stop of the same name). Kitai-gorod, China Town, is where the foreign merchants used to live. Following the Bolshevik Revolution, the area was known as Nogin Square, after the revolutionary figure Viktor Nogin. In 1991, it reverted to its original name. The **Church of All Saints on Kulishki** stands here.

After Prince Dmitri Donskoi defeated the Mongols at Kulikovo in 1380, he erected a wooden church on the *kulishki*, marshy land. It was replaced by the stone church in the l6th century, which has been restored. To the left of the church are the gray buildings of the **Delovoy Dvor**, the business chambers. Built in 1913, they were used for the business operations of the city.

Near the square are the **Ilyinsky Gardens**, with a Monument to the Russian Grenadiers who died in the Battle of Plevna against Turkey in 1877. Along the small side street called Staraya (Old) Prospekt, are buildings that were once used by the Central Committee of the Communist Party. A few minutes' walk away is a 'jewel of merchant architecture,' the five-domed **Church of the Holy Trinity in Nikitniki**. In

1620, Mikhail Romanov hired a wealthy merchant from Yaroslavl, Grigory Nikinikov, to work in the financial administration. Nikinikov named the street after himself and later built this church on the site of the wooden Church of St Nikita (his family saint), which burned down. The oldest icon is St Nikita, which Nikinikov supposedly rescued from the burning church. The icon of the Trinity can be found on the iconostasis, carved in 1640. The burial chapel of the Nikinikovs lies to the right of the altar. To the left, Staraya Prospekt turns into Novaya (New) Prospekt. In the other direction, Staraya Prospekt becomes Solyanka Street. *Sol* means salt, and the old saltyards were along this street in the 17th century. At the time, this area was considered the countryside of Moscow; Ivan the Great had a summer palace near the Convent of St John. Farther up the street is the **Church of St Vladimir in the Old Gardens**. Solyanka intersects with Arkhipov Street, named after the artist, who lived here in 1900. Many middle-class artisans lived in this part of the city. On this street, at number 8, is the **Moscow Synagogue**.

Around the corner, at 6 Furmanny Street, is the **Vasnetsov Museum**, where the artist lived and worked from 1903 to 1933. The museum, which opened in 1965, displays his paintings, drawings, watercolors, sketches and lithographs. It is closed on Mondays and Tuesdays. Another Vasnetsov Museum is located at 13 Vasnetsov Lane (closed Mondays).

The Old Marx Prospekt

In 1991, Prospekt Marxa, the city's busiest avenue, was officially divided into three different streets. From Lubyanka to Teatralnaya Squares, is **Teatralny Proyezd** (past the Bolshoi Theater). From Teatralnaya Square to Pushkinskaya Street is **Okhotny Ryad** (which leads from the Bolshoi Theater to Tverskaya Street and the National Hotel). The rest of the thoroughfare from the Kremlin to Herzen Street is now known as **Mokhovaya Street**.

LUBYANKA SQUARE

Teatralny Proyezd, Theater Passage, begins at this square, where a bronze statue of Felix Dzerzhinsky (1877–1926), a prominent revolutionary leader and founder of the Cheka (the All Russia Extraordinary Commission for Combating Counter-Revolution, Sabotage and Speculation), once stood in the center (earlier called Dzerzhinsky Square). The statue was pulled down after the August 1991 attempted coup. (It now stands in the Park of the Fallen Heroes on the grounds of the State Art Gallery near Gorky Park.) Various graffiti, coup memorabilia and an occasional Orthodox cross decorate the pedestal, which now commemorates all those killed by the KGB. In 1991, the square was given back its historical name of Lubyanka. In the 15th-century, new settlers from Novgorod named the area Lubyanitsa, after a place in their native city.

The Metro station Lubyanka (formerly Dzerzhinskaya) exits on to the square. The large department store on one corner is **Detsky Mir** (Children's World), the largest children's store in Russia. More than half a million shoppers visit daily. Behind it is the Savoy Hotel, and in front are the old KGB Headquarters. A huge local market used to stretch around Detsky Mir, but it has recently been restricted. Dzerzhinsky Street has been renamed Bolshaya Lubyanka.

Standing on the right side of **Lubyanka Square** is the infamous former **KGB Building**, constructed in the early 1900s as the headquarters of the Russian Insurance Firm. It was built on the site of the Royal Secret Dispatch Office, where a dreadful prison was kept in the cellars during the reign of Catherine the Great. After the Revolution, Dzerzhinsky took the building over to house his Cheka police. In the 1930s the building was reconstructed; a new façade was erected, two floors were added and a massive underground prison complex, known as the Lubyanka, was built in the original cellars. In 1954, after the fall of Beria, Krushchev founded the Committee for State Security—the KGB—to establish party control over the secret police after Stalin. When the Communist Party was banned, the KGB tried to improve its image and even held a Ms KGB contest.

With the fall of the Communist government, the organization of the KGB was disbanded; it was split into the Foreign Intelligence Service (SVRR) and the Federal Counterintelligence Service (SVR). The SVRR now handles all intelligence gathering outside of Russia, including the former Soviet republics. Both divisions handle counter-terrorism, illegal arms sales, drug trafficking and smuggling of radioactive materials. It is also now forbidden to use substances (such as poisoned umbrella tips) that could damage human health or to blackmail people into cooperation. After the 1991 attempted coup against Gorbachev, many of the KGB leaders were purged and the agency was turned into the Russian Security Ministry. In December 1991, shortly after his takeover as President, Yeltsin abolished the Security Ministry and split its functions between the two existing agencies. In his decree, Yeltsin harshly spelled out every acronym that the secret police has used since the Bolshevik Revolution: 'The system of the organs of the VChk-OGPU-NKVD-MGB-KGB-MB turned out to be unreformable.'

Today, the two agencies are paralyzed with budget crises, massive reorganizations, a 30 per cent staff cut, and a severe and disorienting change in mission since the end of the Cold War. A paper shortage in the country is even forcing agents to type reports on the back of old documents; many offices still do not have computers

and people are forced to share typewriters. It is now not only difficult to recruit foreigners as (secret) Russian agents, but native Russians as well. The goal of building Communism and the Great Motherland has been usurped by capitalist ideology, and the brightest no longer consider it prestigious to work for intelligence: Registration at the Andropov Red Banner Institute, which trains intelligence recruits, has dropped by more than 75 per cent. The site of the building itself has been the location of nearly 250 years of espionage activity.

Three interesting museums also border the square. The **Mayakovsky Museum** is on the corner of Myasnitskaya (formerly Kirov) Street and 3/6 Serov Passage. The poet lived here for over a decade and committed suicide here in April 1930; many of his works and personal items are on display. Films of Mayakovsky are also shown, along with recordings of him reading his work. The museum is open from 10:00 to 18:00 and is closed on Wednesdays. Check before you go, the museum is sometimes closed for exposition changes.

At 12 Novaya (New) Square Street is the **Museum of the History and Reconstruction of Moscow**, which was founded in 1896. Since 1939, it has been housed in the Church of St John the Divine 'Under the Elm,' built in 1825. It is open daily from 10:00 to 18:00 except Mondays and the last day of each month. Next to it, at 3/4 Novaya Square Street, is the **Polytechnical Museum**; opened in 1872, it was one of Moscow's first museums. The current building, completed in 1907, has 60 halls containing over 100,000 exhibits that trace the history of Russian science and technology.

In the basement is a fabulous collection of old Russian automobiles; the first Russian car was the Pobeda (Victory), manufactured after World War II. Henry Ford also exported his cars to Moscow (through Armand Hammer) until Lenin's death in 1924.

On the top floor is an interesting collection of Russian space capsules and an exhibition on the life of the first Soviet cosmonaut Yuri Gagarin. The library has over three million volumes.

The Polytechnical building was also a popular center for local meetings; writers such as Akhmatova, Gorky and Mayakovsky gave readings here, and Lenin often presented lectures. In 1967, the longest telepathic experiment in history took place between the museum and Leningrad. The sender, Yuri Kamensky, sent telepathic messages from here to the the psychic receiver Karl Nikolayev at Leningrad University. From the 1950s until the 1980s, the Soviets vigorously studied parapsychology and aspects of psychic warfare. The museum is open from 10:00 to 18:00, closed Mondays and the last Thursday of each month. The Statue of Ivan Fyodorov, the first Russian printer, stands a few minutes walk away along the prospekt.

Protestors from the Ukraine in the Arbat, Moscow

TEATRALNY SQUARE

The next section of the old Prospekt Marxa opens on **Ploshchad Teatralnovo,** Theater Square. Until 1991, it was known as Sverdlov Square, after the first President of Soviet Russia, Yakov Sverdlov (1885–1919). The statue of Sverdlov, like that of Dzerzhinsky, now stands in the Park of the Fallen Heroes near Gorky Park. From Theater Square to Red Square, Prospekt Marxa is now known as Okhotny Ryad, Hunter's Row (the passage once led to the countryside and a popular hunting ground). The statue of Karl Marx, inscribed with the words 'Workers of All Countries Unite!' marks the square's center. The Metro stop is Teatralnaya.

On a corner is one of Moscow's finest and most expensive hotels, the **Metropole Hotel,** built in 1903 and magnificently renovated. The mosaic panels on the front were designed by the Russian artist Mikhail Vrubel. Rasputin once had his headquarters here, and entrance plaques honor events of the Revolution. Next door to the hotel is a fascinating antique stop. Facing the hotel to the right are walls of the 16th-century Kitai-gorod.

Up until 1919, this area was known as Theater Square, because two of Moscow's most prominent theaters were built here, the Bolshoi (Big) and the Maly (Small). One of the world's most famous theaters, the **Bolshoi** was built in 1824 by Osip Bovet and Alexander Mikhailov to stage performances of ballet and opera. It was constructed on the original site of the Royal Peter Theater. After a fire in 1856, the Bolshoi was rebuilt by Albert Kavos to coincide with Alexander II's coronation. The stately building, with its large fountain in front, is crowned by the famous four bronze horses pulling the chariot of Apollo, patron of the arts. This is the work of sculptor Pyotr Klodt. The theater's gorgeous interior boasts five tiers of gilded boxes, whose chairs are covered with plush red velvet. The chandelier is made from 13,000 pieces of cut glass. The theater premiered compositions by Tchaikovsky, Glinka, Mussorgsky and Rimsky-Korsakov. After *perestroika,* it even premiered the Orthodox Church's the *Millennium of the Baptism of Rus.* Inquire at your hotel service bureau for tickets to Bolshoi performances.

Opposite the Bolshoi is the light yellow **Maly Drama Theater.** At its entrance stands the statue of Alexander Ostrovsky (1823–86), the outstanding Russian playwright. The theater is nicknamed the Ostrovsky House. Many classic Russian plays are staged here. On the other side of the Bolshoi is the Central Children's Theater, formed in 1921. Across the street from the Maly is the old *Mostorg,* or Moscow Trade. In 1907, when the building was completed, it housed the English department store Muir and Murrilies.

The other end of the square is flanked by the three-story ornamented brick building of the **Central Lenin Museum** (closed on Mondays and the last Tuesday of each month), which marks the entrance to the old Revolution Square. This building, erected in 1892, once housed the Duma (City Hall) of Moscow. In 1936, its 34 halls were converted into the country's, and world's, largest Lenin museum, displaying nearly a million items associated with the revolutionary leader. After the 1991 attempted coup, there was a movement to close the museum, but it was left open to depict a chapter of Russian history. Opposite the museum is the **Moskva Hotel**. Note that the top left of the building's façade is different from the right. In the 1930s, when the architect designed two different fronts for the hotel, he asked Stalin, 'Which one do you like best?' 'Yes,' replied Stalin. Afraid to question the Soviet leader again, the architect built the structure with both designs. On the ground floor of the hotel is the popular Spanish Bar and on the top floor is a disco. Around the corner are Lancômb and Penguin ice-cream. The closest Metro is Okhotny Ryad. Before continuing along the avenue to the main square, some old and interesting side streets off Theater Square merit exploration.

PETROVKA STREET

Ulitsa Petrovka is a small side street that begins in front of the Maly Theater. Three centuries ago, the passage was named after the Petrovsky (St Peter) Monastery, which also served as a protective stronghold and entrance to the town. The monastery was built by Prince Dmitri Donskoi to honor the Mongol defeat in the Battle of Kulikovo in 1380. Much of this monastery has been restored. The **Museum of Literature** (open Tuesday to Saturday, 11:00 to 18:00), located at number 28, traces the history of Russian literature. This neighborhood, once the residence of Moscow's coachmakers, was nicknamed Karetny Ryad, Carriage Row.

The street has long been a popular shopping district with stores selling *podarki* (gifts), *bukinisti* (second-hand books) and *almazi* (diamonds). Next to the Maly is the large central department store, TsUM. The Russikiye Uzory (lace) sells handicrafts, and at number 8 is Chasy, one of Moscow's best watch stores. The Society of World Art had its first exhibition at number 15, displaying the work of Alexander Benois. The writer Anton Chekhov lived at number 19 for many years. The Hermitage Gardens have been here for over a century. The Theater of Miniatures and Maly Concert Hall are located in the gardens.

KUZNETSKY MOST

The poet Vladimir Mayakovsky wrote: 'I love Kuznetsky Most...and then Petrovka.' Petrovka Street leads to Kuznetsky Most, a small lane branching to the right. As far back as the 15th century, the area was the popular residence of Moscow's blacksmiths, who lived along the banks of the Neglinnaya River, which, at the time, flowed through here. Kuznetsky Most means Blacksmith's Bridge.

Almost every building along this steep passage has a fascinating story related to it.

Ballet lessons

It became a highly respected shopping district in the 19th century; items were stamped with 'Bought in Kuznetsky Most.' At number 9 was a restaurant called Yar, which Pushkin and Tolstoy mention in their writings. The Artist Unions have their exhibition halls at number 11. Tolstoy listened to one of the world's first phonographs in the musical shop that was at number 12, and he wrote of Anna Karenina shopping at Gautier's at number 20. The House of Fashion and many airline agencies are also located along this narrow street. At the end is Metro stop Kuznetsky Most.

NEGLINKA STREET

Kuznetsky Most connects with Ulitsa Neglinka, which runs from the old Marx Prospekt to Trubnaya Square on the Boulevard Ring. This street also sprang up alongside the banks of the Neglinnaya River, where many popular shops were located. *Neglinnaya* means without clay. Catherine the Great ordered that the river be diverted underground. In the 19th-century, it was redirected to a larger aqueduct where it flows underground to the Moscow River.

The revolutionary Nikolai Schmit had his furniture store at the corner of Kuznetsky Most. The Moorish-style building of the **Sandunovsky Baths** at number 14 was frequented by Chekhov. This is one of the grandest *banya* in town. The building was bought by the actor Sila Sandunov, who turned it into sauna-baths in the 18th century. The *banya* is still a marbled and gilded extravaganza where one can steam, sweat and swim. Another popular *banya* is the *Tsentralnaya Banya*, the Central Bath-House, located off Okhotny Ryad across from the Metropole Hotel. Also on this street is Moscow's oldest sheet music shop and the Central Bank. At number 29 is the popular Uzbekistan Restaurant.

OKHOTNY RYAD

The continuation of the old Marx Prospekt from Theater Square to the Kremlin is now known as Okhotny Ryad, Hunter's Lane, the name of the old local markets. The main markets of Moscow spread from here to Red Square. Across from the Moskva Hotel is Dom Soyuzov (House of Trade Unions) on the corner of Pushkin and Tverskaya streets. Built in 1784 by Matvei Kazakov, it used to be the Noble's Club. Its Hall of Columns and October Hall hosted social functions. The playwright George Bernard Shaw was honored here on his 75th birthday in 1931. Also past leaders such as Lenin, Stalin and Brezhnev lay in state here before their burials.

Crossing the prospekt via the underpass brings you out in front of the newly renovated **National Hotel.** Built in 1903, it is still one of Moscow's finest hotels.

The Bolshoi Ballet theatre

Lenin stayed in Suite 107, marked by a plaque. Next to the hotel is the Intourist Board of Foreign Tourism; it housed the United States Military Mission during World War II. And next to this is one of the oldest buildings of Moscow University, built between 1786 and 1793 by Kazakov. In the courtyard are two statues of graduates, Nikolai Ogarev and Alexander Herzen.

MOKHOVAYA STREET

From the National Hotel to the end of the prospekt at Borovitskaya Square is Mokhovaya (Moss-Grown) Street. In the center, in Manezhnaya Square, stands the Central Exhibition Hall, which used to be the *manège*, the czar's riding school. It was built in the classical style in 1817 by Augustin Betancourt. Since 1951, Moscow's largest art exhibitions have been shown here. At number 21 is the **Kalinin Museum** (open from 10:00 to 18:00; closed on Mondays), the former mansion of Prince Shakhovsky, built in 1821. Opened on June 30, 1950, the museum traces the life of Party leader Mikhail Kalinin. The statue of Kalinin is in the Park of the Fallen Heroes near Gorky Park.

Mokhovaya ends a few minutes' walk farther down by the **State Public Library** (formerly the Lenin Library), the largest library in Russia with 36 million books. The library orginated in the Rumyantsev House, which the rich aristocrat Pashkov had built in 1786. The mansion had beautiful exotic gardens filled with peacocks that wandered the hills around the Kremlin. In the 18th century, the building housed the famous Rumyantsev collection of books and manuscripts. When Lenin died in 1924, it was renamed the Lenin Library. When the Metro was built in the 1940s, the books were moved into the larger building next door. In 1993, its name was once again changed after extensive restoration. The closest Metro stop is Biblioteka Imeni Lenina.

Across the street, at number 13, is the **Wax Museum**. For a minimum fee, a tour is given. An eclectic group of figures is on display, from Peter the Great and Catherine the Great to Dostoevsky, Stalin, Sakharov and Gorbachev. It is open from 10:00 to 18:00 and is closed on Mondays and Fridays.

PRECHISTENKA STREET

Volkhanka Street begins at the Kremlin's Borovitsky Tower and turns into Prechistenka Ulitsa. The **Pushkin Museum of Fine Arts** is at number 12. The Greek-style building was constructed in 1898 by Roman Klein to house a collection of fine art. It had over 20,000 items on display at its 1912 opening. Today, the museum boasts one of the world's largest collections of ancient, classical, Oriental and Western European art, with over half a million works. Directly behind the Pushkin is the **Marx and Engels Museum** at number 5 Marx and Engels Street. The museum, opened in 1962, is housed in the former 18th-century mansion of the Dolgoruky (whose ancestors founded Moscow). One of the displays is a replica of Karl Marx's study in London. Both museums are open from 11:00 to 18:00 and are closed on Mondays and the last day of each month.

Across from Metro stop Kropotkinskaya, is the heated **Moskva Open-Air Swimming Pool**, which is open year-round. Tickets are bought at the small *kassa* desk next to the main building. Bathing suits, caps and towels can also be rented. Access to the heated pool is gained through a passage from inside the complex. The Cathedral of Christ Our Savior used to stand on the site of the pool. Founded in memory of the Russian victory over Napoleon in 1812, it took 40 years to build, but only one day to destroy. Built by Konstantin Ton, the czar's architect, and opened in 1883, the cathedral's 7,000-person capacity made it Moscow's largest. Seen from miles away, it became one of the city's landmarks, symbolizing the glory of the Russian empire. To perpetuate the glory of the Soviet regime, Stalin decided to build a monumental House of Soviets. The final blueprints of 1934 had the building higher than any American skyscraper at 1,380 feet (420 meters) with a 230-foot (70-meter) statue of Lenin on top. It was to look like an enormous-tiered wedding cake. Stalin selected the cathedral as its site, and then had the building dynamited. Afterwards, it was discovered that the floating bedrock could not support the proposed House of Soviets. In 1959, the pit for the swimming pool was dug on the site of the demolished grounds. It is worth visiting, especially in winter, when semi-naked Russians stand in the mist by the side of the pool and rub snow over their bodies. Other members of the Walrus Club cut ice away and jump into the Moscow River. The complex's observation area provides splendid panoramic views of the Moskva River.

From the Revolution until 1991, the street was called Ulitsa Kropotkinskaya, named after the revolutionary scholar, Pyotr Kropotkin (1842–1921). For centuries, the street was known as Prechistenka (Holy), after the Icon of the Holy Virgin kept in a nearby monastery. Many aristocratic families built their residences along this street. At number 10 lived Count Orlov, a friend of Pushkin's. The mansion now houses the Peace Commission. The writer Turgenev and the poet Zhukovsky also lived on this street. The mansion at number 12 was built by Afanasy Grigorev. It now houses the **Alexander Pushkin Museum**, containing over 80,000 items connected with the poet. It is open from 10:00 to 18:00 and is closed on Mondays and Tuesdays. Across the street at number 11 is the **Leo Tolstoy Museum**, which includes many of the writer's manuscripts, a documentary ('Tolstoy Alive') and recordings of his voice. It is open from 12:00 to 19:00 and is closed on Mondays and the last Friday of the month. (Another Tolstoy museum is on Leo Tolstoy Street.) Outside Moscow, Tolstoy's estate, Yasnaya Polyana (see page 177), can be visited. The poet Denis Davydov lived at number 17 and Prince Dolgorukov (related to Prince Dolgoruky) once lived at

The Conqueror

At ten in the morning of the second of September, Napoleon was standing among his troops on the Poklonny Hill looking at the panorama spread out before him. From the twenty-sixth of August to the Second of September, that is from the battle of Borodino to the entry of the French into Moscow, during the whole of that agitating, memorable week, there had been the extraordinary autumn weather that always comes as a surprise, when the sun hangs low and gives more heat than in spring, when everything shines so brightly in the rare clear atmosphere that the eyes smart, when the lungs are strengthened and refreshed by inhaling the aromatic autumn air, when even the nights are warm, and when in those dark warm nights, golden stars startle and delight us continually by falling from the sky.

The view of the strange city with its peculiar architecture, such as he had never seen before, filled Napoleon with the rather envious and uneasy curiosity men feel when they see an alien form of life. By the indefinite signs which, even at a distance, distinguish a living body from a dead one, Napoleon from the Poklonny Hill perceived the throb of life in the town and felt, as it were, the breathing of that great and beautiful body.

Every Russian looking at Moscow feels her to be mother; every foreigner who sees her, even if ignorant of her significance as the mother city, must feel her feminine character, and Napoleon felt it.

"A town captured by the enemy is like a maid who has lost her honor," thought he, and from that point of view he gazed at the oriental beauty he had not seen before. It seemed strange to him that his long-felt wish, which had seemed unattainable, had at last been realized. In the clear morning light he gazed now at the city and now at the plan, considering its details, and the assurance of possessing it agitated and awed him.

Leo Tolstoy, War and Peace

The Leo Tolstoy Museum

number 21—now the Palace of Fine Arts, which hosts art shows. The famous American ballet dancer Isadora Duncan and her husband, the Russian poet Sergei Yesenin, once lived across the street at number 20. Prechistenka Street ends at the Garden Ring by a statue of Tolstoy.

Across the river at number 10 Lavrushinsky (near Metro Novokuznetskaya) is the **Tretyakov Art Gallery**. In 1856, the brothers Sergei and Pavel Tretyakov, avid art patrons, began to collect the works of Russian artists. In 1892, they founded Russia's first public museum of national art and donated their collection of 3,500 paintings to the city. Today the gallery houses one of the world's largest Russian and Soviet art collections from the tenth to the 20th centuries with well over 50,000 works. These include Rublev's *Icon Trinity*, Ilya Repin's *Ivan the Terrible and his Son Ivan*, Vasily Surikov's *Morning of the Execution of the Streltsy*, and the largest painting in the gallery, Alexander Ivanov's *The Coming of Christ*. It is open daily from 10:00 to 19:00 and is closed on Mondays; check the opening times because the museum is occasionally closed for restoration. A new branch of the Tretyakov (also closed on Mondays) has opened at 10 Krymsky Val. This is opposite Gorky Park near Metro stop Oktyabrskaya.

Tverskaya / Gorky Streets

In the 18th century, **Tverskaya Ulitsa** was the main street of the city; today, it is still one of the busiest in Moscow. The passage was named Tverskaya because it led to the old Russian town of Tver (renamed Kalinin) 160 miles (256 kilometers) north; from there it continued to St Petersburg. From 1932 until 1990, the street was called Gorky, after Maxim Gorky, a famous writer during the Stalinist period (there are two Gorky Museums in Moscow). In 1990, the Moscow City Council voted to restore the street's old name. From the Kremlin to the Garden Ring, the thoroughfare is known as Tverskaya, and from the Garden Ring to Belorussky Train Station, it is called Gorky (or sometimes Yamskaya—in the 17th century, the Yamskaya *Sloboda*, settlement, appeared outside the city's ramparts); from the train station it turns into Leningradsky Prospekt, which leads to the international airport.

In pre-revolutionary days, the street, once winding and narrow, was known for its fashionable shops, luxurious hotels and grandiose aristocratic mansions. The city's first electric lamps were installed here in 1901. The first trams also ran along this street, and the first movie theater opened here. In 1932, when it was renamed Gorky, the thoroughfare was reshaped and widened, and now retains little of its former appearance.

It takes about an hour and a half to stroll the length of Tverskaya Street. You can also ride the Metro to various stops along it—Pushkinskaya, Mayakovskaya and Belorusskaya—to shorten the time.

Tverskaya Street begins in front of Red Square at the **Manezhnaya Square**, known as the 50th Anniversary of the October Revolution Square from 1967 to 1990. The czar had his riding school, the manège, in this area. The Metro stop Okhotny Ryad (formerly Prospekt Marxa) is at the beginning of the street. On the corner is the newly renovated, elegant **National Hotel** with a splendid view of Red Square. Lenin lived here during the Revolution. A small *Beriozka* is inside to the left. The 22-story structure next door is the modern **Intourist Hotel**, opened in 1971. Inside, toward the back, are slot machines; *Beriozkas*, hard-currency and ruble cafés and restaurants can also be found here.

Since *perestroika*, many new shops have opened on Tverskaya, including foreign clothing and cosmetic outlets (many accept hard-currency or credit cards only) and such Russian stores as the Podarki 'gifts' souvenir shop (accepts rubles).

Continuing along the street is the **Yermolova Drama Theater**, named after a famous stage actress. Founded in 1925, the theater moved into the present building, at number 5, in 1946. The Meyerhold Theater occupied the building from 1931 to 1938. It has staged everything from *Mary Poppins to Heartbreak House*. A Yermolova Museum is located at number 11 Tverskoi Boulevard, where the actress lived for 40 years. The museum is closed on Tuesdays. The **Central Telegraph Building**, with its globe and digital clock, is on the corner of Ogareva Street. The building, designed by Ilya Rerberg in 1927, is open 24 hours a day. Telegrams, faxes, and long-distance calls can be made here, but there is usually a wait.

Across the street at 3 Proyezd Khudozhestvennovo Teatra (Arts Passage Street) is the **Moscow Arts Theater**, established by Stanislavsky and Nemirovich-Danchenko in 1896. Here Stanislavsky practiced his 'method-acting' and staged many plays by Gorky and Chekhov. After *The Seagull*, the bird was put on the outside of the building as its emblem. Plays such as *Anna Karenina, Resurrection* and *The Three Sisters* marked a new epoch in the theater. In 1987, the building was reconstructed and now seats 2,000. Today, the theater's repertoire includes such plays as *Uncle Vanya, Bondage of Hypocrites* and *Tartuffe*. Another building of the Moscow Arts Theater is at 22 Tverskoi. Next door at 3A is the Moscow Arts Museum, founded in 1923.

The Aragvi Restaurant (once part of the Dresden Hotel, a favorite of Turgenev and Chekhov), specializing in Georgian cuisine, is on the next corner of Stoleshnikov Lane (right off Tverskaya). Stoleshnikov is designated to become Moscow's second pedestrian lane (the Arbat is already pedestrianized). Craftsmen embroidered table-cloths for the czar's court in this lane over 300 years ago. (*Stoleshnik* means table-

(above and below) Modern Muscovites in a new era

cloth in old Russian.) The Stoleshniki Café, at number 8, is decorated in old-Russian style. It is affectionately known as *U Gilyarovskovo*, in tribute to one of its past regulars, the writer and journalist Gilyarovsky who wrote the popular *Moscow and the Muscovites;* he lived across the street at number 9 for over half a century. Two rooms have been renovated in the café's 17th-century cellars: the Reporter's and Moscow and Muscovites halls. Here Gilyarovsky medals are awarded annually to the writers of the best articles about Moscow. At number 11, the pastry shop still uses old-fashioned ovens built into the walls, and has some of the best cakes in the city. The lane leads to Petrovka Street, a popular shopping area.

The side street to the left, Nezhdanovoi, leads to the **Church of the Resurrection**, founded by Czar Mikhail Romanov. It contains many beautiful 17th-century icons and is open daily for worship.

Sovietskaya Square is marked by the equestrian **Statue of Yuri Dolgoruky**, founder of Moscow. It was erected in 1954 to mark the 800th anniversary of the city. The building behind the square, in the small garden, holds the Party Archives of the Marxism-Leninism Institute, built in 1927. The archives contain more than 6,000 documents of Marx and Engels and over 30,000 of Lenin. In front is a granite statue of Lenin by Sergei Merkurov.

Directly across the street stands the large red-brick and white-columned **Moscow Soviet**, the city's legislature. The architect Matvei Kazakov designed the building as the residence for the first governor-general, appointed by Catherine the Great in 1782. Two of Moscow's governors were Prince Dmitri Golitsyn (1820–44), who paved the streets and installed water pipes, and Vladimir Dolgorukov, a descendent of Yuri Dolgoruky. In 1946, the building was moved back 42 feet (14 meters) and two more stories were added.

Farther up Tverskaya is the Tsentralnaya Hotel at number 10, built in 1911 as the Hotel Liuks. In the same building is the most famous bakery in Moscow, formerly known as Filippov's. Next door is another popular food store, Gastronom Number 1, which recently reverted to its original name of **Yeliseyev's**. Beautiful white sculptures and garlands line the shopfront, and the gilded interior is filled with stained glass and colorful displays. It was named Yeliseyev's after the original owner, who also had a popular gourmet store by the same name in St Petersburg on Nevsky Prospekt which is also still there. The merchant bought the mansion (with a respected salon for artists) from Princess Zinaida Volkonskaya, 'the Queen of Muses,' in 1898 and opened the store in 1901. Even though delicacies are lacking, it is worth a visit to see the interior, see page 305. At 14 Tverskaya is the **Memorial Museum of Nikolai Ostrovsky** (1904–36), who wrote *How the Steel Was Tempered*. The Soviet author's house is now a museum exhibiting his books, photographs and letters. It is open from 10:00 to 18:00 and is closed Mondays and the last day of the month. (Another Ostrovsky

Museum is nearby at 9 Ostrovsky Street, where the writer was born.) Next to the museum is the Central Actors Club and the All-Russia Theatrical Society.

Down the side street, at 6 Stanislavsky, is the **Stanislavsky Memorial House-Museum**. The theater director lived here for 17 years. On display are the living quarters of Stanislavsky and his wife, the opera hall and collections of books, costumes and theatrical props. It is open from 11:00 to 18:00; closed on Mondays and Tuesdays. At Tverskaya and 17 Shchukin Street is the **Sergei Konenkov Studio Museum** (1874–1971), displaying marble and wooden statues by this famous sculptor, who lived here from 1947 to 1971. It is open from 10:00 to 17:00 and is closed on Mondays and Tuesdays. The **Goldenveiser Apartment Museum** is also at number 17, in apartment 110. Goldenveiser was a famous Russian composer, pianist and teacher. The collection includes his musical scores and note library. It is also closed on Mondays and Tuesdays. Nearby is the store Armenia, which specializes in food from the state of the same name.

As Tverskaya crosses the Boulevard Ring, it opens into **Pushkin Square**. In the 16th century, the stone walls of the Beli-gorod, White Town, stretched around what is now the Boulevard Ring; they were torn down in the 18th century. The Strastnoi Convent used to stand on what is now Pushkin Square—the square was originally called Strastnaya (until 1931), after the Convent of the Passion of Our Lord. The convent was demolished in the 1930s; in its place was built the Rossiya Movie Theater and the Izvestia building. In the center of the square stands the **Statue of Alexander Pushkin**, by the sculptor Alexander Opekulin. It was erected in 1880 with funds donated by the public. Pushkin lived over a third of his life in Moscow, where he predicted: 'Word of me shall spread across the Russian land.' Dostoevsky laid a wreath on the statue at its unveiling; today it is always covered with flowers and is a popular spot for open-air readings and political rallies. Under the square are the three Metro stations Tverskaya, Pushkinskaya and Chekhovskaya.

Behind the square is the 3,000-seat Rossiya Cinema, built in 1961 for the 2nd International Moscow Film Festival (the festival is held in Moscow every odd year). This area is also Moscow's major publishing center. Here are the newspaper offices of *Izvestia, Trud, Novosti* (APN) and *Moscow News*. Walking down Chekhov Street (behind *Izvestia*) leads to the tent-shaped **Church of the Nativity**, built between 1649 and 1652. Legend has it that a noblewoman gave birth in her carriage as she passed this spot and later commissioned a church to honor the Nativity. When it burned down, Czar Alexei Romanov donated money to have it rebuilt, along with a chapel dedicated to the icon that prevented fires, Our Lady of the Burning Bush, which is in the chapel.

Across the street from Pushkin Square is a **McDonald's** fast-food outlet, whose queues are sometimes so long that customers must wait literally hours to be served. This is the world's largest McDonald's with 800 seats, 27 cash registers and 250 employees serving up to 50,000 people a day. When the restaurant opened, Russians automatically stood in the longest queue—in Russia, a longer queue is indicative of better quality merchandise. Brochures had to be distributed explaining that each queue gave the same service and food. The chain plans to open a total of 20 restaurants in Moscow; there are already two new ones, another on Tverskaya and one in the Arbat. As part of an agreement with the Moscow City Council, McDonald's was required to purchase or produce its raw materials in Russia, resulting in a vast production and distribution complex on the outskirts of the city.

For a while, there was even a black market for hamburgers. People purchased eight burgers (the maximum allowed per person), ate what they wanted and then sold the rest at a huge profit to those not willing to wait. The grounds surrounding the restaurant are a popular meeting place; small kiosks abound and you can have your picture taken next to cardboard copies of Yeltsin. Bands play here and there are many young people amusing themselves on skateboards and roller blades.

The **Museum of Russian Revolutions** is at 21 Tverskaya Street. This mansion was built for Count Razumovsky in 1780 by the architect Manelas. In 1832, it was rebuilt by Adam Menelaws after a fire, and was bought by the Angliisky (English) Club, formed in 1772 by a group of foreigners residing in Moscow. The club's members (all men) were made up of Russian aristocratic intellectuals and included the best minds in politics, science, art and literature. Tolstoy once lost 1,000 rubles in a card game in the 'infernal' room. Pushkin wrote of the club in his long poem *Evgeny Onegin*. When Tatiana arrived in Moscow, Evgeny described 'the two frivolous-looking lions' at the gates. The last *bolshoi* gala at the club was a banquet thrown for Nicholas II to celebrate the 300th anniversary of the Romanov Dynasty in 1913. The museum, opened in 1924, exhibits over a million items from the 1905 and 1917 revolutions. It was called the Central Museum of the Revolution until 1992. A new hall has opened displaying items from the August 1991 coup attempt. The gun outside was used to shell the White Guards in 1917. Also on display here is a bus that burned during the 1991 attempted coup. The museum is open from 10:00 to 18:00 and is closed on Mondays. Next to the museum, at number 23, is the Stanislavky Drama Theater. Behind it is the Young Spectator's Theater for children. The Baku Restaurant, at number 24, serves delicious Azerbaijani food.

Patriarch's Pond

By McDonald's, off Tverksaya, turn into Bolshaya Bronnaya. This leads to Malaya Bronnaya—if you follow this to number 30, you will come to Patriarch's Pond, one of the oldest and most charming residential areas of Moscow. The area was once known as the Patriarskaya, the Patriarch's land, a place of pastures and fishponds. The writer Bulgakov staged his well-known story *The Master and Margarita* in this area. A mon-

Red Shirts and Black Bread

We plunged into plebeian Moscow, the world of red-shirted workmen and cheap frocked women; low vodka shops and bare, roomy traktirs, where the red-shirted workmen assemble each evening to gossip and swallow astonishing quantities of tea, inferior in quality and very, very weak.

Here was Moscow's social and material contrast to the big houses, with sleeping Dvroniks, and of the silent street of painted house fronts, curtained balcones and all the rest. Though day had not yet dawned for other sections of Moscow, it had long since dawned for the inhabitants of this. Employers of labor in Moscow know nothing of the vexed questions as to eight-hour laws, ten-hour laws, or even laws of twelve. Thousands of red shirts, issuing from the crowded hovels of this quarter, like rats from their hiding places, had scattered over the city long before our arrival on the scene; other thousands were still issuing forth, and streaming along the badly cobbled streets. Under their arms, or in tin pails, were loaves of black rye bread, their food for the day, which would be supplemented at meal times by a salted cucumber, or a slice of melon, from the nearest grocery.

Though Moscow can boast of its electric light as well as gas, it is yet a city of petroleum. Coal is dear, and, in the matter of electric lights and similar innovations from the wide-awake Western world, Moscow is, as ever, doggedly conservative. So repugnant, indeed, to this stronghold of ancient and honourable Muscovite sluggishness, is the necessity of keeping abreast with the spirit modern improvement, that the houses are not yet even numbered. There are no numbers to the houses in Moscow; only the streets are offically known by name. To find anybody's address, you must repair to the street, and inquire of the policeman or drosky driver, who are the most likely persons to know, for the house belonging to Mr. So-and-so, or in which that gentleman lives. It seems odd that in a country where the authorities deem it necessary to know where to put their hand on any person at a moment's notice, the second city of the empire should be, in 1980, without numbers to its houses.

T Stevens, Traveling Through Russia on a Mustang

Crime and Punishment

They use various horrible methods of torture to force out the truth. One of them involves tying the hands behind the back, drawing them up high, and hanging a heavy beam on the feet. The executioner jumps on the beam, thus severely stretching the limbs of the offender from one another. Besides, beneath the victim they set a fire, the heat of which torments the feet, and the smoke the face. Sometimes they shear a bald place on top of the head and allow cold water to fall on it a drop at a time. This is said to be an unbearable torture. Depending on the nature of the case, some may, in addition, be beaten with the knout, after which a red-hot iron is applied to their wounds.

If a case of brawling is being tried, usually the one who struck first is guilty, and he who first brings a complaint is considered in the right. One who commits a murder not in self-defence (they consider the opposite justified), but with premeditation, is thrown into prison, where he must repent under severe conditions for six weeks. Then he is given communion and decapitated.

If someone is accused of robbery and convicted, he is put to torture all the same [to determine] if he has stolen something besides. If he admits nothing more, and this is the first offence, he is beaten with the knout all along the road from the Kremlin to the great square. Here the executioner cuts off one of his ears, and he is put into a dungeon for two years. If he is caught a second time, then in the manner described above, he has the other ear cut off and is installed in his prevous lodging, where he remains until other birds of the kind are found, whereupon they are all sent to Siberia. However, no one pays with his life for robbery, unless a murder is committed along with it. If, under torture, the thief names those to whom he sold the stolen goods, the buyers are brought to court and orderd to make restoration to the complainant. They call such payment vyt, and on its account many are constrained against purchasing suspicious things.

Olearius, Travels in Seventeenth-Century Russia

ument to Krylov, the fable writer, stands in the square. In winter, there is ice-skating and in summer boating. Across the street from the pond, at number 28, is the popular Café At Margareta's. It is open daily from noon until 22:00 (closed between 16:00 and 20:00). The area was once occupied by artisans—the *bronnaya*, armorers, and the *kozia*, wool-spinners.

The **Moscow Drama Theater** is at 4 Malaya Bronnaya. Formed in 1950, the theater seats 850. Across the street at number 27 is the Dutch store Markt A, which sells many foreign products. Nearby, the newly renovated Marco Polo Hotel has a good restaurant. A short walk away at 6/2 Kachalova Street is the **Maxim Gorky House-Museum** where the writer lived with his family from 1931 to 1936. It is worth visiting just to see the architecture. The house, designed by Shekhte, was built by the Russian industrialist Ryabushinsky in art-nouveau style in 1900 with stained-glass windows, wooden carvings and a glass roof. The exquisite staircase, constructed in the Spanish-Gaudi style, resembles a giant crashing wave. The library has over 10,000 volumes and the parlor looks as it did when Gorky lived here. A superb collection of carved ivory is in his bedroom, and many of his books and letters are also on display. Stalin gave Gorky this house as a meeting place for writers and artists, but the writer felt uncomfortable here, saying that he 'felt like a bird in a golden cage.' The museum is open Wednesdays and Fridays from noon to 19:00; Thursdays, Saturdays and Sundays from 10:00 to 17:00. It is closed on Mondays and Tuesdays, and the last Thursday of each month.

Next to the Gorky House is the **Tolstoy House-Museum.** This is not the Leo Tolstoy of *War and Peace*, but Alexei Tolstoy, another Russian writer, who lived here for several years; the museum displays his books and personal belongings. His books include *Ivan the Terrible* and *Peter the Great*. It is open Thursdays, Saturdays and Sundays from 11:00 to 18:00 (11:00 to 16:00 in winter), on Wednesdays and Fridays from 13:00 to 20:00 (12:00 to 16:00 in winter); it is closed on Mondays and Tuesdays, and the last day of each month. Across the street from the Gorky House stands the white **Church of the Ascension**. It was here, in 1831, that Alexander Pushkin married Nathalie Gancharova (who, later, was the cause of the St Petersburg duel in which Pushkin was killed). The church is open, though restoration is in progress. Behind is the 17th-century Fyodor Studit Church.

GORKY STREET

Passing the Minsk Hotel, whose restaurant specializes in Byelorussian cuisine, and some shops brings you to the corner of Tverskaya (here Tverskaya becomes Gorky) and the Sadovoye Koltso (Garden Ring). On the corner of **Mayakovsky Square** stands a large building with ten columns, the **Tchaikovsky Concert Hall** (built for Meyerhold's Theater in the 1930s), where orchestras and dance ensembles perform. The Moscow Stars and Winter Festivals also take place here. The Mayakovsky Metro station is in front. Directly behind the Hall, at number 18, is the circular-domed building of the **Moscow Satire Theater**, founded in 1924, whose productions have ranged from *The Cherry Orchard* to the *Three-Penny Opera*. The Aquarium gardens are next and the Mossoviet Theater, at 16 Bolshaya Sadovaya Street. Also nearby, at 19 Chistoprudny, is the **Sovremennik Theater**, which stages contemporary plays. Across the street is the **Peking Hotel**, housing one of the few Chinese restaurants in town.

A statue of the poet Vladimir Mayakovsky (1893–1930) stands in **Mayakovsky Square**. On the other side of the square is the Sofia Restaurant, which serves Bulgarian food. To the right is the Moskva Cinema. At number 43 is the House of Children's Books, and at number 46 the Exhibition Hall of Artist Unions. A few minutes walk to 4 Fedeyeva Street is the **Glinka Music Museum**, opened in 1943. The museum has a large collection of musical instruments, rare recordings and unique manuscripts of famous composers, such as Tchaikovsky, Shostakovich and Glinka; it is closed on Mondays.

Gorky Street ends at Byelorusskaya Square, also called Zastava (Gate) Square, which was the old site of the Kamer-Kollezhsky gates on the road to Tver. At the center of the square is a **Monument to Maxim Gorky** (1868–1935), erected in 1951. The trains from the 120-year-old **Byelorusskaya Railway Station** journey to points west, including Warsaw, Berlin, Paris and London. The Metro station Byelorusskaya is in front. Here Gorky Street turns into Leningradsky Prospekt, which runs all the way to the international airport, Sheremetyevo. On the next side street are the offices of the newspaper *Pravda*, whose circulation was once 10 million. After the 1991 attempted putsch, the offices were shut down for the first time in its history. There was no money (Communist Party funds had been frozen) to continue operations. A few months later the newspaper was back in business, but it was asking for donations and the price of the paper had increased.

Along Begovaya (Running) Street is the **Moscow Hippodrome**, a race course. It was built a century ago and frequented by the Russian aristocracy. Today, the Hippodrome is rather run-down, but is open three or four times weekly, drawing up to 20,000 people for the nine daily races. During off-hours, horses can be hired. The **Casino Royale** is now located in the Hippodrome's Central Hall. This was the idea of renowned eye-surgeon Svyatoslav Fyodorov, who developed the famous daisy-wheel operating room technique—operating on up to 10 patients in one room at a time; Fyodorov also breeds horses. A little farther up, at 32 Leningradsky, is the Hotel Sovietskaya and the **Romany Gypsy Theater**. Seating over 800, the theater focuses on gypsy national culture. The Moscow Chamber Musical Theater is at 71 Leningradsky Prospekt.

From here, take the Metro into the city center or continue by bus along Leningradsky Prospekt.

The Old Kalinin Prospekt

In 1991, Kalinin Prospekt was divided into two different streets. Vozdvizhenka Street (the name stems from the 16th-century Krestovovozdvizhensky or Church of the Exaltation) runs from the Kremlin's Kutafya Tower (by the Alexandrov Gardens) to Arbat Square. Novy Arbat begins at Arbat Square and continues to the Kalinin Bridge. Here Novy Arbat turns into Kutuzovsky Prospekt and later the Minsk Highway.

The old route was known as Novodvizhenskaya; it stretched from the Kremlin to the outer walls of the city. A new thoroughfare was built along this former road; from 1963 to 1991, it was named Kalinin, after a leader of the Communist Party, Mikhail Kalinin. The old section of the prospekt runs from the Kremlin to the Boulevard Ring, where the more modern part begins.

The road starts by a large grey building off of Mokhovaya (the old Marx Prospekt), the **State Public Library** (formerly the Lenin Library). The library opened in the 1800s, when the book collector Nikolai Rumyantsev moved his collection from St Petersburg to a Moscow mansion opposite the Kremlin. A new building was constructed on the site in 1940, and now houses the largest collection of books in the country, over 36 million. The first part of the street still contains a few 18th-century buildings. At number 7 is the former **Monastery of the Holy Cross**. The house at number 9 belonged to Tolstoy's grandfather, Count Volkonsky, upon whom he based a character in *War and Peace*.

At the corner of Granovsky (named after the celebrated historian) is an early 18th-century mansion that belonged to the wealthy Count Sheremetev. Across the street, at number 5, is an old mansion of the Tolyzin estate, built by Kazakov. It now houses the **Alexei Shchusev Museum of Architecture**, which features the history of Russian and Soviet architecture (mainly after 1917). It is open from 11:00 to 19:00 and is closed on Mondays and Fridays. The nearest Metro stop is Alexandrovsky Sad (formerly Kalininskaya). Krushchev, Kosygin, Frunze and Voroshilov all lived on this street.

At number 16 is the white, medieval former mansion of the merchant Morozov, who hired the designer Marizin in 1899 to model his residence after a Moorish castle. After the Revolution it was turned over to the Union of Anarchists. In 1959, it became the **House of Friendship**, where delegations of foreign friendship societies meet. Nearby, the eight-story building with one turret was built in the 1920s as the first Soviet skyscraper in constructivist style. Near the Metro stop Arbatskaya, on the side street Suvorov, is the Journalist Club. Opposite the club is a monument to Gogol, standing in front of the house where the writer lived. On this corner is the large **Dom Svyazi** (House of Communications) with a post office, telephone center and video-phone links to some other Russian cities.

THE ARBAT

On the corner opposite the Dom Svyazi is the Prague Restaurant, marking the entrance to one of the city's oldest sections, the **Arbat**. Long ago, the Arbat Gates led into Moscow. *Arbad* is an old Russian word meaning beyond the town walls. Some believe the word could still further stem from the Mongol word *arba*, a sack to collect tributes; the ancient 'Arab' settlements; or the Latin *arbutum*, cherry, because of the cherry orchards that were once in the area. There is one other proposed origin: A creek named *Chertory*, the Devil's Creek, once meandered or 'hunchbacked' through the vicinity, which was quite damp and boggy. When a small one-kopek candle started a fire in the All Saints Church and burnt it and the rest of Moscow to the ground in 1365, many thought the area cursed. The Russian word *khorbaty* means hunchbacked place.

The area was first mentioned in 15th-century chronicles. It lay along the Smolensk Road, making it a busy trade center. Many court artisans lived here in the 16th century; in the 19th century, many wealthy and educated people chose to live in the Arbat. Today the street is a cobbled pedestrian thoroughfare about one kilometer long, and one of the most popular meeting and shopping spots in Moscow. Along with its shops, cafés, art galleries, concert and theater halls and a museum tracing the history of the area, are portrait painters, performance artists and even demonstrators. It is also a frequent site for festivals and carnivals. Chekhov once said that 'the Arbat is one of the most pleasant spots on Earth.' It is definitely worth a stroll.

The colorful buildings lining the pedestrian mall and its side streets have a rich and romantic history. Many poems, songs and novels, such as Anatoly Rybakov's *Children of the Arbat*, have been written about this area. The czar's stablemen once lived along Starokonivshenny, Old Stable Lane. An old church stood on the corner of Spasopekovsky (Savior-on-Sand) Lane. Other small streets have the names Serebryany (Silversmith), Plotnikov (Carpenter) and Kalashny (Pastrycook). Pushkin rented a house at 53 Arbat in 1831 and lived there with his new bride, Natalia Goncharova. The house is now the **Pushkin Museum**. It is open Wednesday to Friday from 12:00 to 18:00 and on Saturdays and Sundays from 11:00 to 17:00. The writer Herzen, the composer Scriabin and the sculptress Golubkina also lived in the Arbat neighborhood.

At 27 Sivtsev Vrazhek Pereulok (*vrazhek* means gully; once the River Sivtsev ran through a gully in this location) is the **Herzen Museum**, where the writer lived from 1843 to 1846. Here he wrote *Dr Krupov*, *Magpie the Thief* and his famous novel *Who is to Blame?* His 'Letters on Nature,' according to Lenin, 'put him [Herzen] in one row with the most prominent thinkers of his time.' The museum is open on Wednesdays and Fridays from 14:00 to 19:30, on other days from 10:00 to 17:30, and is closed on Mondays. In the same lane at number 30 is the **Aksakov Museum**, where the Russian writer lived (it is closed on Mondays and Tuesdays). The writer Mikhail Sholokhov,

(above, top) Colourful Matrushka dolls, (bottom) Along the Arbat
(opposite, top) Cartoon stall along the Arbat, (bottom) Icons for Sale

who wrote *Quiet Flows the Don*, lived at number 33. The millionare Maecenas Schiukin's home with his large collection of European paintings was at 35 Starokoniushenny Pereulok. After Schiukin presented the city with his art in 1918, the collection was moved to the Pushkin Art Museum. The **Scriabin Museum** is nearby at 11 Vakhatanova Street. The famous composer lived here from 1912 to 1922. His concert programs, photographs and books are on display, along with recordings of his music, the museum is closed on Mondays and Tuesdays. The **Golubkina Studio Museum** is at 12 Shchukina Street, where the sculptress' work is on exhibit. It is also closed on Mondays and Tuesdays. At the end of Spasopeskhovsky Street is the **Spasso House**, part of the US embassy, which was originally built by the banker Ftorov in 1913.

In the Arbat, at number 7, is the Literary Café, a favorite of Mayakovsky and Isadora Duncan's husband, the Russian poet Yesenin, in the 1920s. The niece of Leo Tolstoy, Obolenskaya, lived at number 9. The 1,000-seat Vakhtangov Theater is at number 26. It was founded in 1921 by the director Vakhtangov. The Ministry of Culture, at number 35, is decorated with statues of knights. On the first floor is the Samotsvety (Precious stones) shop. The Georgian Center or *Mziuri* is at number 42, where Georgian souvenirs are sold and a Georgian restaurant is in the basement. A number of excellent antique shops are at 6 Arbat and 5 Vakhtangova Street. After a leisurely stroll to Smolensky Square, you will better understand the lyrics to a popular song: 'Oy, Arbat, a whole lifetime is not enough to travel through your length!'

Novy Arbat

The avenue from Arbat Square on the Boulevard Ring to the Kalinin Bridge is better known as the Novy (New) Arbat, the main western thoroughfare of the city. The shops and flats in this area were built during Khrushchev's regime in the l960s; they were designed by Moscow's chief architect, Mikhail Posokhin. Across the street from the Prague Restaurant (one of the oldest in Moscow) is the **Church of Simon Stylites**, now an exhibition hall. Down the side street, behind the church, at 2 Malaya Molchanovka, is the **House-Museum of Lermontov**. During the poet's habitation here from 1829 to 1832, he wrote about 100 poems and plays. It is open on Saturdays, Sundays and Thursdays from 11:00 to 18:00; on Wednesdays and Fridays from 14:00 to 21:00; and is closed on Mondays and Tuesdays.

Next to the church, on Novy Arbat, is **Dom Knigi** (House of Books), the city's largest bookstore. Here books, posters, and even antiques and icons (for rubles only) are for sale. The Malachite Casket Jewelry Shop is also in this building. On the same side of the street is the Melodia Record Shop and the 3,000-seat Oktyabr Cinema.

A series of shops and cafés line the left side of Novy Arbat. On the second floor is the **Irish House**, a hard-currency store where you can find most Western food products and the **Irish Bar**, which is open daily from 09:00 to 20:00. Other shops include the Moskvichka (Miss Moscow) Fashion Shop, Sintetika Department Store, Metelitsa (Snowball) Ice Cream Café, Charodeika (Sorceress) Beauty Shop, Jazz Café Pechora and the Podarki (Gift) Shop. The block ends at the 2,000-seat Arbat Restaurant, which has a large globe on its roof.

Novy Arbat crosses the Garden Ring at Novinsky Bulvar (formerly Tchaikovsky Street) and ends at the river. Before Kalinin Bridge, on the right, stands the 30-story **CMEA/COMECON** building, headquarters of the East European economic trade community. The Hotel Mir (Peace) is behind it. Farther down, on the same side of the river, is the Sovincenter and the **Mezhdunarodny** (International) **Hotel**, built with the help of Armand Hammer and used by foreign firms. Before more hotels were built in Moscow, the Mezhdunarodny was the international businessman's hotel of choice. It has a number of restaurants, cafés and shops, a health center with sauna and pool, a pharmacy, an Aeroflot ticket office and a food *Beriozka* on the second floor. Next door, in the **Sovincenter** office building, are many other airline offices, and Federal Express is on the ground floor.

Kutuzovsky Prospekt

After crossing the Kalinin Bridge, the Novy Arbat turns into Kutuzovsky Prospekt, named after the Russian General Mikhail Kutuzov (1745–1813), who fought against Napoleon. The building on the right with the star-spire is the Ukraine Hotel, which has a *Beriozka* and a Ukrainian restaurant. (This is one of Stalin's seven Gothic structures.) A statue to the Ukrainian poet Taras Shevchenko stands in front. The White House, the Russian Parliament Building and scene of the two latest coup attempts, can be seen from the hotel. Parts of the barricades from the 1991 attempted putsch have been left to honor the citizens who helped Yeltsin in his famous stand-off. Nearby is the House of Toys. Across the street at number 6 is the Central Art Fund, which occasionally sells local handicrafts and artwork. At the next corner is the Hero City of Moscow Obelisk. Troops left from this point in 1941 to fight the advancing German army. At number 26, a plaque marks the 30-year residence of Leonid Brezhnev; Yuri Andropov also lived here.

The obelisk stands at the entrance of Bolshaya Dorogomilovskaya, along which are the **Kievskaya Railway Station** (with a Metro stop) and the **Sadko** hard-currency food *Beriozka* at number 16; it is open daily from 10:00 to 20:00, on Sundays until 18:00, and is closed from 15:00 to 16:00. Around the corner from Sadko is **Pizza Hut** (another is on Tverskaya), with ruble and hard-currency sides. A notable Russian souvenir store (rubles only) is a few blocks away at number 9; it is open from 11:00

ALL ABOARD THE BOLSHOI EXPRESS — Amanda Reynolds Leung

Although today the Commonwealth of Independent States has one of the world's largest rail networks and arguably the most famous of train journeys—the Trans-Siberian—for years it actually lagged behind the railway systems of other European powers. Fourteen years after George Stephenson began building his proto-railway from Stockton to Darlington, and eight years after the engineer's locomotive, *Rocket*, was built, Tsar Nicholas I reluctantly opened Russia's first railroad. The Pushkin to St Petersburg line, inaugurated in 1837, was succeeded by additional tracks including a St Petersburg to Moscow service in 1851. Yet by this date the country could still only boast some 770 miles (1,240 kilometers) of tracks.

Russia's transport and military supply service was shown to be woefully inadequate in 1854 when British, French and Turkish armies inflicted a humiliating defeat on the country in the Crimean War. Historians have noted that more Russian troops died on the freezing foot march to the Crimea, and from disease, than perished in battle.

The reforming Tsar Alexander II instituted a programme of modernisation which included railway building, often inspired by military campaigns. The St Petersburg to Warsaw line was initiated in 1861; a decade later iron sleepers reached the Volga. At the time of his death in 1881, Russia had 14,000 miles (22,530 kilometers) of track. In 1892 the Trans-Siberian route started from Chelyabinsk, it reached Irkutsk in 1898 and the last leg to the port city of Vladivostock was broached in 1916. Until this point, passengers traveled by boat in summer (and sleigh in winter) across Lake Baikal.

The railroads had an enormous economic and strategic importance for the country. The Trans-Caspian line to Central Asia was part of a military campaign to conquer the territory. As the sleepers snaked their way from the Baltic sea through the rolling heartland of Russia and on across the Siberian wilderness ploughing the deserts of Uzbekistan and Kazakstan, markets and trade opened up almost overnight. The railways were responsible for Russia's first speculative boom.

Today, the CIS's network carries some 11 million travelers every day on some 145,000 miles (233,355 kilometers) of rails. Thanks to Lenin's prognosis that Communism was Soviet power plus the electrification of the whole country, a third of the network is now electrified. The most heavily used route is between St Petersburg and Moscow where express trains run the distance in about four hours. The most interesting way is to take the overnight Red Arrow service which departs at midnight and arrives in time for breakfast next morning.

And those travelers who long to recapture the golden era of railway travel and enjoy the sights and history of the CIS can now do so with Cox and Kings' specialized tours. Aiming to revive the stately pace of travel of the Tsars and Grand Dukes who traveled annually left St Petersburg for the South of France, Cox and Kings Travel Ltd bought up a series of carriages built in the 1950s.

Named the Bolshoi Express, this special train, which began serving tourists in 1993, comprises 16 maroon carriages. In addition to six sleeping carriages, travelers can relax in three dining cars decorated in Baltic, Ukrainian and Georgian styles and a 1920's style saloon car with wooden parquet floor. The sleeping cars feature double-berth compartments with brass, oak and mahogany fittings. Thanks to the additional space available on the Russian broad (1.524 metres) gauge track, each room has an armchair, writing table and sofa, with an adjoining small bathroom containing shower and washbasin. For the ultimate in luxury, each carriage has a centrally located suite of two rooms plus bathroom.

Measuring 800 metres in length, the imposing Bolshoi Express makes a lasting impression as it sweeps out of the station to the strains of a jazz band on the platform and passengers tinkling champagne glasses—part of the celebration which accompanies every gracious departure. One of the tour's original features is the use of steam engines for part of each journey transporting travelers back to the golden era of rail travel. En route, travelers are entertained nightly by the train's musicians who play classical and folk music during and after dinner in the saloon and restaurant cars.

Passengers can select between four-day sight-seeing weekends in St Petersburg and Moscow with two nights aboard the locomotive and an optional detour to take in the twelfth-century city of Novgorod or an eight-day tour of the duchies and principalities of ancient Muscovy and medieval Russia—the famed Golden Ring—which takes in Suzdal, Rostov and Yaroslavl as well as the premier cities.

Those with more time on their hands can take the 14-day, 5,000-kilometer ride from St Petersburg through Central Asia to Tashkent. This fascinating journey on the Bolshoi Express was filmed by the BBC as part of its *Great Railway Journeys of the World* series aired in early 1994. The train carried prima ballerina Natalia Makarova on a nostalgic visit through her homeland. The tour takes in the city of Volgograd (formerly Stalingrad) before coasting the Volga delta, settled by the Mongol-Turkic Khazar tribes, to the Caspian Sea for a visit to the Tartar capital, Astrakhan, and on to the deserts of Central Asia. The trip takes in the ancient Silk Road cities of Khiva, legendary Tamerlaine's Samarkand and Bukhara.

Options include a ten-day circular tour starting from St Petersburg and taking in the Baltic states of Estonia, Latvia and Lithuania before reaching Moscow, or an in-depth ride from Moscow to the well- and lesser-known Golden Ring historical and religious centres of imperial Russia—Rostov the Great, Yaroslavl on the Volga, Kostroma, Ivanovo and Suzdal.

The famous Trans-Siberian route which stretches 5,787 miles (9,313 kilometers) from European Russia to the Sea of Japan is often no more than a dream for all but hardy travelers who take the state trains. However, the Bolshoi Express made its inaugural trip to Vladivostock in August 1994.

Cox & Kings Travel Ltd, St James Court, 45 Buckingham Gate, London SW1E 6AF. Tel: 071 873 5003, fax 071 630 6038, telex 23378 COXKIN G.

THE RUSSIAN CIRCUS

'Oh, how I love the Circus,' bellows Alexander Frish, a charismatic and eccentric clown, who has been clowning around in the Russian Circus for over 20 years. Frish believes that 'the circus is the universal language of joy and laughter that lets us all become children again.'

The Russian Circus is a world of vibrant artistry, precision and grace. Throughout the country, the circus is a highly respected art form taken as seriously as classical ballet. It is also the most popular entertainment: more than 100 million Russians attend performances each year. The Circus employs more than 25,000 people, including 6,000 performing artists and 7,000 animals. Seventy permanent circus buildings, including ice and aquatic circuses, are scattered from Moscow to Siberia—more than in the rest of the world combined. Over 100 circus troupes (many are government regulated, others private collectives) give up to nine performances a week in over 30 countries a year.

The early traditions of the circus go back over three centuries. The first formalized circus was created in England in 1770 by an ex-cavalry officer and showman named Philip Astley. It consisted mostly of trick riding, rope dancers, tumblers and jugglers, staged within a circular ring. In 1793, one of Astley's horsemen and later competitors, Charles Hughes, introduced this novel form of entertainment to Russia, with a private circus for Catherine the Great in the Royal Palace at St Petersburg. (In the same year, Hughes' pupil, John Bill Ricketts, introduced modern circus to American audiences in Philadelphia.)

Russia's first permanent circus building was built in St Petersburg in 1877 by Gaetano Ciniselli, an equestrian entrepreneur from Milan. The Ciniselli Circus was the center of performance activitity up to the Revolution, and this classic building still houses today's St Petersburg Circus. The second oldest circus was the Old Circus in Moscow (a new Old Circus has been built on the site where the original once stood). Moscow also boasts the New Circus and the summer tent circuses.

Nowhere in Europe were circus performers as politically active as in turn-of-the-century Russia. The circus became a sort of political sanctuary where sketches depicting the tumultuous state of Russia were tolerated. The clowns, especially, took every opportunity to satirize the czars, landowners and merchants. Many of the performers participated in active demonstra-

(following pages) The thrills of the Russian Circus

tions with organized parades through the cities. Lunacharksy, the head of the Circus House that organized performers, encouraged their participation: 'Here it will be possible to have fiery Revolutionary speeches, declarative couplets and clowns doing caricatures on enemy forces.' The artists performed on small flatbed stages that were rolled through the streets of Moscow. Vladimir Durov, with trained animals, joined the merry cavalcade, as did the most popular clown of the era, Vitaly Lazarenko, on stilts! Taking up the Bolshevik cause, the acts were now catalysts for social reform. The circus had become a political hotbed.

The poet Mayakovsky wrote for the circus. In one of his most famous skits, *Moscow Burning*, he wrote: 'Proud of the year 1917/Don't forget about 1905./A year of undying glory and fame/When the dream of the land came alive.../Comrade Circus, where's your grin?/Here's a sight to tickle us/Look and see who's trotting in/The Dynasty of Czar Nicholas !!!'

During these years of intellectual and political intensity, some of Russia's finest writers and directors, such as Gorky, Chekhov, and Stanislavsky, turned their attention to the circus. In one of his short stories, Maxim Gorky wrote: 'Everything I see in the arena blends into something triumphant, where skill and strength celebrate their victory over mortal danger.' Later, even Lenin took time off from the Revolution to nationalize the circus: on September 22, 1919, the world's first government circus began its operations.

In order to provide a consistently high standard of training in the circus arts, the government founded the first professional circus school in 1927. Today, at hundreds of circus schools throughout the country, students train for up to four years, studying all facets of circus life. During his final year, the student creates his own act and utilizes the services of circus producers, directors and choreographers. Once the act is approved by a circus board, the performer's prefessional career begins—the State supplies everything needed, from costumes and equipment to animals and special effects. Employment for the State circus artist is guaranteed for 20 years with a full pension upon retirement.

The emblem of the Russian Circus depicts a circus performer reaching for the stars. The language of the circus is without words, as beauty, courage and skill bridge the gap between generations and nationalities. The circus is the universal language of the heart.

to 20:00 and is closed on Sundays. A *Beriozka* is next door selling fur hats and clothing. At number 26 is the Art Salon, which sells art supplies. Nearby is Baskin-Robbins ice cream. Stalin's *dacha* was out here, where he died in 1953.

The prospekt ends at the **Triumphal Arch** in **Victory Square**, designed by Osip Bovet in 1829 to honor Russia's victory in the War of 1812. It originally stood in front of the Belorusskaya Train Station and was moved to this spot in 1968, when Tverskaya Street was widened. It is decorated with the coats-of-arms of Russia's provinces. Here on Poklonaya Hill, Napoleon waited for Moscow's citizens to bow to him and relinquish the keys to the city. From the hill is a magnificent view of Moscow; Anton Chekhov once said: 'Those who want to understand Russia should look at Moscow from Poklonaya Hill.' Between the Kutuzovskaya Metro station and the arch is the **Statue of Mikhail Kutuzov** by Nikolas Tomsky and an obelisk that marks the common graves of 300 men who died in the War of 1812.

The large circular building at number 38 is the **Battle of Borodino Museum**, which is closed on Fridays. The 68 cannons in front were captured from Napoleon. In 1912, to commemorate the 100th anniversary of the war, Franz Rouband was commissioned to paint scenes of the Battle of Borodino, which took place on August 26, 1812 (September 7 on the new calendar). The large murals are displayed in the museum, which was constructed in 1962 to honor the 150th anniversary. Behind is the **Kutuzov Hut**. Here on September 1, 1812, as the French invaded Moscow, Kutuzov and the Military Council decided to abandon the city. The Hut is closed Mondays and Fridays. The actual site of the Battle of Borodino is about 75 miles (120 kilometers) outside of Moscow, see page 172.

From here, Kutuzovsky Prospekt turns into the Mokhaiskoye Chausee and then the Minsk Highway, along which is the Mozhaisky Hotel and campgrounds. In the village of Fili, at 6 Novozavodskaya Street, is the 17th-century Naryshkin-baroque **Pokrov Church**. The highway, of course, leads to the city of Minsk in Byelorussia.

The Boulevard Ring

During the 16th and 17th centuries, the stone walls of the Beligorod (White Town), stretched around the area now known as the Boulevard Ring. During the Time of Troubles at the end of the 17th century, Boris Godunov fortified the walls and built 37 towers and gates. By 1800 the walls were taken down and the area was planted with trees and gardens, divided by a series of small connected boulevards. Ten *bulvari* make up the Bulvarnoye Koltso, the Boulevard Ring, actually a horseshoe shape that begins in the southwest off Prechistenka Street and circles around to the back of the Rossiya Hotel on the other side of the Kremlin. Some of the squares still bear the name of the old gate towers. Frequent buses run around the ring, stopping off at each intersecting boulevard.

THE TEN BOULEVARDS

The first bears the name of the writer Nikolai Gogol. **Gogolevsky Bulvar** stretches from the Moskva open-air swimming pool to Arbat Square. It was known as the Immaculate Virgin Boulevard, *Prechistensky Bulvar*, until 1924; the first square is still called Prechistensky Vorota (Gates) with the Metro stop Kropotkinskaya nearby. The right side of the street is lined with mansions dating back to the 1800s. In the 19th century, the aristocratic Naryshkin family had their estate at number 10. At number 14 is the Central Chess Club. The next square is Arbatskaya, which leads into the old Arbat district (Metro Arbatskaya). A side-street leading to the Kremlin is Znamenka, which dates back to the 13th century. It means The Sign, taking its name at the time from the Church of the Virgin Icon. In the 17th century, the czar's apothecary was nearby; medicinal herbs were planted on Vagankovsky Hill.

Nikitsky Boulevard extends from Novy Arbat to Herzen Street. Until 1992, it was named after the famous Russian army commander Alexander Suvorov, who lived at the thoroughfare's end. The Nikitskiye Gates used to stand at the junction of the boulevard and Herzen Street, which is named Nikitskaya Square after a monastery that was in the area. Gogol lived at number seven; increasingly despondent in his later years, Gogol burned the second volume of his novel *Dead Souls* in this house, and died here in 1852. A monument to Nikolai Gogol, upon which characters from his books are depicted, stands in front. The Union of Journalists, opened in 1920, is at number 8. The Lunin House, at number 12, was built by Gilliardi in Russian-empire style with eight Corinthian columns in 1823. It is now the **Museum of Oriental Art**; it is open from 11:00 to 19:00 and is closed on Mondays. The museum has displays from Asian countries and former Soviet republics.

Ulitsa Gerzena, Herzen Street, named after the revolutionary writer Alexander Herzen, extends from the Kremlin's Manezhnaya Square (between Tverskaya and Novy Arbat streets) to the Boulevard Ring. In the 15th century, this was the route to the town of Novgorod. At number 13 is the Moscow Conservatory Grand Hall, built in 1901. The conservatory was founded in 1866 by Rubenstein. A statue of Tchaikovsky stands before it. Count Menschikov once lived in the palace at number 12. At number 19 is the Mayakovsky Theater, and at number 6 the **Zoological Museum**. It is one of Moscow's oldest museums, founded in 1791 as a natural history project of Moscow University. It was opened to the public in 1805; the present building was completed in 1902. The museum has a collection of more than a million vertebrates and invertebrates, with over 10,000 animals from around the world. It is open from 10:00 to 17:00 on Saturdays, Sundays, Tuesdays and Thursdays, and from 12:00 to

20:00 on Wednesdays and Fridays; it is closed on Mondays.

Tverskoi Boulevard begins with the Monument to Kliment Timiryazev, a prominent Russian botanist. Built in 1796, it is the oldest boulevard on the ring, and was once a very fashionable promenade. Pushkin, Turgenev and Tolstoy all mentioned the Tverskoi in their writings. Number 11, where the great Russian actress Yermolova lived, is now the **Maria Yermolova Museum**. It is open from 13:00 to 20:00 on Wednesdays, Thursdays and Fridays, from 12:00 to 19:00 on Saturdays and Sundays, and is closed on Mondays and Tuesdays. At number 23 is the Pushkin Drama Theater, and at number 25 the Gorky Literature Institute. Across the street is the Theater of Friendship of the Peoples of the Commonwealth. On the corner of Bogoslovsky Lane is the oldest architectural monument on the boulevard, the 17th-century Church of St John the Divine. The new Moscow Art Theater, standing where the boulevard crosses Tverskaya Street, was built in 1973. Tverskoi ends at Pushkin Square and the Metro Pushkinskaya.

The Strastnoi (Passion) Monastery used to be in the area of the **Strastnoi Boulevard**, which begins with the Statue of Pushkin. On Pushkin's birthday, June 6, many people crowd the square to honor the poet. Pushkin and Chekhov streets branch out from the center. At 2 Dostoevsky Street is the **Dostoevsky Museum**, which is open on Saturdays, Sundays and Thursdays from 11:00 to 18:00, on Wednesdays and Fridays from 14:00 to 20:00, and is closed on Mondays and Tuesdays. Strastnoi is one of the shortest and widest parts of the Boulevard Ring. The city hospital, with 12 Ionic columns, is at number 15; it was once the Palace of the Gagarin Princes and later the English Club from 1802 to 1812.

The Petrovskiye Gates used to stand at what is now the beginning of **Petrovsky Boulevard**, which runs from Petrovsky Street to Trubnaya Square. It is one of the few areas on the ring whose appearance has hardly changed since the 1800s. Some buildings still remain from the 14th-century Vysoko-Petrovsky (St Peter's) Monastery, which once stood on the banks of the (now underground) Neglinnaya River. Trubnaya originates from the Russian word *truba*, meaning pipe; the river was diverted through a pipe under this square. Many of the old mansions on this boulevard were converted into hospitals and schools after the Revolution. At the end of Petrovsky stands the building of the former Hermitage Hotel; its restaurant was once the most popular in Moscow—Turgenev, Dostoevsky and Tchaikovsky all ate here. After the Revolution, it became the House of the Collective Farmer, and today is a theater.

Branching off to the left from Petrovsky is Tsvetnoi Boulevard, named after the flower, *tsveti*, market that used to be here. At number 13 is the **Old Circus**. It was established by Salamonsky for his private circus, the first in Moscow. After the Revolution it was turned into the State Circus. Not long ago a new circus was built on the site to match the original building. The new Old Circus was reopened in 1989. Tickets can be purchased at the building itself or at your hotel's Service desk. Some kiosks on the street also sell tickets. Take the Metro to Tvesnoi Bulvar. Make sure you buy tickets for the Old Circus, *Stary Tsirk*, since the New Circus, *Novy Tsirk*, is near Moscow University. In summer, tent circuses are set up in Gorky and Izmailovo parks. Next to the Old Circus is the Tsentralny Rinok, Central Market, the best stocked *rinok* in the city.

Rozhdestvensky (Nativity) **Boulevard** ends at Sretenka Street, a popular shopping area. On the right are the l4th-century walls of the Convent of the Nativity of God. This complex also includes other churches and the nun cells with a belfry. An exhibit of the Soviet fleet is sometimes in the l5th-century Church of the Assumption. Recently, it has been used as a refuge by the homeless. At the corner of Rozhdestvensky and Pushechnaya streets is one of Moscow's best hotels, the Savoy. Built in 1913 by the architect Velichkin, it was renamed the Hotel Berlin after the war. After major restoration, it was reopened under its original name.

The **Statue to Nadezhda Krupskaya** (1869–1939), Lenin's wife, marks the beginning of **Sretensky Boulevard**, the shortest boulevard with a length of 700 feet (215 meters). The old Russian word *vstreteniye* meant meeting. In 1395, the Vladimir Icon of the Mother of God was brought to Moscow and was met here at the gate of the White Town on its way to the Kremlin. Lining the boulevard's right side are early 20th-century homes, distinguished by their original façades. In 1885, Moscow named its first public library, located here, after the writer Turgenev. Nearby, in Bolshaya Lubyanka (formerly Dzerzhinsky) Street is the 14th-century Cathedral of the Sretenka Monastery. At the beginning of Sretenka Street is the 17th-century Church of the Dormition at Pechatniki. The Central Post Office is on Myasnitskaya (formerly Kirov) Street. To the right, in Telegrafny Lane, one can make out the tower of the Church of the Archangel Gabriel. Prince Alexander Menschikov ordered it built on his estate in 1707; he wanted it to be taller than the Kremlin's Ivan the Great Bell tower. In 1723, the archangel at the top was struck by lightning; so, for a while, the tower was the second largest structure in Moscow. Today it is known as the **Menschikov Tower**. The boulevard ends on Turgenevskaya Square with a Metro stop.

A Statue of the writer Griboyedov (1795–1829) marks the beginning of **Chistoprudny Boulevard**. Its name, Clear Pond, comes from the pond at its center, which offers boating and ice skating in winter. (The Rachka river was diverted underground.) The Sovremennik (Contemporary) Theater (called the Moscow Workers' Theater of the Prolekult in the 1930s) is at number 19.

Pokrovsky (Intercession) **Boulevard** begins at Chernyshevsky Street. The 18th-century buildings on the left used to serve as the Pokrovsky barracks. A highly decorative rococo-style house built here in 1766 was known as the Chest of Drawers. The czars often took this route to their estate in **Izmailovo**, now a popular 3,000-acre park with a theater, amusement park and summer tent-circus. The estate, situated on an artificial island, dates back to the 14th century, and was the property of the Romanovs. Peter the Great staged mock battle maneuvers here. The 17th-century churches of the Nativity and Protecting Veil survive, along with some of the gates and a three-tiered bridge. It is worth visiting on weekends. A huge market stretches across the park with thousands of people selling a wide variety of goods—it is a marvelous place to shop and bargain. It can be reached from Metro stop Izmailovo Park. At 39 Izmailovsky Bulvar is the Theater of Mimicry and Gesture, whose company is peopled by deaf actors.

The **Yauzsky Boulevard** is the last and narrowest section of the Boulevard Ring. This ends by Yauzsky Gate Square and the Yauza River, where it joins the Moskva River. A few 18th-century mansions remain in this area. Branching off to Petropavlovsky Lane brings you to the 18th-century baroque Church of Sts Peter and Paul. The 17th-century Trinity Church is located in Serebryanichesky (Silversmiths) Lane, named after the jewelers' quarter. Across the river lies Moscow's old Zayauzye district, once the home to artisans and tailors. Continuing along the banks of the Moskva, past another of Stalin's Gothic skyscrapers, leads you to the back of the Kremlin. One of the best views of the Kremlin is from the **Bolshoi Kammeni Most** (Large Stone Bridge).

The Garden Ring

After much of Moscow burned in the great fire of 1812 (over 7,000 buildings were destroyed), it was decided to tear down all the old earthen ramparts and in their place build a circular road around the city. Anyone who had a house along the ring was required to plant a *sad*, garden; thus the thoroughfare was named Sadovaya Koltso, Garden Ring. The ring, Moscow's widest avenue, stretches for ten miles (16 kilometers) around the city, with the Kremlin's bell tower at midpoint. It is less than a mile (two kilometers) from the Boulevard Ring. The 16 squares and streets that make up this ring each have a garden in their name, such as Big Garden and Sloping Garden. Buses, trolleys and the Koltso Metro circle the route. Along the way, 18th- and 19th-century mansions and old manor houses are interspersed amongst the modern buildings.

Beginning by the river, near the Metro stop Park Kultury and Gorky Park, is Krymskaya (Crimean) Square, surrounded by very old classically designed provisional warehouses, built by Stasov between 1832 and 1835. Nearby is the Olympic Press Center, Novosti Press Agency and Progress Publishers, which publishes books in foreign languages.

At Zubovsky Square, Bolshaya Pirogovskaya (named after Nikolai Pirogov, a renowned surgeon) leads to Novodevichy Monastery. Many of Moscow's clinics and research institutes are located here. **Zubovsky Bulvar** begins at Devichye Park, Maiden's Field, where carnivals were held and maidens danced to Russian folk tunes. To the right, Prechistenka Street leads to the Kremlin. The area between the Boulevard and Garden rings was once an aristocratic residential district; many old mansions are still in the area. At number 18 is the former estate of the wealthy merchant Morozov.

On **Smolensky Bulvar** (formerly called Sennaya, the Haymarket) is the tall Ministry of Foreign Affairs. Nearby is the Belgrade Hotel. Novinsky (a composer) Street branches off the square. From 1940 to 1992 the street was named after Tchaikovsky. The poet Alexander Griboyedov grew up at number 17. The great singer Fyodor Chaliapin (1873–1938) lived at number 25 for over a decade. The American Embassy is at number 19–32.

The next square, **Vosstaniya** (Uprising), was named after the heavy fighting that took place here during the revolutions of 1905 and 1917. The street is still known as Kudrinskaya, after the local village of Kudrino. The square is surrounded by large apartment complexes, except for the 18th-century Widow's House, the residence of widows and orphans of czarist officers killed in battle. It used to be the home of writer Alexander Kuprin; it is now a medical institute.

Before the square, to the right, is Vorovsky Street, once one of the most fashionable areas of the city. Centuries ago, when the czar's servants and cooks lived in this area, the street was known as Povarskaya, Cook. Other side streets were Khlebny (Bread), Nozhevoy (Knife), and Chashechny (Cup). The two lanes Skaterny, Tablecloth, and Stolovoy, Table, still branch off the street. In *War and Peace*, Tolstoy described the Rostov's estate at 52 Povarskaya Street, where there is now a statue of Tolstoy. Next door is the Writer's Club, named after the Soviet writer Alexander Fadeyev. The **Maxim Gorky Museum** at number 25, recognizable by the statue of Gorky at the front, chronicles the life of the Russian writer. It is open on Thursdays, Saturdays and Sundays from 10:00 to 18:00, on Wednesdays and Fridays from 12:00 to 19:00 and is closed on Mondays and Tuesdays. Gorky also spent his last years in a house on the neighboring street of Kachalov at number 6, which is also a museum (see Patriarch's Pond, page 125).

On the other side of Vosstaniya Square is Barrikadnaya Street, with a Metro stop of the same name. The Planetarium and Zoo are in the area. This street leads into Krasnaya Presnya, once a working-class district and the scene of many revolutionary battles. On the nearby side street of Bolshevistskaya, at number 4, the **Krasnaya**

Presnya Historical Revolutionary Museum traces the history of the area. It is open from 11:00 to 18:00; closed on Mondays. l905 Street leads to the International Trade Center, along the Krasnopresnenskaya Embankment. It was built with the cooperation of the American firms Occidental Petroleum and Welton-Becket to promote cultural relations and international exhibits. Anton Chekhov lived in the small red house at 6 Sadovaya Kudrinskaya, now the **Chekhov House-Museum**. It is open on Saturdays, Sundays, Tuesdays and Thursdays from 11:00 to 18:00, on Wednesdays and Fridays from 14:00 to 20:00 and is closed on Mondays.

Bolshaya Sadovaya (Great Garden) Street once had a triumphal arch through which troops returned to Moscow. The next street is **Sad Triumfalnaya**. Past Mayakovsky Square (with a Metro stop of the same name) is the **All Russia Museum of Decorative, Applied and Folk Art** at 31 Delegatskaya Street. The museum exhibits Bogorodsky toys, birch-bark weavings, embroidery, folk costumes, lace, porcelain, pottery, trays, *samovars* and wood cuttings. It is open on Saturdays, Sundays, Mondays and Wednesdays from 11:00 to 18:00, on Tuesdays and Thursdays from 12:30 to 20:00 and is closed on Fridays. Along the next street at 3 **Sadovaya Samotyochnaya** is the **Central Puppet Theater**, better known as the Obraztsov, after its founder. The puppet clock on the front of the building has 12 little houses with a tiny rooster on top; every hour, one house opens. At noon, all the boxes open, each with an animal puppet dancing to an old Russian folk song. On Tsvetnoi (Flower) Boulevard, branching off the square, are the Old Circus and popular Tsentralny Rinok, Central Market. Nearby is the Army Museum and Theater.

The next street and square returned to their original names of **Sukharevskaya** in 1992; they are named after Sukhorov, a popular commander of the czar's *streltsy* guards who were quartered here. After the Revolution the street and square were called Kolkhoznaya, Collective-Farm. Peter the Great opened Russia's first navigational school in the center of the square where the Sukharov Tower had stood. Prospekt Mira, Peace, leads to the **Exhibition Park of Economic Achievements**. Prospekt Mira's original name was Meshchanskaya Sloboda, Commoner's Quarters; immigrant settlements were concentrated here. At 5 Prospekt Mira is the Perlov House, the former home of an old tea merchant family of the same name. At number 18 is the **Wedding Palace**, an 18th-century structure designed by Bazhenov. Opposite the palace are the headquarters of Vyacheslav Zaitsev, Moscow's top fashion designer. At number 28 are the oldest botanical gardens in the city, known in Peter the Great's time as the **Apothecary**; the Metro stop is Botanichesky Sad. At number 94, near the Rizhskaya (Riga) Railway Station (with a Metro stop of the same name), is the Rizhsky marketplace, which the city has lately clamped down on because of blackmarket activity. Near the Metro Prospekt Mira is the Olympic Sports Complex, built in the late 1970s. In front of it is the the 18th-century Church of St Filipp (once the Metropolitan of Moscow). The **Museum of Cosmonautics** is on the Alley of Cosmonauts. It is open on Tuesdays, Wednesdays and Thursdays from 12:00 to 20:00, on Fridays, Saturdays and Sundays from 11:00 to 17:30 and is closed on Mondays. Prospekt Mira led to the old towns of Rostov and Suzdal; it now turns into the Yaroslavl Highway, which runs to Yaroslavl in the Golden Ring.

The next square, **Lermontovskaya**, is named after the Russian poet Lermontov, who was born in a house near the square on October 3, 1814; a plaque on a building marks where the house stood. The plaque is inscribed with Lermontov's words: 'Moscow, Moscow, I love you deeply as a son, passionately and tenderly.' The square was known as Krasniye Vorota , Red Gate, because red gates once marked the entrance to the square. The Metro station was given this name. The czar's kitchen gardens were in this area. Nearby is the Academy of Agriculture, housed in a 17th-century mansion once owned by Count Yusupov, a descendent of a Mongol Khan.

Zemlyanoi Val, Earthen rampart, is the longest street on the ring, once named after the pilot Valeri Chakalov, who made the first non-stop flight over the North Pole from the USSR to America in 1936. At numbers 14 to 16 lived the poet Marshak, the composer Prokofiev and the violinist Oistrach. Tchaikovsky once lived at number 47. Behind the Kursky Railway Station is an 18th-century stone mansion, the Naidyonov Estate. Gilliardi and Grigorev built the estate, whose gardens stretch down to the Yauza River; it is now a sanatorium. After crossing the Yauza River, the ring becomes Taganskaya Square (with a Metro stop of the same name), where the popular avant-garde theater **Taganka** is located at number 76. The Bolshaya Krasnokholmsky Bridge crosses the Moskva River off of Zetsepsky Street. Near the Pavletskaya Metro stop is Bakhrushina Street. At number 31 is the **Bakhrushkin Theatrical Museum** (closed Tuesdays) with collections on the history of Russian theater. It is named after the merchant Alexei Bakhruskin, who opened the museum in 1894. A separate exhibition hall is also located at 11 Tverskoi Boulevard.

Dobryninskaya Square was named after the revolutionary Dobrynin, who was killed in the 1917 Revolution. The next square, Oktyabrskaya, leads to the entrance of **Gorky Park**, with two large ferris wheels. The nearby chocolate factory of Krasny Oktyabr, Red October, has been making chocolate here for over 125 years. Across from the park is the **State Art Gallery** (a branch of the Tretyakov, closed on Mondays) and the **Complex of Arts**. In the grounds is the newly formed **Park of the Fallen Heroes,** where statues of revolutionary figures now lie, sit and stand. The statue of Felix Dzerzhinsky, toppled during the 1991 attempted coup, is here, along with the statues of Kalinin, Sverdlov, Krushchev and Stalin. Krimsky Val, Crimean Rampart, is the last section of the ring. It crosses the Moskva River by way of the Krymsky suspension bridge that brings you back to Gorky Park.

When strolling along the Garden or Boulevard Ring, pay attention to the traffic.

Even 150 years ago, Nikolai Gogol wrote: 'What Russian doesn't like fast driving?' And this is just as true today. Traffic accidents have multiplied; cars often use sidewalks as passing lanes; and at night, headlights are not normally used. Many *yama*, potholes, are left unrepaired, so that getting splashed with rain and mud during a rainfall is likely.

The Lenin Hills

The Lenin Hills, in the southwest, are the highest point in Moscow and provide one of the best views of the city. Group tours usually include a stop on the hills, or they can easily be reached by taking the Metro to Leninskiye Gory, Lenin Hills. The Metro here rides above ground and crosses the Moskva River; pedestrian walkways are on each side of the bridge.

A short walk from the Metro is a glass-enclosed escalator to the top of the hill. The avenue to the right leads to an observation platform, about a 15-minute walk. The platform provides a spectacular view of the city; in good weather the golden domes of the Kremlin are visible. If you stand with the Moskva River behind you, you can see a massive 36-story building. This is Lomonosov University, more widely known as **Moscow University**, founded in 1755 by Russian scientist Mikhail Lomonosov. This university building was erected between 1949 and 1953 by Stalin, who had six other similar Gothic-style structures built throughout the city. The top of the university's main tower is crowned by a golden star in the shape of ears of corn. It is the largest university in Russia, with students from over 100 countries. The campus comprises 40 buildings, including sports centers, an observatory, botanical gardens and a park. The Gorky Library has over six million volumes. Gorbachev graduated from Moscow University with a degree in law, and his wife Raisa with a degree in Leninist philosophy. Recently Moscow University became independent from the Ministry of Education. Lomonosov Prospekt extends from behind the university, and Universitetsky Prospekt lies in front.

A few blocks to the left, between the Vernadksy and Lomonosov prospekts, is the circular building of the **Novi Tsirk**, New Circus. The circus is one of the most popular forms of entertainment in Russia, and the Moscow Circus is famous throughout the world. This circus building, opened in 1971, seats 3,400. Its ring has four interchangeable floors that can be switched in less than five minutes. One is the regular ring, another a special ring for magicians, and the others are a pool for the aquatic circus and a rink for the ice ballet. The Universitet Metro station is directly behind the Circus. The other main circus of Moscow is the **Stari Tsirk**, Old Circus, at 13 Tsvetnoi Boulevard.

Moscow Burning

Narychkine invited a guest to meet me at lunch next day—the Moscow Chief of Police, Schetchinsky by name. Before we had been more than 10 minutes at table a wild-looking police officer rushed in unannounced and uttered one word—"Pajare!"—"Quick!" The Chief of Police sprang from his seat while Narychkine and Jenny, with one voice, exclaimed: "A fire? Where?" A fire is no rare event in Moscow and is always a serious matter, for of the 11,000 houses in the centre of Moscow only 3,500 are of stone, the rest are of wood. Just as St. Petersburg counts its disasters in floods, Moscow numbers the fires that have reduced great stretches of the city to ashes, the most terrible being, of course in 1812, when barely 6,000 buildings remained standing.

I was seized with a sudden urge to see this fire for myself.

"Can I come with you?" I begged the Chief of Police.

"If you promise not to delay me a single second."

I seized my hat as we ran together to the door. His troika, with its three mettlesome black horses, was waiting. We jumped in and shot off like lightning while the messenger, already in the saddle, spurred his own mount and led the way. I had no conception of how fast a troika can move behind three galloping horses, and for a moment I could not even draw breath. Dust from the macadamised country road billowed up in clouds above our heads; then, as we skimmed over the pointed cobbles of Moscow's streets, sparks struck by our flying hooves fell around us like rain and clung desperately to the iron strut while the Chief of Police yelled: "Faster! Faster!"

As soon as we left Petrovsky Park we could see smoke hanging like an umbrella—fortunately there was no wind. In the town there were dense crowds, but the messenger, riding a horse's length ahead, cleared a path for us, using his knout on any bystanders who did not move fast enough to please him, and we passed between ranks of people like lightning between clouds. Every moment I feared that someone would be run over, but by some miracle no one was even touched and five minutes later we were facing the fire, our horses trembling, their legs folding beneath them. A whole island of houses was burning fiercely. By good fortune the road in front of it was fifteen or twenty yards wide, but on every other side only narrow alleys separated it from neighbouring dwellings. Into one of these alleys rushed M. Schetchinsky, I at his heels. He urged me back—in vain. "Then hold fast to my sword-belt," he cried, "and don't let go!" For several seconds I was in the midst of flames and thought I would suffocate. My very lungs seemed on fire as I gasped for breath. Luckily another alley led off to our right. the Chief of Police ran into it, I followed and we both sank on a baulk of timber. "You've lost your hat," he laughed. "D'you feel inclined to go back for it?"

"God! No! Let it lie! All I want is a drink."

At a gesture from my companion a woman standing by went back in to her house and brought out a pitcher of water. Never did the finest wine taste so good! As I drank, we heard a rumble like thunder. The fire-engines had arrived!

Moscow's Fire Service is very well organised, and each of the 21 districts has its own engines. A man is stationed on the highest tower in the area, on the watch day and night, and at the first sign of fire he sets in motion a system of globes to indicate exactly where smoke is rising. So the engines arrive without losing a second, as they did on this occasion, but the fire was quicker still. It had started in the coutyard of an inn, where a carter had carelessly lit a cigar near a heap of straw. I looked into that courtyard. It was an inferno!

To my amazement, M. Schetchinsky directed the hoses not on the fire itself but on the roofs of the nearby houses. He explained that there could be no hope of of saving the houses that were actually burning, but if the sheets of iron on neighbouring rooftops could be prevented from getting red hot there might be a chance of saving the homes they covered.

The only source of water in the district was 300 yards away, and soon the engines were racing to it to refill their tanks. "Why don't the people make a chain?" I asked.

"What is that?"

"In France, everyone in the street would volunteer to pass along buckets of water so that the engines could go on pumping."

"That's a very good idea! I can see how useful that would be. But we have no law to make people do that."

"Nor have we, but everyone rushes to lend a hand. When the Théâtre Italien caught fire I saw princes working in the chain."

"My dear M. Dumas," said the Chief of Police, "that's your French fraternity in action. The people of Russia haven't reached that stage yet."

"What about the firemen?"

"They are under orders. Go and see how they are working and tell me what you think of them."

They were indeed working desperately hard. They had climbed into the attics of the nearby houses and with hatchets and levers, their left hands protected by gloves, they were trying to dislodge the metal roofing sheets, but they were too late. Smoke was already pouring from the top storey of the corner house and its roof glowed red. Still the men persisted like soldiers attacking an enemy position. They were really wonderful, quite unlike our French firemen who attack the destructive element on their own initiative, each finding his own way to conquer the flames. No! Theirs was a passive obedience, complete and unquestioning. If their chief had said "Jump in the fire!" they would have done so with the same devotion to duty, though they well knew that it meant certain death to no purpose.

Brave? Yes, indeed, and bravery in action is always inspiring to see. But I was the only one to appreciate it. Three or four thousand people stood there watching, but they showed not the slightest concern at this great devastation, no sign of admiration for the courage of the firemen. In France there would have been cries of horror, encouragement, applause, pity, despair, but here—nothing! Complete silence, not of consternation but of utter indifference, and I realised the profound truth of M. Schetchinsky's comment that as yet the Russians have no conception of fraternity as we know it, no idea of brotherhood between man and his fellows. God! How many revolutions must a people endure before they can reach our level of understanding?

Alexandre Dumas, Adventures in Czarist Russia

On the right side of this prospekt are what were known as the Vorobiev, Sparrow Hills, in the 15th century. Peter the Great and Catherine the Great had their country palaces in this area. Many *dacha*, country homes, are still situated here. Stalin ordered Moscow University built on the highest point of the Sparrow Hills.

In front of the New Circus is the Moscow Palace of Young Pioneers, sometimes referred to as **Pioneerland**. This is a large club and recreational center for children. Before the Communist Party was banned in 1991, children who belonged to the Communist Youth Organization were known as Young Pioneers. Older members belonged to the Young Komsomol League. During the last years of Communist rule, over 25 million members were in the Young Pioneers, and over 39 million in the Komsomol. The 400 rooms in the palace include clubs, laboratories and workshops. It also has its own concert hall, sports stadium, gardens, and even an artificial lake for learning how to row and sail. There are over 35 youth house branches in Moscow. The entrance to the palace is marked by the Statue of Malchish-Kibalchish, a character from a popular children's book. On the corner is the Children's Musical Theater.

The Lenin Hill Ski Jump is on your left. The hills are a favorite spot for picnics in summer, and in winter there is skiing and tobogganing. Across the river are the white buildings of the **Central (Lenin) Stadium** in the wide meadow area known as Luzhniki. *Lug* means meadow. The complex consists of the **Stadium** (seating 100,000), the Palace of Sport, the Swimming and Tennis stadiums, the Friendship Hall and the Museum of Physical Culture. Many events of the Moscow 1980 Olympics were held here. The Olympic Village was built behind the University on Lomonosov Prospekt. Glancing to the left of the stadium, you can make out the golden domes of the Novodevichy Convent. To the right of the stadium, on Komsomolky Prospekt, is the Church of St Nicholas at Khamovniki, built in 1682. In the past, weavers lived in this area. The old Russian word for weavers is *khamovniki*. A side street off the prospekt near the Garden Ring is Leo Tolstoy Street, where the Russian writer lived for 19 years. Two of the works that he wrote while living in the house at number 21 are *Power of Darkness* and *Resurrection*. The **Leo Tolstoy Museum** is open on Sundays, Wednesdays, Thursdays and Fridays from 11:00 to 17:00, on Saturdays from 10:00 to 16:00 and is closed on Mondays and Tuesdays.

NOVODEVICHY CONVENT

Ride the Metro one stop from Lenin Hills back across the river to Sportivnaya and get off in front of the Stadium. Walking a few blocks along Fruzenskaya Street will bring you to one of the oldest religious complexes in the city, the New Maiden Convent, a baroque-style complex of 15 buildings and 16 gilded domes dating from the 16th and 17th centuries. Grand-Prince Vasily III founded the convent in 1514 to commemorate the capture of Smolensk from Lithuania, which had controlled the area for over a century (the convent was built on the road to Smolensk). The convent was also one in the group of fortified monasteries that surrounded Moscow. Novodevichy served mainly as a religious retreat for Russian noblewomen. Peter the Great banished his half-sister Sophia and first wife Evdokia to the convent and forced them to wear the veil. Boris Godunov was crowned here in 1598. Napoleon tried to blow up the convent before he fled the city, but a nun pulled out the fuses. The convent was converted into a museum in 1922.

The five-domed Smolensky Cathedral was the convent's first stone building and lies at its center. It was dedicated to the Virgin of Smolensk, a much revered 16th-century icon, and modeled on the Kremlin's Uspensky Cathedral. Many 16th-century interior frescoes portray the life of Vasily III (the father of Ivan the Terrible). A copy of the *Icon of Our Lady of Smolenskaya* hangs over the altar. Many of the icons were painted by Simon Ushakov. The beautiful five-tiered iconostasis (1683–86) was presented by Sophia; its wooden columns, decorated with climbing grapevines, are made out of whole tree trunks. Ivan the Terrible's daughter Anna, Sophia and Evdokia are some of the noblewomen in the burial vault. There are two Gate Churches: the Transfiguration Gate Church at the northern entrance and the Church of Pokrov at the southern. Other structures include the Refectory Church (1685–87), Bell Tower (1690) and four nun's residences. The Miloslavsky Chambers are named after Sophia's sister Maria Miloslavskaya, who lived here until her death. Sofia's Chamber Prison is where Peter the Great imprisoned his half-sister when he deposed her as Regent and took the throne. Irina Godunova had her chamber here. She was the sister of Boris Godunov and was married to Czar Fedor. When Fedor died, Irina refused the throne and her brother Boris was elected czar. Peter the Great's first wife, Evdokia Lopukhina, lived in the Lopukhina Chamber. The Convent (with a large *Beriozka* next door) is open daily from 10:00 to 17:30 and is closed on Tuesdays.

Many notable Russian personalities are buried in the Novodevichy's two cemeteries. Within the convent grounds are the graves of princes, wealthy merchants, clergymen and war heroes. Behind the southern wall, the 19th-century cemetery has been been the burial site of many of Russia's most prominent statemen, artists and scientists. These include Chekhov, Eisenstein, Gogol, Krushchev, Mayakovsky, Prokofiev, Scriabin, Serov, Shostokovich, Stanislavsky and Stalin's first wife. During periods of restoration, it is closed to the public (it used always to be closed to the public).

GORKY PARK

Gorky Park lies a few minutes' walk over the Moskva River from the Park Kultury Metro station in the Frunze District. It can also be reached from the other side of the river at Metro stop Oktyabrskaya, which features a bronze statue of Lenin. A large archway marks the entrance to the park. In this vast park are amusement rides, boats for hire and the Zelyoni (Green) open-air theater. In summer, the park is teeming with strollers, performance artists and circus performers of the Tent Circus. In winter, the popular ice skating rink is in operation. The park is open daily from 09:00 to midnight. Also part of the park are the Neskuchny Sadi, Not-Boring Gardens, originally part of the Alexandrov Estate and now used by the Academy of Sciences. The estate is part of the Main Botanical Gardens (with a collection of over 16,000 varieties of rose) that stretch as far as the river.

DONSKOI MONASTERY

Not far from Gorky Park near the Shabolovskaya Metro station is the **Donskoi Monastery**. This monastery and seven churches were founded by Czar Fedor and Boris Godunov in 1591, on the site of the Russian Army's line of defense against the invading Mongols. Legend claims that the city was protected by the Donskaya Virgin Icon, the icon that Prince Donskoi took for protection in the battle against the Tatars in 1380. In the 16th century, six fortified monasteries formed a ring to defend the city from the Mongols. The monasteries were connected by an earthen rampart, today's Garden Ring. The Donskoi Monastery houses a branch of the **Shchusev Museum of Architecture**, opened in 1934 (closed Mondays and Fridays); it has exhibits of pre-revolutionary Russian architecture. The Old Cathedral of the Donskaya Virgin was the first building of the monastery. The cube roof and onion domes are topped with golden half-moon crosses that symbolize the Christian victory over Islam. A copy of the Donskaya Virgin Icon is on the eight-tiered iconostasis; the original is in the Tretyakov Gallery. Patriarch Tikhon, who was appointed the head of the Orthodox Church on the eve of the October 1917 Revolution, is buried in a marble tomb at the southern wall.

The Naryshkin-baroque style New Cathedral of the Donskaya Virgin was commissioned a century later by Peter the Great's sister. The interior frescoes were painted by the Italian artist Antonio Claudio between 1782 and 1785. At the southwestern corner of the monastery is the classical Church of the Archangel Michael, built between 1806 and 1809. The church served as a memorial chapel for the Golitsyn family. Mikhail Golitsyn (1681–1764) was Peter the Great's star general who began his career as a service drummer. Fourteen Golitsyns are buried here, including Dmitri and his wife Natalia, who is the subject of Pushkin's novel *Queen of Spades*. The Church is now the Museum of Monumental Sculpture. Some pieces include the *Sitting Christ* by Antokolsky and two lions from the old English Club. Some of the people buried in the cemetery are Turgenev, the architect Bovet, and Zhukovsky, the father of Russian aviation. Other buildings include the Tikhvin Gate Church, the Abbot's residence, a bell tower and the 20th-century Church of St Seraphim, now a

A New World Indeed

And then the Gypsy Restaurant. I know it has another name but I do not know what it is, or where it is. But since it is a night restaurant of sorts— the only place where a little public night gayety is to be found in Moscow— it will not be hard for anyone who knows Moscow to identify it.

I was taken there by Reswick, the representative of the Associated Press, and we timed ourselves to arrive at midnight, previously taking the trouble to telephone for a table. And knowing the economic and social restrictions of the Soviet Empire at the time, I was more cheered than not, for I had expected so little. It is so in Russia. You know that all bourgeois gayety is suspect, and certainly a night restaurant of any description is bourgeois— and so is likely to be patronized by conniving capitalists, concessionaries, money hoarders or grafters who are not in sympathy with the Communistic ideal, and so not entitled to gayety, or indeed relaxation in any form. Yet such is the nature of man, as well as all Russians, that it is difficult to taboo quite everything. The heart of him is unregenerate. And being so, some bits of compromise must be made here and there. Only then, a resort such as this becomes a kind of Communist trap. For it tends to draw these unregenerate, and eke secretly gilded flies, out into the light, where they can be pounced upon by the virtuous and self-sacrificing. Ha! Ha! You will hoard money, will you? You will graft or profiteer and then come to such a place as this to make merry! Very good, come to the Cheka! Come to the office of the G.P.U. We will look into your affairs. Perhaps you have not paid all your dues, accounted for all of your takings.

So, as I say, I was not a little pleased to find a quite cheery room, not badly lighted; the food, as it proved, good; the music consisting of ten genuine gypsies of assorted ages and sizes all sitting on a platform, tambours or castanets in hand, and indulging at intervals in various spirited and yet invariably mournful airs, which recited, as I was told, how love, and spring, come early and are soon over—how follow the brief, scorching days of passion and then the sad, brown leaves of autumn and the snows of winter.

'Gather ye rosebuds while ye may.' And yet, so different is the Russian temperament from ours that it finds nothing incongruous in a night restaurant where the music is furnished by ten none-too-attractive and, in certain instances withered and wrinkled gypsies, their ears dangling bangles, their brown, clawy hands thrumming tambours or strings, their throats chanting wistful and yet defiant tunes of sorrows that befall us all. Indeed, my friend, who was surely a Russian man of the world, was enthusiastic in his praise, beating time with his hands and stamping with his feet and saying how lovely the old sad airs were—how wistful and tearful and hence wonderful. And all the other diners equally loud in their approval.

'Yet imagine this in New York or Chicago,' I thought! 'Imagine any night club employing such a world-worn and sinister group as this! Imagine! 'Tis Russia, and none other than Russia.'

But I am running ahead of myself. What really interested me at first, and after, were the patrons themselves. Here we were, now in the only public night resort of any consequence, and yet see how it was—low-ceilinged and decorated not at all, the furniture of that same mixed and au contraire character that marked the Restaurant Tolstoi. And apart from a few men and women in evening dress (how very few, indeed!), an assortment of garments that left me breathless. Upon my word, this is the new, free, different world, this Russia of to-day. For here now comes a strapping young fellow, his plump, pasty-faced girl on his arm, and while she is in flouncy white and wears high-heeled slippers, he is in the standardized dark blue blouse and leather belt, his hair combed backward in long graceful lines over his ears. And behind him, at another table, with his girl, as dark and curly as an Italian Juliet, a blondish youth in a light summer suit far from new and such as one might wear in July—never in December—yet as swagger as you please on account of it. For mark you, these western suits of whatever vintage, even with an occasional patch, are not to be had in Russia at all. They do not make such cloth—(too luxurious as yet)—and they cannot afford to import it. The cheaper grades cost plenty here, God knows! And so, should a foreigner arrive and sell such a suit or leave it indifferently behind—Presto! a Russian, below the rank of an official, say, in a new and smart outfit! And the wonder of it, English or American! Cut right, and with a distinctive pattern. Ha! Ha! And yet, as you say to yourself, the knees bag, and surely the thing doesn't fit as well as it should. But who are you to judge? Are not you the outsider? It is the Russian, the insider, who will be impressed by this. And so...no wonder he is applauding loudly, and the girl, too.

But our evening is young. Wait! Here comes a Kalmuk, with an overcoat that I swear has somehow the look of a corset attached to a hoopskirt—(the skeleton frame, I mean), and with a fur hat that has the dimensions of a very, very, very wide and decidedly truncated dish pan. And with him his girl or wife—small, brown, black-eyed, intense, and even a little savage-looking, and in a combination of things half silk, half linen, that are green, yellow, brown, black, purple. You gaze and are impressed. For after all, if this were a stage—the chorus of some colorful show—it could not be so much better.

And then next, a really portly Russian, of perhaps the trader or bloodsucker type—fat, red-cheeked, double-chinned, puffy-necked, a really beastlike type. And with him two attractive and yet semi-obese girls or women of not over twenty-six or seven, with a heavy, meaty sensuality radiating from every pore. The white flabby double chins and crinkled necks. The small and yet fat and even puffy hands. The little, shrewd, greedy eyes, half concealed by fat lids. And yet they too are moved by those gypsy laments, and sing or beat time with their heavily bejeweled fingers. Surely some Cheka agent or G.P.U. will see and call our fat friend to an accounting on the morrow. Surely, surely.

But along with these the artist types. And writers. Ho, should they be excluded? And why, pray? The outer door is heard to close and here enters, as brisk and flippant as the chill wind he brings with him, Ivan Ivanovitch, say—painter or sculptor or poet, and looking all three. That flaring chrysanthemum hair. The thin, yellow, downy mustaches. The long, waxy, artistic, and yet vital hands. The swagger and even defiant or tolerant air. You think perhaps that he is to be overawed by poverty, or defeated by the gayety of this place. Go to! Heigh, ho! We artists will show you what art and poverty are like, and genius also! And so, an overcoat! (I am not over exaggerating. God forgive me, should I!) And so an overcoat (and in this Moscow weather no less), of nothing other than cretonne or its loom sister—a vari-colored and flaring, posterish thing of quite Chinese exuberances, as who should say the more of this, the better. And to top the thing off—yellow gloves. And worn with what an air! Surely in this case it is the manner and not the clothes that make the man. But with his girl on his arm or preceeding him, in a trim English walking suit, which has been come by God knows how! Yet not expensive. No, no. A thing like that could be picked up in London for twenty shillings, or in New York on Fourteenth Street for nine or ten dollars. But here in Moscow, heigh,ho!

Indeed I might continue this for pages. For Moscow, and all Russia for that matter, is to-day picturesque if poor—all the more so because it is poor. And patches and rags and makeshift and mixtures of the most amazing character are the veriest commonplaces of the hour. Yet as for being deplored—nonsense! Who is rich? Who can be rich? And as for bourgeois, capitalist, fashions, pouf! Also tush! We will do these things as we wish, devise new ways and means. And so you yourself, fresh from London, or New York, and with all your capitalistic and other class notions still strong upon you are suddenly swept into the newness, the strangeness, the freshness of it all. Heigh ho! Bully for a new day! Bully for a new idea! To hell with fashion plates, with what the west, or the north, or the south, may think! This is Russia. This is the new, shifting, shimmering, changeful, colorful, classless day of a new social order. A new world indeed. A fresh deal. Verily. Selah. And let us hope that no real harm comes to it, lest something fresh and strange and new and of glorious promise pass from the eyes and the minds and the hopes of men.

Theodore Dreiser, Dreiser Looks at Russia, 1928

Restoration work at Novodevichy Convent, Moscow

Novodevichy Cemetery

crematorium. Outside the gates is the Church of Rizpolozhenie, whose priests also conduct mass in the Old Cathedral on Sundays and holidays.

At 56 Donskaya Street is the Moscow baroque Church of the Deposition of the Lord's Robe, built in 1701. The Church is filled with interesting cherubs and contains a copy of the *Icon of the Deposition of the Lord's Robe* under a gilded canopy. In 1625, an envoy of a Persian shah presented Czar Mikhail Romanov and the Patriarch Filaret with a fragment of Jesus' robe. Filaret had an icon painted and declared a new church holiday. The icon shows Romanov and Filaret placing the gold box, containing the piece of cloth, on the altar of the Kremlin's Uspensky Cathedral. The original icon is now in the Tretyakov Gallery.

DANILOVSKY MONASTERY

The St Daniil Monastery lies south of the Donskoi, it was founded in 1276 by Prince Daniil (the youngest son of Alexander Nevsky), who is buried in a golden coffin in the Cathedral of the Holy Fathers of the Seven Ecumenical Councils. This cathedral was built by Ivan the Terrible in 1565 on the original site of St Daniil's Church. Daniil is the only Moscow Prince to be canonized by the Russian Church.The fresco of St Daniil is the oldest in the cathedral, which was closed down after the Revolution; it was later used as a prison. In 1985, the Soviet government returned the monastery to the Orthodox Church. In 1988, to celebrate the Millennium of the Baptism of Rus, the Patriarch Pimen chose St Daniil Monastery for the celebrations. It is now the residency of the Moscow Patriarch, along with the administrative bodies of the Holy Synod. It is currently undergoing restoration.

Leninsky Prospekt runs in front of the Donskoi Monastery along the river and leads into Moscow's modern southwestern district, which consists mostly of residential housing. It winds past the Academy of Sciences, formerly Neskuchny (Not-Boring) Castle, and Gagarin Square, which features a titanium-cast monument of Yuri Gagarin, the first Soviet in space. At the base of the monument is a replica of the space capsule Vostok, East, in which Gagarin traveled on April 12, 1961. (Gagarin died in a plane crash in 1968.) This square used to mark the city limits in the 1950s. The prospekt continues past many department stores to the Lumumba People's Friendship University, with 6,000 students from around the world. It eventually turns into the Kievsky Highway and ends at the Vnukovo local airport.

SPASO-ANDRONIKOV MONASTERY

This monastery, at 10 Pryamikova Square, is situated along the River Yauza, a tributary of the Moskva, in the southeastern part of the city, near the Metro station Ploshchad Ilicha. It was founded in 1359 by the Metropolitan Alexei during the reign of Prince Donskoi and has quite an interesting history. After Alexei was confirmed by the Byzantine Patriarch in Constaninople, a heavy storm occurred at sea during his return journey. Alexei promised God, if he should live, to build a monastery dedicated to the saint, whose feast day was celebrated on the day of his safe arrival in Moscow. Alexei returned on August 16, the Saviour Day, or Vernicle. When the Mongol Khan suddenly summoned Alexei to help his ailing wife in the south, the Metropolitan appointed Andronik, a monk at Sergiyev Posad's Trinity-Sergius Monastery, to oversee the complex's construction in his absence. The monastery was named the Spaso-Andronikov after the Saviour and its first abbot; it later became the stronghold of the Old Believers.

This is the oldest architectural complex in Moscow after the Kremlin. The white Cathedral of the Saviour was built between 1420 and 1427; the iconist Andrei Rublev, who also trained as a monk at the Trinity-St Sergius Monastery, painted many of the interior frescoes (it was here that Rublev painted his famous *Old Testament Trinity* icon, now in the Tretyakov Gallery); he is also buried in the monastery. The baroque Church of the Archangel Michael was commissioned by Ustinia Lopukhina in 1694 to celebrate the birth of her grandson Alexei, son of Peter the Great, and her daughter Evdokia. Peter later banished Evdokia to Novodevichy Monastery (a form of divorce in those days) and the Lopukhinas to Siberia. The church is now an icon restoration studio.

The **Andrei Rublev Museum of Religious Art** is housed in three separate buildings. They are located immediately beyond the main gate. The former Seminary Building contains many 15th- and early 16th-century icons by Rublev and his students. Some of the icons include St Sergius, St George, John the Baptist and the Saviour. Many of the icons found in the Monks' Quarters (behind the Saviour Cathedral) were painted in Novgorod in the 17th century. Nearby is a new Exhibition Hall of mainly 17th- and 18th-century icons that include Our Lady of Tikhvin. There are also displays of other paintings, sculpture, embroidery, old books and chronicles. The museum is open daily, except Wednesdays, from 11:00 to 18:00.

Exhibition of Economic Achievements

Known in Russian as *Vy'stavka Dostizhen'ii Narod'novo Khozyai'stva* (VDNKh), the exhibition (opened in 1959) is worth visiting if time permits; most group tours make a stop. The park is situated on the opposite side of the street to the **Kosmos Hotel** at the end of Prospekt Mira, near the Metro station VDNKh. Nearly 100,000 objects representing the latest achievements in science, industry, transport, building and culture are exhibited in 300 buildings and 80 pavilions, which cover an area of 545 acres. The first monuments that come into view are the 315-foot- (96-meter-) high **Sputnik Rocket** (1964) that appears to shoot into space, and the Soviet-realist **Monument to the Worker and Collective Farm Girl** (1937). Pavilions include the **Atomic Energy**, **Agriculture** and **Culture pavilions**. The most interesting, located at the end of the park, is the **Kosmos Pavilion**. In front of it stands a replica of the Vostok rocket that carried Yuri Gagarin into space in 1961. Inside are displays of rockets and space capsules, including the first Sputnik, Lunnik and Soyuz rockets, and Salyut space stations. A display also honors Konstantin Tsiolkovsky, the father of the Russian Space program. He invented the first wind tunnel and outlined the principle of the reactor rocket; he once said: 'This planet is the cradle of the human mind, but one cannot spend one's life in a cradle.' Lining the walls are photographs of Yuri Gargarin, Valentin Tereshkova (the first woman in space), Alexi Leonov (who took the first space walk), and Laika, Belka and Strelka (the first dogs in space). One exhibit chronicles the first joint US–USSR space mission, Soyuz–Apollo, undertaken in July 1975. The first Russian cosmonaut flew in the American Space Shuttle in February 1994. Other buildings include an open-air theater, small zoo, amusement park, shopping center, the Circorama (standing-only) circular movie theater and restaurants. You can hire boats and go fishing in the ponds; fishing tackle can be rented from booths along the bank. In winter, especially during the Winter Festival, there is plenty of entertainment, including ice-skating and troika rides. The park is open on weekdays from 10:00 to 22:00, and on weekends from 10:00 to 23:00; the pavilions are open from 10:00 to 19:00. A half-hour tour of the park can be taken on electric trams.

Ostankino

Not far from Metro stop VDNKh near the Exhibition Park is the **Ostankino Palace**. At the close of the 18th century, Nikolai Sheremetev built a palace on the grounds of his family's Ostankino estate. The palace (1792–97) was built of wood, but painted to resemble bricks and stone. Interesting rooms are the Blue Room, Egyptian Ballroom, Italian Reception Room and the Picture Gallery and Theater, which had over 200 serf actors, dancers and musicians. The palace also houses the **Museum of Serf Art**. The beautiful serf-actress Prashkovya Kovalyova-Zhemchugova later became the count's wife. One of the streets in Ostankino bears her name. The Trinity Church adjoins the palace. The museum is open daily, except Tuesdays and Wednesdays, from 10:00 to 17:00; in winter from 10:00 to 15:00. A short walk away is the **Ostankino TV Tower**, 160 feet (540 meters) high. The tower has an observation deck and a rotating restaurant called Sedmoye Nebo, Seventh Heaven.

Down The Moskva River

The Moskva River winds through the city for about 30 miles (48 kilometers). If your tour does not include a trip on the river, the best **boat cruises** leave from Kievsky Railway Station and run eastward to Novospassky Bridge (May to October). To get

The Emperor Cannon, the world's largest, in the Moscow Kremlin

there, take the Metro to Kievskaya, not far from Hotel Ukrainia. The boat pier is located on the Berezhkovskaya Embankment at one end of Borodinsky Bridge. The *Rocket* hydrofoil also leaves from Gorky Park to Novospassky Bridge in warmer months. Some sites along the way are the Novodevichy Monastery, Lenin Hills and Stadium, Gorky Park, Srelka Rowing Club, Moscow Open-Air Pool, the Kremlin, Hotel Rossiya, and many estates, palaces and churches. The tour takes about 80 minutes and ends at the **Novospassky Monastery**, founded in the 15th century by Ivan the Great. The 17th-century Cathedral of the Transfiguration of the Savior became the burial site of the czar's relatives; the inner vaults were painted by masters from the Kremlin armory. The bell tower, gates and stone walls also date from the 17th century. Today, the New Monastery of the Savior is a restoration institute. Also lying on the banks of the Moskva River are the 17th-century **Kruititskoye Metropolitans' Residence** (*krutitsy* are small hills), and the **Simonov Monastery**, founded by the monk Simon in the 14th century; it was built as a defensive fortress to protect the southern end of Moscow from the invading Mongols. A second boat also leaves from the same pier and runs westward to Kuntsevo-Krylatskoye in Fili-Kuntsevo Park, which has a river beach. This trip lasts about an hour.

TSARITSYNO

In the 16th century, the Czarina Irina had her country estate here and had the Tsaritsyno, czarina, ponds dug. Later, it was a favorite of the Golitsyn princes; in 1712, Peter the Great presented the estate to a Moldavian count.

After Catherine the Great remodeled the Winter Palace and Hermitage in St Petersburg, she turned her attention to Moscow. She bought the estate in the wooded countryside southeast of Moscow, complete with a palace and miniature opera house. It was known as *Chorny Graz*, Black Mud; Catherine renamed it Tsaritsyno. Her architect, Vasily Bazhenov, was commissioned to transform the main building into a Moorish-Gothic-style palace. After ten years, Bazhenov completed the work and Catherine came from St Petersburg to inspect it. After looking it over, she commanded that all work be stopped and the main palace be torn down. Soon after, Bazhenov's pupil and rival, Kazakov, was asked to build a new one; these are the buildings we see today, begun in 1786. Some speculate that Catherine had the original palace demolished because she had had it constructed in two parts—one for herself and one for her son Paul—connected by a common corridor After a decade, however, she had come to abhor her son, who held equal contempt for her, so she no longer wanted anything associated with him. She also hated all the Freemason motifs; Catherine disliked the Freemasons. The rebuilding was halted when Catherine died, and parts of it were never completed.

Walk along the causeway and over the Figurny Bridge (with stone Maltese crosses—motifs of the Freemasons), which separate Tsaritsyno's two lakes, and climb the stairs that lead through the woods. The main building, through the Grapevine entrance gate, looks more like a cathedral than a palace. Its windows are broken and its roof crumbling—in the 19th century, a local factory needed roofing materials and demolished it. The palace has never been lived in and has stood empty for more than two centuries. The strange deserted buildings are fun to explore, and strolling around the grounds is delightful, especially in summer. In 1988, the Russian Church was allowed to build a church nearby, to commemorate the Millennium of the Baptism of Rus; it was the first church allowed to be built in Moscow during the Soviet era. The old palace can be reached by getting off at Metro stop Tsaritsyno in the southern part of Moscow.

Vicinity of Moscow

The privileged classes of Russia used to build their summer residences in the countryside around Moscow. Many of these palaces and parks have been preserved and converted into museums. They are easily reached by Metro, bus or car. Excursions can also be booked through the Service Bureau at your hotel; they include transportation and a tour of the sights.

ABRAMTSEVO

The **Abramtsevo Estate Museum** is located along the Yaroslavsky Highway near the town of Sergiyev Posad, 37 miles (60 kilometers) north of Moscow. It is about an hour's journey by train from the Yaroslavsky Railway Station. In 1843, the Russian writer Sergei Aksakov bought the country estate (built in the 1770s); over the next 15 years it was frequented by many prominent writers, such as Gogol, Tyutchev and Turgenev. Here Gogol gave a reading of the first chapter from his second volume of *Dead Souls*, which he later burned at his home in Moscow. In 1870, the art patron Savva Mamontov bought the estate and turned it into a popular meeting place and artist colony. Art, theater, writing and pottery workshops were held, and Serov, Vrubel, Repin, Chaliapin and Stanislavsky all lived and worked here. The 12th century-style Orthodox church in the park was designed by Victor Vasnetsov and painted by Polenov and Repin. Vasnetsov also built the park's 'Hut on Chick Legs,' based on a popular fairy-tale. Abramtsevo, now a museum, displays rooms as they were used by Aksakov and Mamontov. Paintings and other art work executed on the estate, including many by Vrubel, are exhibited in the art studio. The museum is open daily, except Tuesdays and Wednesdays, from 11:00 to 17:00.

(top right) Playing chess in the park, (bottom right) Reading the daily newspaper, (left) The famous foodstore, Yeliseyev's

ARKHANGELSKOYE ESTATE MUSEUM

This museum lies in the village of Arkhangelskoye, ten miles (16 kilometers) west of Moscow. Take the Volokolamskoye Highway and then the left road toward Petrovo-Dalniye. The closest Metro station is Tushinskaya; then proceed by bus. The estate, situated along the banks of the Moskva River, took 40 years to complete. Prince Golitsyn originally founded the estate at the end of the l8th century. The mansion and park were designed in French style by the architect Chevalier de Huerne and built by serf craftsmen. In l810, the estate passed into the hands of the wealthy land-owner Prince Yusupov (a descendent of one of the Khans—not the one who killed Rasputin) who was the director of the Hermitage Museum and Imperial Theater. He turned the classical palace into his own personal art museum. Today the palace (made into a State museum in l919) contains works by such artists as Boucher, Hubert Robert, Roslin and Van Dyck. The rooms and halls are beautifully decorated with antique furniture, marble sculptures, tapestries, porcelain and chandeliers; much of the china and glassware was produced on the estate. The palace is surrounded on three sides by a park, lined with sculptures, pavilions and arbors. The Temple to the Memory of Catherine the Great depicts her as Themis, Goddess of Justice. There is also a monument to Pushkin, who enjoyed visiting the grounds. The triumphal arch over the entrance was built in l817.

A short distance from the palace is the wooden **Serf Theater**, exhibiting theatrical and original set designs by Pietro Gottardo Gonzaga. Built in l819 by the serf-architect Ivanov, the theater had one of the largest companies of serf actors. Nearby is the Russkaya Izba (Russian Cottage) Restaurant, fashioned after Russian peasant rooms. The cooking is also Old Russian; the menu offers bear meat and venison along with *kvas*, mead, and tea served from a bubbling *samovar*. Call ahead to make reservations (tel. 561-4244); the address is Ilyinskoye village. Arkhangelskoye is open daily, except on Mondays, Tuesdays and the last Friday of each month, from 11:00 to 18:00. Check before you go; Arkhangelskoye is occasionally closed for restoration. Not long ago, a war sanatorium was located on the premises, but only parts of the estate were closed to tourists.

BORODINO

Borodino, site of the most famous battle in the War of 1812, lies on the Moscow–Minsk Road, 75 miles (120 kilometers) from Moscow. On August 26, l812, Napoleon's troops fought the Russian Army, commanded by Mikhail Kutuzov, on a large field near the village. Napoleon's army numbered 135,000 soldiers and 600 guns. After 15 hours of fighting, Napoleon was forced to retreat. The Battle of Borodino was the turning point of the war. In l912, to mark the 100th anniversary, 34 monuments were erected throughout the battlefield. The polished granite obelisk (l966) crowned by a bronze eagle is dedicated to Field-Marshall Kutuzov. Leo Tolstoy visited the battlefield in l876 while writing *War and Peace*. Other memorials commemorate World War II battles that took place here in l941. Every year the anniversary of the 1812 battle is celebrated by a Borodino Field Day, when the battle is actually re-enacted. People playing the French and Russian soldiers dress in period uniforms, cannons roar and smoke rises from the battlefield. Today, a religious ceremony is held after the battle to give thanks for Napolean's defeat. The **Borodino Military History Museum**, with exhibits of the Battle of Borodino, is open from 10:00 to 18:00; it is closed on Mondays and the last Friday of each month. (Another Battle of Borodino Museum is in Moscow at 38 Kutuzovsky Prospekt; open 10:30 to 16:00, closed on Fridays.)

Istra River Museum of Wooden Architecture

The museum is located 35 miles (56kilometers) west of Moscow near the Novoyerusalimsky (New Jerusalem) Monastery. The main building in the monastery is the Resurrection Cathedral (1656–85), built as an exact replica of the Christian church in Jerusalem. A collection of Russian paintings and porcelain is on display in the Refectory. The **Museum of Wooden Architecture** in the park along the River Istra contains a wooden 17th-century church and farmstead, cottages, granaries and windmills brought in from nearby areas. The museums are open from 10:00 to 18:00 and are closed on Mondays and the last Friday of each month.

Klin

The old Russian town of Klin, founded on the banks of the Sestra River (a tributary of the Volga) in 1318, is located 50 miles (80 kilometers) northwest of Moscow along the Leningrad Highway. Only two Naryshkin baroque-style churches remain of the town's monastery. Klin is widely known as the home of the great Russian composer Pyotr Tchaikovsky (l840–93). His house, surrounded by a charming garden, is now a museum containing his personal belongings and grand piano. Here, Tchaikovsky composed *The Nutcracker, Sleeping Beauty*, and the Fifth and Sixth Symphonies. On his birthday, May 7, the winners of the Moscow Tchaikovsky International Competition play works on his grand piano. Concerts are also given year-round in a hall near the museum. The museum is open on Saturdays, Sundays, Mondays, Tuesdays and Fridays from 10:00 to 18:00; it is closed on Wednesdays, Thursdays and the last Monday of each month.

Kolomenskoye Museum Preserve

This preserve is on the southern side of Moscow on the banks of the Moskva River and can be reached from the Metro station Proletarsky (39 Andropov Prospekt). Kolomenskoye was once the country estate of numerous Russian princes and czars,

(following pages) Inside the Kremlin; (left and top right) Cathedral of the Annunciation, (bottom right) Cathedral of the Assumption

including Ivan the Terrible and Peter the Great. The name of the area dates from the 13th century, when villagers from the town of Kolomna settled here. It is now an open-air museum of 16th- and 17th-century architecture. When it was built in 1532, the tent-shaped Church of the Ascension, decorated with *kokoshnik* gables, was the highest structure in Moscow at 189 feet (60 meters); it also acted as a watchtower. Next to it is the 16th-century Church of St George the Victorious; nearby is the five-domed Church of St John the Baptist. Other structures of interest are the Dyako-vskaya and Kazanskaya churches (open for services), the water and clock towers, a Siberian watch tower (1631), and a cottage (1702) used by Peter the Great, which was brought from Arkhangelskoye. Also noteworthy is a replica of Czar Alexei's wooden palace, made by the carver Smirnov in the 19th century. The museum was founded in 1923, and from the 1930s until the 1950s, monuments of Russian architecture were brought here from different regions of the country. These buildings now exhibit 16th- to 19th-century Russian applied and decorative art, including collections of paintings, ceramics, woodcarvings and clocks. It is a favorite wooded area for picnics; one of the oak trees is thought to date back to the 14th century, during the rule of Ivan Kalita. The museum is open from September to April, from 11:00 to 17:00; from May to August, from 13:00 to 20:00 on Wednesdays and Thursdays, and from 11:00 to 17:00 on other days; it is closed on Mondays and Tuesdays.

KUSKOVO PALACE MUSEUM

This museum is located within the city limits and can be reached easily from Metro station Zhdanovskaya. The Kuskovo Estate was in the Sheremetev family since the 16th century. In the early 18th century, Count Pyotr Sheremetev, who had over 200,000 serfs, transformed Kuskovo into his summer residence. His wooden man-sion (1769–75), designed by Karl Blank and the serf-architect Alexei Mironov, is faced with white stone and decorated with parquet floors, antique furniture and crystal chandeliers; it also houses an excellent collection of 18th-century Russian art. The **Ceramics Museum** exhibits a fine collection of Russian and European porcelain, faïence and glass. The museum is open from 11:00 to 19:00 or 10:00 to 16:00, de-pending on the time of year; it is closed on Mondays, Tuesdays and the last Wednes-day of each month.

MOSCOW COUNTRY CLUB (NAHABINO)

Located about 18 miles (28 kilometers) northwest of Moscow in Nahabino, is the Mos-cow Country Club (formerly known as Nahabino), Russia's first 18-hole championship golf course. Opened in 1993, the Moscow Country Club is an 18-hole, 7,000-plus-yard, (6,735-meter) par-72 championship course, with an adjoining sports and hotel com-plex. In September 1993, Moscow held its first Golf-Open Championship here. The

Russians hope that the Moscow Country Club will ultimately be a venue for European tour play. The Moscow Country Club Hotel is open to tourists; in Moscow telephone 561-2975 for reservations and to book a game (currently no clubs are rented).

PEREDELKINO

A few stops from Moscow's Kievsky Railway Station is Peredelkino. Here you can visit the estate and grave of the great Russian writer and Nobel laureate Boris Pasternak, who wrote *Dr Zhivago*. From the train station, walk up the road to the top of the hill where the church stands. Following the path to the left of the church brings you to Pasternak's grave, bordered by three pines. Other writers are also buried in the cemetery. Peredelkino has always been an artist's and writer's community, filled with many beautiful *dacha*. It is a fine place to stroll through the countryside; nordic-skiing and ice fishing are possible in winter. Pasternak wrote of Moscow:

> For the dreamer and the night-bird
> Moscow is dearer than all else in the world.
> It is at the hearth, the source
> Of everything that the century will live for.

YASNAYA POLYANA

This town lies south of Moscow along the Simferopolskoye Highway. The great Russian writer Leo Tolstoy was born in Yasnaya Polyana, Clear Glade, in 1828, and lived and worked here for over 60 years. Everything on the estate has been preserved as he left it — his study, library and parlor, where his wife Sofia Andreyevna meticulously copied his manuscripts. Here he wrote *Anna Karenina*, *War and Peace* (which his wife recopied by hand nine times) and chapters of *The Resurrection*. Peasants would gather under the 'Tree of the Poor' to ask his advice. Nearby, Tolstoy opened a school for peasant children. Today, this houses the Literary Museum. Here he also developed a philosophy of Christianity so potent that the Russian Church excommunicated him. Yasnaya Polyana, on 1,100 acres, was the main source of creative inspiration for Tolstoy, and the location is reflected in many of his works. Late in his life, Tolstoy wrote: 'It is difficult for me to imagine Russia without my Yasnaya Polyana.' Here, he wanted to create a utopian miniature of Russian society. In 1910, at the age of 82, Tolstoy left the estate to embark on a solitary journey on foot. He turned up at a railway station more than 200 miles away, where he died. He was buried on the estate grounds. Tolstoy's wife and then his daughters managed the estate until 1956, when it fell under State control. Now it is the center of a political and historical wrangle. Accusing the government of severe neglect, Tolstoy's great-great grandson, Vladimir, is attempting to take over the estate's daily management and have it returned to the Tolstoy family (there are now over 200 relatives scattered around six countries). The museum is open daily, except on Mondays and Tuesdays, from 10:00 to 17:30.

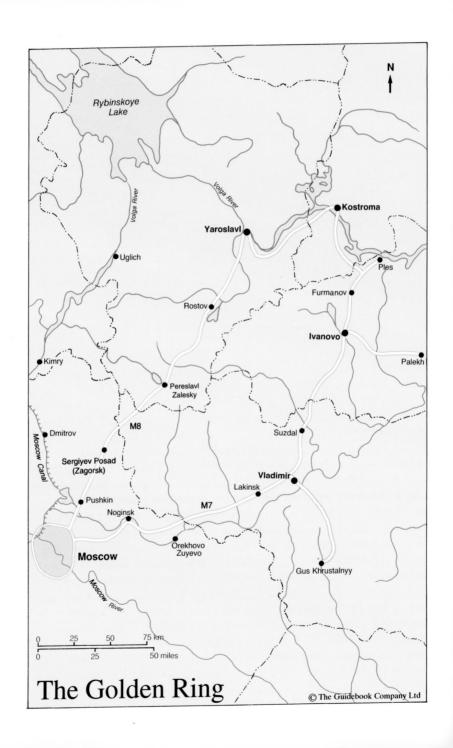

The Golden Ring

© The Guidebook Company Ltd

The Golden Ring

The ancient towns of the Golden Ring, built between the 11th and 17th centuries, are the cradle of Russian culture. During Russia's early history, the two most important cities were Kiev in the south and Novgorod in the north. Both, situated in what is now western Russia, lay along important commerce routes to the Black and Baltic seas. The settlements that sprang up along the trade routes between these two cities prospered and grew into large towns of major political and religious importance. From the 11th to 15th centuries, the towns of Rostov, Yaroslavl, Vladimir and Suzdal became capitals of the northern principalities, and Sergiyev Posad (Zagorsk) served as the center of Russian Orthodoxy. In the 12th century, Moscow was established as a small protective outpost of the Rostov-Suzdal principality. By the 16th century, Moscow had grown so big and affluent that it was named the capital of the Russian empire. At the turn of the 18th century, St Petersburg became the center of Russian power. The prominent towns that lay in a circular formation between Moscow and St Petersburg became known as the Golden Ring.

The Russian Town

Up to the end of the 18th century, a typical Russian town consisted of a *kremlin*, a protective fortress surrounding the area. Watchtowers were built in strategic points along the *kremlin* wall and contained vaulted carriageways, which served as the gates to the city. The 'timber town' within the *kremin* contained the governmental and administrative offices. The b*oyars*, noble class, had homes here too that were used only in time of war—otherwise they lived outside the town on their own country estates, where the peasants or serfs worked the land. The p*osad*, earth town, was the settlement of traders and craftsmen. The *posad* also contained the *rinoks*—the markets and bazaars, as well as the storage-houses for the town. The merchants and *boyars* used their wealth to help build the churches and commissioned artists to paint elaborate frescoes and icons. The number of churches and monasteries mirrored the prosperity of the town. The rest of the townspeople lived in settlements known as the *slobody* around the *kremlin*. The historical nucleus and heart of the town was known as the *strelka*. The regions were separated into principalities with their own governing princes. The ruler of the united principalities was known as the Grand-Prince and later Czar. The head of the Orthodox Church was called the Metropolitan or Patriarch.

The Golden Ring area provides an excellent opportunity to view typical old Russian towns, which are still surrounded by ancient *kremlins*, churches and monasteries. The towns of Rostov, Vladimir, Suzdal and Pereslavl-Zalessky retain much of their original layouts. Outside Suzdal and Kostroma are open-air architectural museums—entire wooden villages built to typify old Russian life. All the towns of the Golden Ring have been well-restored, and many of the buildings are now museums that trace the history of the area that was the center of the Golden Age of Rus for more than four centuries.

Religion and the Church

Before Prince Vladimir introduced Byzantine Christianity to the Kievan principality in AD 988, Russia was a pagan state; the people of Rus worshipped numerous gods. Festivals were held according to the seasons, planting and harvest cycles, and life passages. Special offerings of eggs, wheat and honey were presented to the gods of water, soil and sun. Carved figures of mermaids and suns adorned the roofs of houses. When Prince Vladimir married the sister of the Byzantine Emperor and introduced Christianity, Russia finally united under one God, and Kiev became the center of the Orthodox Church. But it took almost a century to convert the many pagan areas, especially in the north. Early church architecture (11th-century) was based on the Byzantine cube-shaped building with one low rounded cupola on the roof bearing an Orthodox cross facing east. The domes gradually evolved into helmet drums on tent-shaped or square sloping roofs. These drums eventually took on the distinctive onion shape suitable to the heavy snowfalls. By the end of the 16th century, three or five domes, with one dominant central dome, were commonly installed atop Orthodox places of worship. The next two centuries witnessed classical and baroque influences, and the onion domes become elaborately shaped and decorated. During your tour of the Golden Ring, try dating the churches by the shapes of their domes.

The outer walls of churches were divided into three sections by protruding vertical strips, which indicated the position of the piers inside. A few centuries later, the churches expanded considerably, and were built from white stone or brick instead of wood. (Unfortunately, many of the wooden buildings did not survive and stone churches were built on their original sites.) The main body of the church was tiered into different levels and adjoined by chapels, galleries and porches. A large tent-shaped bell tower usually dominated one side.

During the two and a half centuries of Mongol occupation (beginning in the mid-13th century), Russia was cut off from any outside influence. Monasteries united the Russian people and acted as shelters and fortresses against attacks. They became the educational centers and housed the historical manuscripts, which monks wrote on birch-bark parchment. During this period, Russian church architecture developed a unique style. Some distinctive features were the decorative *zakomara*, semi-circular arches, that lined the tops of the outer walls where they joined the roof. The *trapeza* porch was built outside the western entrance of the church and other carved designs were copied from the decorations on peasant houses. Elaborate carved gables around doors, windows and archways were called *kokoshnik*, named after the large headdresses worn by young married women. Even though, through the years, the architecture took on elements of European classical, Gothic and baroque elements, the designs always retained a distinctive Russian flair. Each entrance of the *kremlin* had its own Gate Church. The most elaborate stood by the Holy Gates, the main entrance to the town. Many cathedrals took years to build and twin churches were also a common sight—one was used in winter and the other, more elaborate, for summer services and festivals.

The interior of the church was highly decorated with frescoes. Images of Christ were painted inside the central dome, surrounded by angels. Beneath the dome came the pictures of saints, apostles and prophets. Images of the patron saint of the church might appear on the pillars. Special religious scenes and the earthly life of Christ or the Virgin Mary were depicted on the walls and vaults. The Transfiguration was usually painted on the east wall by the altar and scenes from the Last Judgment and Old Testament were illustrated on the west wall, where the people would exit the church. The iconostasis was an elaborate tiered structure, filled with icons, that stretched behind the altar from the floor toward the ceiling. The top tiers held Christ, the middle the saints and prophets, and the lower tiers were reserved for scenes from church history.

Fresco painting was a highly respected skill and many master craftsmen, such as Andrei Rublev and Daniil Chorny, produced beautiful works of art. The plaster was applied to the wall of the church, and then the artists would sketch the main outline of the fresco right onto the damp plaster. The master supervised the work and filled in the more intricate and important parts of the composition, while the apprentices added the background detail.

The building of elaborate churches and painting of exquisite icons and frescoes reached its zenith in the prosperous towns of the Golden Ring. Even cathedrals in the Moscow Kremlin were copied from church designs that originated in Rostov, Vladimir and Suzdal. Today these churches and works of art stand as monuments to an extraordinary era of Russian history.

Religion after the Revolution

For nearly 1,000 years, the Russian Orthodox Church dominated the life of Russia and, as Tolstoy observed, for most of the Russian people 'faith was the force of life.' But after the 1917 Revolution, when Marx proclaimed that 'religion is the opium of the people,' all churches were closed to religious use and their property confiscated and redistributed by the government—even though Article 124 of the Soviet Constitution stated that 'church is separate from state' and provided 'freedom of worship for all citizens.' Before the Revolution, Russia had almost 100,000 churches and monasteries; Moscow alone had more than 500. By the time of the purges in the 1930s, only 100 still functioned officially in the entire Soviet Union. Churches were turned into swimming pools, ice-skating rinks and restaurants. Moscow's Danilovsky Monastery was used as a prison. The Church of St Nicholas became a gas station. Today the country has less than 10,000 (with an increase of 3,000 only in the last few years) that are open for religious activities. There are about 50 million Orthodox believers, 25 per cent of whom are regular church attendants. St Petersburg, a city of nearly six million people, has only about 20 churches, but now many are in the process of being restored. Moscow now supports over 130 active churches.

In 1988, the Millennium of Russian Christianity was officially celebrated throughout the former Soviet Union, and government decrees provided a new legal status for the Orthodox Church and other religions. The Russian Orthodox Church remained headed by the Patriarch and assisted by the Holy Synod, whose seats are in Sergiyev Posad and Moscow respectively. But the government continued to control and dictate the moves of the Church, while the topic of religion was discussed in meetings of the Supreme Soviet. Positive signs of increased religious tolerance and freedom slowly emerged, and a small number of churches were eventually given back for religious use.

During the period of *perestroika*, the process of renewal of Soviet society brought about major changes in the relations between Church and State and believers and non-believers. On April 29, 1988, the Eve of the Millennium of Russian Orthodoxy, Gorbachev received the Patriarch of Moscow and All Russia and members of the Synod in the Yekaterininsky Hall in the Kremlin. Gorbachev stated: 'Believers are Soviet people; they are workers and patriots and they have a full right to adequately express their convictions. The reforms of *perestroika* and *glasnost* concern them also without any limitations.' On October 13, 1989, a Thanksgiving Service was held in the Kremlin's Assumption Cathedral, the first service to take place there in 71 years. The last Mass held there had been at Easter in 1918. The government also returned the Danilovsky Monastery to the Orthodox Church. In 1988 alone some 900 build-

A rural wooden church

ings were returned to the Church, and religious figures were even elected to the Congress of Peoples' Deputies. On December 1, 1989, Gorbachev became the first Soviet leader to set foot in the Vatican.

Today, more people, especially the younger generation, are attending religious services and being baptized. Theological seminaries are training monks and priests and church charity organizations are now permitted to help the poor, unemployed and homeless.

One well-respected St Petersburg rector of the Orthodox Church and city seminary (who was allowed to visit Rome for an audience with the Pope during *perestroika*) remarked: 'I am an optimist. People are not only interested in bettering themselves economically, but also morally and spiritually. The powers of the Communist State could never extend to the soul. And in these uncertain times, we would like to help the new generation find its way.'

Since the collapse of the Soviet Union, the Patriarch of All Russia is now the head of the Russian Orthodox Church, and the Church is separate from the State. In 1992, Boris Yeltsin became the first Russian leader since the 1917 Bolshevik Revolution to attend Easter ceremonies in an Orthodox Church. Yeltsin, who was baptized, told Patriarch Alexei: 'It is time for Russia to return to her strong religious heritage.' On November 4, 1993, Yeltsin attended the consecration of the newly restored Kazan Cathedral in Red Square. During the stand-off siege of 1993 in the White House, the Patriarch was called in to help arbitrate between the hardliners and Yeltsin. However, another battle is being waged: to determine whether the government, museums or the Church owns religious art. In 1993, Yeltsin signed orders to transfer two famous icons by Andrei Rublev in the Tretyakov Gallery to the Orthodox Church.

Many other religious groups are also enjoying a new period of openness. There are 1.5 million officially registered Jews (given as their nationality), four million Roman Catholics, five million Uniates (Catholics of Eastern Rite), over one million Baptists, two million Lutherans, 250,000 Pentecostalists, and 50,000 each of Mennonites, Seventh-Day Adventists and Jehovah's Witnesses. Other groups such as Scientologists, Sikhs and Hari Krishnas have also established themselves in Russia. There are also half a million Buddhists, 5.5 million Moslems and about one million Old Believers, a sect resulting from the 1666 schism of the Orthodox Church. Such religious tolerance in Russia has not been known since Peter the Great.

Getting There

Many travel organizations offer package tours specifically to the Golden Ring area that include stops in Moscow and St Petersburg; most tour the Golden Ring by bus, which is also an ideal way to see the Russian countryside. Your hotel Service desk can help book excursions to cities along the Golden Ring route from Moscow or St Petersburg once you are in Russia—they also add the towns to your visa. Some places, such as Sergiyev Posad (Zagorsk), can be visited in a day from Moscow. In others you can stay overnight, so long as you have prebooked the hotel. You can travel quite comfortably to the areas via bus, train or car. There are restaurants along the way, but take some food and drinks for the journeys.

The Golden Ring area is still not easily accessible to the independent traveler. Since the towns are popular, most hotels have been prebooked by groups. To travel off the beaten track, outside a group tour, plan an itinerary, prebook hotels through your hotel Service desk, and then go by car; either rent a car and driver or go with friends. You could even bargain with a taxi driver or an owner of a private car.

You can also take the *elektrichka* (electric) trains from Moscow's Yaroslavsky station to Sergiyev Posad, or from the Kursk station to Vladimir. The ride takes only an hour and stops in the center of town. It is better to go during weekdays since trains are crowded on summer weekends.

Note: Today, some of the street and square names of the towns in the Golden Ring area are in the process of being changed—often back to what they were before the Revolution. Since the government currently does not have the funds to change all the signs, and put out new maps, many have still not been officially changed. Because name changes have been in flux since the fall of Communism, the names of streets and squares have been referred to here as they were during the Soviet Union, even though some locals may refer to certain areas by another appellation, especially streets with names like Lenin or Engels. The town councils are also trying to decide what Communist names should be left for the sake of history and posterity. If there is any confusion, ask.

The towns of the Golden Ring are a majestic mirror of Russia's past grandeur. The churches and monasteries are beautifully preserved and their frescoes and icons have been painstakingly restored. Many of the churches still hold religious services, which you are welcome to attend, as long as you are not wearing shorts or sleeveless shirts. Other religious buildings have been converted into museums that house the art and historical artifacts of the regions.

A splendid skyline of golden-domed churches, tent-shaped towers, ornamental belfries, picturesque old wooden buildings and rolling countryside dotted with birch trees greets you—as it did the visitor more than seven centuries ago.

(following pages) A variety of church architecture
in the Golden Ring

Sergiyev Posad (Zagorsk)

A 45-mile (70-kilometer) ride north of Moscow on the Yaroslavskoye Highway (or an hour-long train journey from Moscow's Yaroslavsky Station) leads to Sergiyev Posad, the most popular town on the Golden Ring route. As soon as the road leaves Moscow, it winds back in time through dense forests of spruce and birch, past old wooden *dacha*, country homes, and collective farms, and eventually opens onto a magical view, upon which fairy-tales are based. Once upon a time on a hilltop in a large white fortress surrounded by the rivers Koshura and Glimitza and filled with star-studded golden onion domes, sparkling in the sunlight and dusted lightly with glistening snow, an obscure monk, who was destined to become a saint, founded the small settlement of Sergiev Posad and a monastery that was to be the center of Russian Orthodoxy for centuries to come. Sergiyev Posad, the jewel of old Russian towns, gives the visitor a marvelous glimpse of Russian life six centuries ago.

HISTORY

In the early 14th century, two brothers from Radonezh, Stefan and Varfolomei, built a small wooden church in the area. The latter took his monk vows as Sergius and headed the small monastery. To unify the Russian territories during the Mongol invasions (which began in the 13th century), Sergius and his pupils went on to establish 23 other monasteries across Russia that also acted as regional strongholds. Moscow princes, czars and rich *boyars* contributed heavily to the establishment of the Troitse-Sergiyev Lavra until the monastery became not only the wealthiest in all Russia, but also the most revered pilgrimage shrine in Moscovy. For centuries, the Trinity-St Sergius Monastery was the center of the Church and today is still the seat of the Patriarch of the Orthodox Faith. After his death, Sergius was canonized; he is buried in the Trinity Church on the monastery grounds.

Grand-Prince Dmitri Donskoi, blessed before battle by Sergius himself, defeated the Khan Mamai's hordes in 1380. At the monastery, one of St Sergius' pupils, the famous iconist Andrei Rublev, painted the Old *Testament Trinity* (now in Moscow's Tretyakov Gallery) to commemorate this famous battle at Kulikovo on the Don. The town's name of Sergiyev Posad (Settlement of Sergius) was changed to Zagorsk, after the revolutionary Vladimir Zagorsk, in 1930. The town reverted to its orginal name of Sergiyev Posad in 1990; but people still refer to it by both names. Sergiyev Posad has a population of over 100,000.

The art of carving wooden toys has long been a tradition here; the first toys were made and distributed by St Sergius to the children of the town. Many painters, sculptors and folk artists trace their heritage back to the 17th century, when the first toy

Sergiyev Posad (Zagorsk)

© The Guidebook Company Ltd

and craft workshops were set up in the town. The *Beriozka*, to the left as you pass through the main gates, sells many locally made wooden toys.

The thick *kremlin* walls were built around the monastery in 1540 during the reign of Ivan the Terrible to protect it from attack. A half-century later, the *Lavra* (the word stems from the Greek, meaning most important monastery; there were only four *lavra* in all of Russia) withstood a 16-month siege by Polish forces; it was protected by over 3,000 monks. The monastery complex was such an important center for the Russian people that its fall would have meant the end of Rus. The monastery remained an important fortress that defended Moscow well into the 17th century. Eleven octagonal towers were built into the walls as key defense points. The most famous, the northeast tower, is known as the Utichya (Duck) Tower; the duck atop its spire symbolizes Peter the Great's hunting expeditions in Sergiyev Posad. The place also played an important cultural role; the manuscript-writing and color-miniature painting sections date back to the 15th century. Today, the Trinity-St Sergius Monastery is the largest *lavra* run by the Orthodox Church, with over 100 monks. The monastery remains a place of devoted pilgrimage, and believers from all over the country continue to pay homage to 'the saint and guardian of the Russian land.' The town receives nearly a million visitors a year.

SIGHTS

The parking square, near the main gates of the monastery complex, looks out over many ancient settlements that dot the landscape, and the large *kremlin* citadel that houses priceless relics of old Russian architecture. Enter the main gates at the eastern entrance through the Pilgrim Tower; paintings of the Holy Pilgrims depict the life of Sergius Radonezhsky (from the town of Radonezh), the 14th-century monk who established the Troitse-Sergiyev Lavra—the Trinity Monastery of St Sergius, lying beyond the gates. The small **Church of St John the Baptist**, built in 1693 by the wealthy and princely Stroganov family, stands over the main or Holy Gates.

The first large structure that catches the eye is the monastery's main **Assumption (Uspensky) Cathedral**. This blue and gold-starred, five-domed church with elegant sloping *zakomara* archways was consecrated in 1585 to commemorate Ivan the Terrible's defeat of the Mongols in the Asian territory of Astrakhan. Yaroslavl artists, whose names are inscribed on the west wall, painted the interior frescoes in 1684. The burial chambers of the Godunov family (Boris Godunov was czar from 1598 to 1605) are located in the northwestern corner. Its design resembles the Kremlin's Uspensky Cathedral. By the south wall is the Sergius Church (1686–92). Many of these churches are open for worship and conduct services throughout the day. Respectfully-dressed visitors are welcome. Picture-taking without flash is usually permitted.

The brightly painted **Chapel-over-the-Well**, located outside by the cathedral's west wall, is built in the Naryshkin cube-shaped octagonal style. Near the riverbank stands the **Sergius Well Chapel**. It was customary for small chapels to be built over sacred wells; today, pilgrims still bring bottles to fill with holy water.

Directly beyond the cathedral is the five-tiered turquoise and white baroque bell tower (285 feet,

Sergiyev Posad Monastery

87 meters, high), designed by Prince Ukhtomsky (1740–70) and Rastrelli. Topped with a dome in the form of a crown, it once held 40 bells.

Head directly left of the cathedral to the southern end of the complex. A stroll in this direction to the Refectory may lead past long-bearded monks dressed in the traditional black robes and *klobuki* tall hats. The **Refectory**, rebuilt in 1686, is painted in colorful checkerboard patterns of red, blue, green and yellow. It has a large open gallery with 19th-century paintings and wide staircases, and is decorated with carved columns and gables.

The small chapel at the end of the hall has a carved iconostasis by the altar and a beautiful red jasper inlaid floor. Another quaint church, standing next to the Refectory, is the **Church of St Micah** (1734).

Behind the Refectory, in the southwestern corner, is the oldest building in the monastery, the one-domed **Trinity Cathedral**, which the Abbot Nikon erected over the site of the original Church of St Sergius in 1422 (the year Sergius was canonized). Pilgrims still visit the remains of St Sergius of Radonezh, which lie in a silver sarcophagus donated by Ivan the Terrible. An embroidered portrait of St Sergius that covered his coffin is now preserved in the History and Art Museum, a short walk away. In 1425, Andrei Rublev and Daniil Chorny painted the icons on the cathedral's iconostasis, which include a copy of Rublev's *Holy Testament Trinity* (the original is now in Moscow's Tretyakov Gallery). The cathedral contains 42 works by Rublev and is joined by the smaller **Church of St Nikon** (1548).

Across from the cathedral is the slender **Church of the Holy Spirit** with a long bell tower under its dome. It was built in 1746 by stone masons from Pskov.

Behind this church stands the **Trinity Monastery of St Sergius**, one of the most important monuments of medieval Russia. The **Metropolitan's House**, vestry and adjoining monastery buildings now house the **History and Art Museum**. The museum, which displays gifts in the order presented to the monastery, contains one of Russia's richest collections of early religious art. The exhibits include icons from the 14th to 19th centuries, and portraits, chalices, china, crowns, furniture, jewelry and handicrafts from the 14th to 20th centuries. The museum is open daily from 10:00 to 17:00 and is closed on Mondays.

The monastery also served as the town's hospital and school. Next to the museum is the red brick, yellow-and-white sandstone hospital building with the adjoining all-white tent-roofed **Church of Sts Zosimus and Savvaty** (1635).

In the opposite, northeastern, corner, behind the Duck Tower, is the colorfully painted and tiled **Chertogi Palace**, built at the end of the 17th century for Czar Alexei, who often came to Sergiyev Posad with an entourage of over 500 people. One of the ceilings in the palace is covered with paintings that honor his son's (Peter the Great) victories in battle. It now houses the Theological College. The seminary, founded in 1742, and the Academy, founded in 1812, now have over 500 students.

Exiting through the main gate turn right and walk toward the **Kelarskiye Ponds**, situated beyond the southeastern Pyatnitskaya Tower. There you may find artists sketching and people strolling among the old garden walls. Two churches built in 1547 stand outside the walls—the **Church of St Parasceva Pyatnitsa** and the **Church of the Presentation of the Mother of God**, nearest the pond. The Zolotoye Koltso, Golden Ring Restaurant, is only a few minutes' walk away.

The craft of wood carving remains alive in Sergiyev Posad. The famous *matryoshka*, the nest of carved dolls, has its origins here. First appearing in Russia in the 1890s, the *matryona* doll was later called by its diminutive form, *matryoshka*, representing peasant girls. The dolls were carved from wood and painted in traditional

Russian dress, with *sarafan* jumpers, embroidered blouses and *kokoshniki* headdresses. Up to 24 smaller dolls could be nested within the largest, including Russian lads or fairy-tale figures. The doll first attained popularity at the 1900 World Exposition in Paris. Today, there are even Yeltsin (containing past leaders from Gorbachev down to Nicholas II) and Clinton *matryoshki*. The history of toys and folk art can be viewed at the **Toy Museum** at 136 Krasnoi Armii Prospekt. The Art Workshop Collective continues to produce wooden folk art. A special souvenir section contains carved wooden dolls, boxes and jewelry.

VICINITY OF SERGIYEV POSAD

Not far outside Sergiyev Posad is the small town of **Alexandrov**, whose history is connected with Ivan the Terrible. The Alexandrova Sloboda was a residence of Ivan the Terrible for 17 years and one of the headquarters for his select army of *oprichniki*. The oldest buildings in the village are the (non-functioning) convent and **Trinity Cathedral** that women helped build in the 15th century. After Ivan's *oprichniki* sacked Novgorod, he brought the golden oak doors from the Hagia Sophia Cathedral to adorn the Trinity's entrance. The daughters of Czar Alexei are buried in the Church of the Purification. The Church of the Intercession was Ivan the Terrible's court chapel. Next to this chapel is a bell tower and residential quarters, where Marfa, who was forced to take the veil by her step-brother Peter the Great, was exiled from 1698 to 1707. The future Empress Elizabeth was also banished to the Alexandrova Sloboda for nine years.

Pereslavl-Zalessky

The tranquil town of Pereslavl-Zalessky is situated on a hilltop by the southeastern shores of Lake Pleshcheyevo about 35 miles (56 kilometers) northeast of Sergiyev Posad. Approaching Pereslavl from the road, pleasantly scented by the surrounding groves of pine and birch, you have an enchanting view of the shimmering azure waters of the lake, three old monasteries on the side of the road, and golden crosses on top of painted onion domes that loom up from sprawling green fields dusted with blue and yellow wildflowers. Young boys wave at passersby as they fish in the lake with long reed poles. The River Trubezh meanders through the old earthen *kremlin* that winds around the center of town. These ramparts date back over eight centuries. One of Russia's most ancient towns, Pereslavl-Zalessky is a charming place, scattered with well-preserved churches and monasteries that at once numbered over 50. After checking into your hotel and having a meal at the *Skazka* (Fairy Tale) Restaurant, take a pleasant walk along the dirt roads and imagine that Peter the Great may have traversed the same footpaths before you.

HISTORY

Pereslavl-Zalessky's long and fascinating history traces back to the year 1152, when Prince Yuri Dolgoruky (who founded Moscow five years earlier) fortified the small village of Kleschchin on the banks of the Trubezh and renamed it Pereslavl after an old Kievan town. Situated in an area on the *zalasye* (beyond the dense woods of Moscow), it became known as Pereslavl-Zalessky. The area was an important outpost of Moscow; Prince Alexander Nevsky set out from Pereslavl to win his decisive battle against the Swedes in 1240. Since the town also lay on important

White Sea trade routes, it quickly prospered; by 1302, Pereslavl had grown large enough to be annexed to the principality of Moscovy.

SIGHTS

Ivan the Terrible later consolidated Pereslavl, along with the nearby village of Alexandrov, into a strategic military outpost to headquarter his *oprichniki* bodyguards. In 1688, the young Czar Peter I came here from Moscow to build his first *poteshny* (amusement) boats on Lake Pleshcheyevo. It was in a small shed near the lake that Peter discovered a wrecked English boat, which he learned to sail against the wind. In 1692, Peter paraded these boats (forerunners of the Russian fleet) before members of the Moscow court. One of them, the *Fortuna*, can be found in the **Botik Museum**, which lies about two miles (three kilometers) from Pereslavl (by the south bank of the lake) near the village of Veskovo. Other relics from the Russian flotilla are also displayed here. Two large anchors mark the entrance and a monument to Peter the Great by Campioni stands nearby. It is open from 10:00 to 16:00 and is closed on Tuesdays.

Make your way to the central Krasnaya Square. The small grassy hills around you are the remains of the town's 12th-century earthen protective walls. In front of the **Statue of Alexander Nevsky** (who was born in Pereslavl) is the white stone **Cathedral of the Transfiguration**, the oldest architectural monument in northeastern Russia. Yuri Dolgoruky himself laid the foundations of this church, which was completed by his son, Andrei Bogoliubsky (God-Loving), in 1157. This refined structure with its one massive fringed dome became the burial place for the local princes. Each side of the cathedral is decorated with simple friezes. The *zakomara*, the semi-circular rounded shape of the upper walls, distinguish the Russian style from the original simpler cube-shaped Byzantine design. Frescoes and icons from inside the cathedral, like the 14th-century *Transfiguration* by Theophanes the Greek and Yuri Dolgoruky's silver chalice, are now in Moscow's Tretyakov Gallery and Kremlin Armory. The other frescoes were executed during the cathedral's restoration in 1894. Across from the cathedral is the **Church of St Peter the Metropolitan**. Built in 1585 (with a 19th-century bell tower), the octagonal frame is topped with a long white tent-shaped roof. This design in stone and brick was copied from the traditional Russian log-cabin churches of the north.

In the distance, over the river, is the **Church of St Semion** (1771). Between this church and the Lenin Monument on Svoboda Street are the early 19th-century shopping arcades Gostiny Dvor. Religious services are held at the **Church of the Intercession** on Pleshcheyevskaya Street.

Take a leisurely stroll towards the river and follow it down to the lake. Scattered along the paths are brightly painted wooden *dacha* with carved windows covered by lace curtains. Children can be found playing outside with their kittens or a *babushka* (accent on first syllable) hauling water from the well. Many times the *dedushka* is picking apples and wild strawberries or carving a small toy for his grandchildren out of wood. Stop for a chat; it is amazing how far a few common words can go—an invitation for chai may soon follow. At

(opposite and right) At the Sergiyev Posad Monastery Complex

the point where the Trubezh flows into the lake stands the **Church of the Forty Saints** (1781) on Ribnaya (Fish) Sloboda, the old fish quarter. With a little bargaining or a smile, get a rowing boat to go out on the lake or go out with the fishermen. On a warm day, it is a perfect place for a picnic; you may even want to take a dip.

On a little side trip out of the town are a number of monasteries and chapels that you may have glimpsed if you arrived from Sergiyev Posad. The four monasteries lining the road into and out of Pereslavl also acted as protective strongholds, guarding the town from invasions. The one farthest away is the **Convent of St Theodore**, about four miles (6.5 kilometers) south on Sovetskaya Street. Ivan the Terrible built this convent and the **Chapel of St Theodore** to honor his wife Anastasia, who gave birth to their first son, Fedor (Theodore), in 1557. Ivan often stopped at the shrine to pray when he visited his bodyguard army, which resided in Pereslavl-Zalessky.

About a mile closer to the town is the memorial **Church of Alexander Nevsky** (1778). A few minutes' walk from this church, set in a woody rustic setting, is the **Danilov Monastery**. A few buildings remain of this 16th-century structure. The **Trinity Cathedral** was commissioned by Grand-Prince Vasily III in 1532. The single-domed cathedral, with 17th-century frescoes by renowned Kostroma artists Nikitin and Savin, was built by Rostov architect Grigory Borisov in honor of Vasily's son, Ivan the Terrible. The Abbot Daniel, who founded the monastery in 1508, was in charge of the cathedral's construction and present at Ivan's christening. The smaller **Church of All Saints** was built in 1687 by Prince Bariatinsky, who later became a monk (Ephriam) at the monastery and was buried near the south wall. Other surviving structures are the two-story Refectory (1695) and the large tent-roofed bell tower (1689), whose bell is now in the Moscow Kremlin's Ivan the Great Bell Tower.

On the other side of the road, behind the **Monument to Yuri Dolgoruky**, is the **Goritsky Monastery**, surrounded by a large red-brick *kremlin*. On the hilltop, a mass of sparkling onion domes rise up from inside the fortified walls. The monastery is now the **Museum of History and Art** (open from 10:00 to 16:00, closed on Tuesdays). The monastery, founded during the reign of Ivan I in the 14th century (rebuilt in the 18th), is a fine example of medieval architecture with its octagonal towers, large cube-shaped walls and ornamental stone entrance gates The tiny white gate-church next to the gatekeeper's lodge was once known as the 'casket studded with precious stones,' for it was richly decorated with gilded carvings and colorful tiles. The large seven-domed **Cathedral of the Assumption** was built in 1757. The exquisite golden-framed and figured iconostasis, designed by Karl Blank, was carved and painted by the same team of artists who decorated the churches in the Moscow Kremlin.

The monastery, with 47 rooms filled with local treasures, is now one of the largest regional museums in Russia. The rooms include a unique collection of ancient

Russian art, sculptures and rare books. The museum also exhibits the plaster face mask of Peter the Great by Rastrelli (1719) and Falconnet's original model of the Bronze Horseman. The elaborately carved wooden gates from the Church of the Presentation won the Gold Medal at the 1867 Paris World Exhibition. May 2nd is a town holiday, Museum Day, at the Goritsky Monastery.

Heading north toward Rostov and Yaroslavl, you will find the last monument structure of Pereslavl-Zalessky, the 12th-century **Monastery of St Nicetas**, encased in a long white-bricked *kremlin*. In 1561, Ivan the Terrible added stone buildings and the five-domed cathedral. He intended to convert the Monastery into the headquarters of his *oprichniki*, but later transferred their residence to the village of Alexandrov.

Rostov Veliky

Approaching Rostov on the road from Moscow (34 miles, 54 kilometers, north of Pereslavl-Zalessky), the visitor is greeted with a breathtaking view of silvery aspen domes, white stone churches and high *kremlin* towers. Rostov is one of Russia's ancient towns and has stood along the picturesque banks of Lake Nero for more than 11 centuries. It was once marveled as 'a reflection of heaven on the ground.' Named after Prince Rosta, a powerful governing lord, the town was mentioned in chronicles as far back as AD 862. Rostov's size and splendor grew to equal the two great towns of Novgorod and Kiev. By the 12th century, Rostov was named *Veliky* 'The Great' and became the capital of the Russian north. Rostov later came under the jurisdiction of Moscow and lost its importance as a cultural center by the end of the 18th century.

Today Rostov is the district center of the Yaroslavl region, and considered a historical preserve, heralding the glory of old Russian art and architecture. The town, with a population of about 50,000, has been restored to much of its original grandeur after a tornado destroyed many of the buildings in 1953. The oldest section of the town, set by the lake, is still surrounded by low earthen walls, built around 1630. From the main hotel and restaurant on Karl Marx Street, it is just a few minutes' walk to the ancient cathedrals inside the *kremlin*.

History

Rostov Veliky was one of the wealthiest towns in all Russia and the most important trade center between Kiev and the White Sea. Rostov became not only the capital of its own principality, but also the northern ecclesiastical center of early Christianity and the seat of the Metropolitan, head of the Orthodox Church. In the 17th century, the Metropolitans Jonah and Ion Sisoyevich built a large number of magnificent

The Old Aristocracy

Wealth was measured in those times by the number of "souls" which a landed proprietor owned. So many "souls" meant so many male serfs: women did not count. My father, who owned nearly twelve hundred souls, in three different provinces, and who had, in addition to his peasants' holdings, large tacts of land which were cultivated by these peasants, was accounted a rich man. He lived up to his reputation, which meant that his house was open to any number of visitors, and that he kept a very large household.

We were a family of eight, occasionally ten or twelve; but fifty servants at Moscow, and half as many more in the country, were considered not one too may. Four coachmen to attend a dozen horses, three cooks for the masters and two more for the servants, a dozen men to wait upon us at dinner-time (one man, plate in hand, standing behind each person seated at the table), and girls innumerable in the maid-servants' room,—how could anyone do with less than this?

Besides, the ambition of every landed proprietor was that everything required for his household should be made at home by is own men.

"How nicely your piano is always tuned! I suppose Herr Schimmel must be your tuner?" perhaps a visitor would remark.

To be able to answer, "I have my own piano-tuner," was in those times the correct thing.

"What a beautiful pastry!" the guests would exclaim, when a work of art, composed of ices and pastry, appeared toward the end of the dinner. "Confess, prince, that it comes from Tremblé" (the fashionable pastry cook).

"It is by my own confectioner, a pupil of Tremblé, whom I have allowed to show what he can do," was a reply which elicited general admiration.

As soon as the children of the servants attained the age of ten, they were sent as apprentices to the fashionable shops, where they were obliged to spend five or seven years chiefly in sweeping, in receiving an incredible number of thrashings, and in running about town on errands of all sorts. I must own that few of them became masters of their respective arts. The tailors and the shoemakers were found only skillful enough to make clothes or shoes for the servants, and when a really good pastry was required for a dinner-party it was ordered at Tremblé's, while our own confectioner was beating the drum in the music band.

That band was another of my father's ambitions, and almost every one of his male servants, in addition to other accomplishments, was a bass-viol or a clarinet in the band. Makar, the piano-tuner, alias under-butler, was also a flautist; Andrei, the tailor, played the French horn; the confectioner was first put to beat the drum, but misused his instrument to such a deafening degree that a tremendous trumpet was bought for him, in the hope that his lungs would not have the power to make the same noise as his hands; when, however, this last hope had to be abandoned, he was sent to be a soldier. As to "spotted Tikhon", in addition to his numerous functions in the household as lamp-cleaner, floor-polisher, and, footman he made himself useful in the band—today as trombone, tomorrow as bassoon, and occasionally as second violin...

Dancing-parties were not infrequent, to say nothing of obligatory balls every winter. Father's way, in such cases, was to have everything done in good style, whatever the expense. But at the same time such niggardliness was practised in our house in daily life that if I were to recount it, I should be accused of exaggeration. However, in the Old Equerries' Quarter such a mode of life only raised my father in public esteem. "The old prince," it was said, "seems to be sharp over money at home; but knows how a nobleman ought to live".

Prince Peter Kropotkin, Memoirs of a Revolutionist, *1899* cathedrals and church residences, decorated with the Byzantine influence of icons and frescoes. The many religious shrines of a Russian town symbolized its wealth and status. Unlike other Russian towns, the Rostov kremlin was not originally built as a protective fortress, but served as a decorative feature that surrounded the palace of the Metropolitan. Also, the main cathedral stood outside the kremlin walls and not in the town's center.

SIGHTS

The kremlin itself, built in 1670, has 11 rounded towers and encompasses an area of about 5 acres. At the west gate is the **Church of St John Divine** (1683). The five-domed **Church of the Resurrection** (1670) at the northern gates is designed with intricate white-stone patterns and the classic Russian *zakomara*, forming the 24 slopes of the roof. The towers on either side of both churches are made from aspen, and sparkle with a silken sheen. Stone iconostasis (instead of traditional wooden ones) inside both churches are decorated with beautiful frescoes painted by the artists Nikitin and Savin from the Golden Ring town of Kostroma. The Church of the Resurrection stands over the Holy Gates, so named because the Metropolitan passed through them on the way from his residence inside the kremlin to the main cathedral.

The first stone of the massive **Cathedral of the Assumption** was laid by Prince Andrei Bogoliubsky (son of Yuri Dolgoruky who founded Moscow) in 1162. Bogoliubsky ruled the Russian north from Rostov. The 11th-century Vladimir Virgin hangs to the left of the Holy Doors. A few of the 12th-century frescoes have survived, along with the original lion mask handles that guard the western doors. Rostov frescoes were known for their soft color combinations of turquoise, blue, yellow and white. Five large aspen-hewn onion domes and beautiful white-stone friezes decorate the outside of the structure. The four-tiered bell tower (1687), standing atop the Assumption Cathedral, was the most famous in all Russia. Bells played an important role in the life of Russian towns. The 13 bells (the heaviest, the Sysoi, weighs 32 tons) can be heard 15 miles away.

Other churches inside the kremlin include the one-domed **Church of the Savior-on-the-Marketplace** (1690) that stands across 25th October Street; it is now the town library. In the northeast, at the end of Karl Marx Street, is the five-domed **Church of St Isodore the Blessed** (1566), built during the reign of Ivan the Terrible. Directly behind this church, on the other side of the earthen walls, stands the **Church of St Nicholas-in-the-Field** (1830) on Gogol Street. This is one of the few places in town open for religious services. At the southeastern end by the water is the **Church of the Nativity**. *Gostiny Dvor* (Traders' Row) marks the town's center. This long yellow arcade, with its many carved white archways, is still the shopping and market district of Rostov.

The large main complex at the western end by the Cathedral of the Assumption is the **Metropolitan's Palace** (1680), containing the highly decorated Otdatochnaya Hall; here people gathered to pay their respects to the prince and Metropolitan. The **White Chambers** were built for the prince and, later, visiting czars. The **Red Chambers** accommodated other church and civil dignitaries. This complex of buildings now houses the **Rostov Museum Preserve of Art and Architecture**. The chambers are filled with collections of icons, woodcarvings and enamels from the 14th to 20th centuries. Rostov enamels were famous throughout Russia. Craftsmen painted miniature icons and other decorative enamels for church books and clergy robes. Today, Rostov craftsmen still produce elegant enamel jewelry, ornaments and small paintings that are sold in *Beriozkas*.

Heading west out of the *kremlin* along Lenin Street brings you to the small three-domed **Church of the Savior-on-the-Sands**. This is all that has survived of a monastery built by Princess Maria, whose husband was killed by invading Mongols in the 14th century. Princess Maria and other noblewomen of Rostov chronicled many of the events of medieval Russia. During the 17th century, the library of Countess Irina Musina-Pushkina was one of the largest in Russia.

On the banks of **Lake Nero** are the 17th-century remains of **St Jacob's Monastery of Our Savior**; the original walls are still standing. The Immaculate Conception Cathedral (1686) and Church of St Demetrius (1800) are designed in the Russian classical style. Along the water is a park, where boats can be rented. Fishing is also a pleasant pastime.

Along the shores of the lake at the eastern end of town (at the end of Proletarskaya Street) is the **Church of Sts Cosma and Damian** (1775). Next to this small church stands the larger **Epiphany Cathedral** (1553), part of the **Monastery of St Barlaam** (Abraham); this is one of the oldest surviving monasteries in Russia, dating back to the 11th century.

Outside of Rostov, in the northwestern suburbs of the village of Bogoslov, is the lovely red **Church of St John upon Ishnya**, one of the last wooden churches left in the region. It stands on the River Ishnya and legend has it that it miraculously appeared from the lake and was washed up on the shores of its present location. It is open daily for visits and closed on Wednesdays.

VICINITY OF ROSTOV VELIKY

About 15 miles (24 kilometers) outside of Rostov Veliky on the way to Yaroslavl lies the **Borisoglebsky Monastery**. Built in the early 16th century, it was later surrounded by a fortified *kremlin* during the reign of Boris Godunov to protect it from Polish invasions. The famous Rostov architect Grigory Borisov built the **Cathedral of Sts Boris and Gleb** in 1524 and decorated it with colorful tiles. Boris and Gleb, sons of

Prince Vladimir (who introduced Christianity to Russia in AD 988), were the first saints of Russia. As political and religious turmoil swept Kiev, they passively accepted their deaths without fighting, believing in Christ's redemption. Borisov also built the five-domed Gate Church of St Sergius (1545) and the Church of the Annunciation (1526).

Yaroslavl

The English writer and adventurer Robert Byron wrote of his first visit to Yaroslavl in the early 1930s:

While Veliki Novgorod retains something of the character of early Russia before the Tatar invasion, the monuments of Yaroslavl commemorate the expansion of commerce that marked the 17th century... The English built a shipyard here; Dutch, Germans, French and Spaniards followed them. Great prosperity came to the town, and found expression in a series of churches whose spacious proportions and richness of architectural decoration had no rival in the Russia of their time.

Today Yaroslavl, lying 175 miles (280 kilometers) northeast of Moscow on the M8 Highway (and by train from Moscow's Yaroslavl Station), is still an important commercial center with a population of almost a million. It occupies the land on both sides of the Volga, where the River Kotorosl flows into it. Yaroslavl, the oldest city on the Volga, celebrated its 975th anniversary in 1985, commemorated by a monument in the city center. The seven-ton Ice Age boulder was unearthed on the site of the Strelka and the inscription reads,: 'On this spot in 1010 Yaroslavl the Wise founded Yaroslavl.' The oldest part of town, located at the confluence of the two rivers, contains many grandiose churches and residencies, erected by the many prosperous merchants. Not far from the city is the Estate-Museum of the poet Nekrasov and the Cosmos Museum, dedicated to the first Soviet woman cosmonaut, Valentina Tereshkova.

HISTORY

On the city's crest is the symbol of a bear, which was worshipped by pagan inhabitants as their sacred animal. In the ninth century, a small outpost arose on the right bank of the Volga River and became known as Bear Corner, forming the northern border of the Rostov region. When Kievan Grand-Prince Yaroslavl the Wise visited the settlement in 1010, its named was changed to honor the Grand Prince. It grew as large as Rostov; an early chronicle entry stated that in one great fire 17 churches burned to the ground. By the 13th century, Yaroslavl had become the capital of its

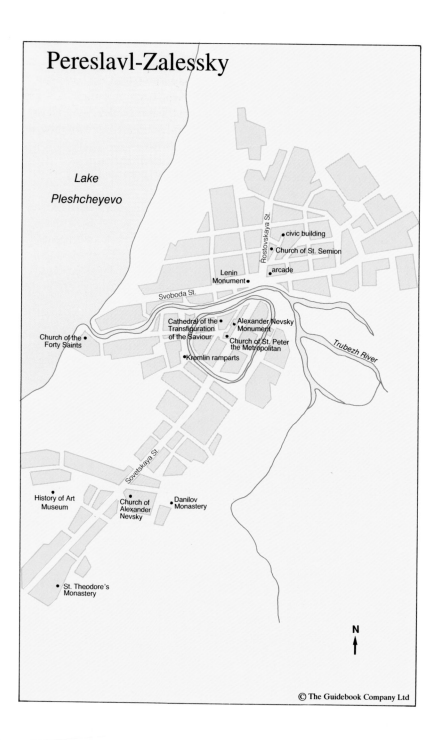

Pereslavl-Zalessky

Lake

Pleshcheyevo

Rostovskaya St.

• civic building

• Church of St. Semion

Lenin
Monument •

• arcade

Svoboda St.

Cathedral of the
Transfiguration
of the Saviour •

• Alexander Nevsky
Monument

Church of the •
Forty Saints

• Church of St. Peter
the Metropolitan

• Kremlin ramparts

Trubezh River

Sovetskaya St.

History of Art
Museum •

• Church of
Alexander
Nevsky

• Danilov
Monastery

• St. Theodore's
Monastery

N

© The Guidebook Company Ltd

own principality along the Volga and remained politically independent for another 250 years.

The hordes of the Mongol Khan Batu invaded in 1238 and destroyed a great part of the city. Later, in 1463, when Prince Alexander handed over his ancestral lands to the Grand-Prince of Moscow, Ivan III, Yaroslavl was finally annexed to the Moscovy principality. For a short time, Yaroslavl regained its political importance when it was made the temporary capital during the Time of Troubles from 1598 to 1613; it was the main trading post between Moscow and Archangel.

The city reached the height of its prosperity in the 17th century when it became known for its handicrafts. Located along important trade routes, merchants journeyed from as far away as England and the Netherlands to purchase leather goods, silverware, woodcarvings and fabrics. At one point, one-sixth of Russia's most prosperous merchant families lived in Yaroslavl, which was the second most populated city in the country. These families, in turn, put their wealth back into the city; by the middle of the 17th century, more than 30 new churches had been built. Yaroslavl was also Moscow's Volga port until the Moscow-Volga canal was built in 1937.

The *burlaki* (barge haulers) were a common sight, as portrayed in Repin's famous Barge Haulers on the Volga. (Merchants would travel along the Volga and River Kotorosl to Rostov, and then along a system of rivers and dry land, *volokoi*, on to Vladimir.) In 1795, Count Musin-Pushkin discovered, in the Savior Monastery, the famous 12th-century chronicle The *Lay of Igor's Host*, which was based on the fighting campaigns of *Prince Igor* of Novgorod who, in the words of the chronicle, 'did not let loose ten falcons on a flock of swans, but laid down his own wizard fingers on living strings, which themselves throbbed out praises...' Later Borodin composed the opera *Prince Igor* based on this chronicle.

SIGHTS

A tour of Yaroslavl, known as the 'Florence of Russia,' begins at the oldest part of town, the Strelka, (arrow or spit of land), lying along the right bank of the Volga, where the Kotorosl empties into it; the Bear Ravine, now Peace Boulevard, once separated the Timber Town from the *posad*, Earth Town.

By the Kotorosl, on Podbelskov Square, is the oldest surviving structure in Yaroslavl, the **Transfiguration of Our Savior Monastery**, founded at the end of the 12th century. It grew into a large feudal power; by the end of the 16th century, the monastery was one of the strongest fortresses in the northern states with a permanent garrison of its own *streltsy*, musketeer marksmen, to protect it. The *kremlin* walls were fortified to nine feet (three meters) thick in 1621. During an attack, the defenders would pour boiling water or hot tar on their enemies.

The Holy Gates of the monastery were built at the southern entrance in 1516. The archway frescoes include details from the Apocalypse. The 16th-century bell tower stands in front of the gates; climb up to the observation platform along its upper tier for a breathtaking panorama of the city.

The monastery's gold-domed **Cathedral of the Transfiguration of the Savior** (1506) was one of the wealthiest churches in all Russia. The frescoes that cover the entire interior are the oldest wall paintings in Yaroslavl. The fresco of the *Last Judgment*, painted in 1564, is on the west wall; the east side contains scenes of the *Transfiguration and Adoration of the Virgin*. It served as the burial chamber for the Yaroslavl princes. The vestry exhibits icons and old vestments that were used during church rituals and services.

Behind the bell-clock tower are two buildings, the Refectory and the Chambers of the Father Superior and Monks, which now house branches of the **Yaroslavl museums of Art, History and Architecture**. The museums are open daily from 10:00 to 17:00 and are closed on Mondays and the first Wednesday of each month. The Refectory exhibits the history of the Yaroslavl region up to the present day. The monk cells contain collections of Old Russian art, including icons, folk-art, manuscripts, costumes, armor and jewelry. Here also is the **Museum of The Lay of Igor's Host**. The story of this famous epic, along with ancient birch-bark documents and early printed books, is on display. Twelve years after Count Musin-Pushkin discovered the epic and other old rare manuscripts in the monastery library, the great fire of Moscow, during Napoleon's invasion, destroyed all the originals. The **Church of the Yaroslavl Miracle Workers** (1827), at the southern end of the cathedral, is the museum's cinema and lecture hall.

The red-brick and blue five-domed **Church of the Ephiphany** (1684) stands on the square behind the monastery. The church is open from May 1 to October 1 from 10:00 to 17:00 and is closed on Tuesdays. It is festively decorated with *kokoshniki* and glazed colored tiles, a tradition of Yaroslavl church architecture. The interior is a rich tapestry of frescoes illustrating the life of Christ; they were painted by Yaroslavl artists in 1692. It also has an impressive gilded seven-tiered iconostasis.

Crossing the square and walking up Pervomaiskaya Street (away from the Volga) leads to the early 19th-century **Central Bazaar**. Today this area is still a busy shopping district. A short walk behind the walls of the arcade brings you to the Znamenskaya (Sign) Tower of the *kremlin*. Towers in Russia were usually named after the icon that was displayed over their entrance. This tower once held the *Sign of the Mother of God* Icon.

Directly behind the tower on Ushinskov Street is the Yaroslavl Hotel. Here you can stop at the café and have a quick cup of *chai* or a meal in the Medvyed (Bear)

Rostov Veliky

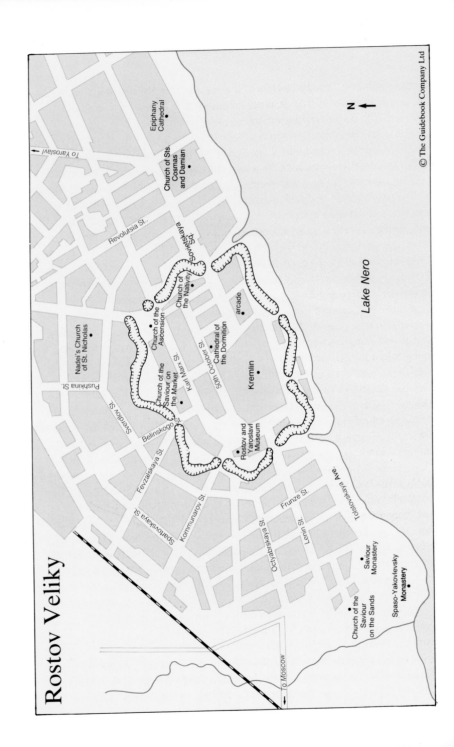

N

To Yaroslavl

Epiphany Cathedral

Church of Sts. Cosmas and Damian

Revolutsia St.

Nadei's Church of St. Nicholas

Pushkina St.

Sverdlov St.

Belinskogo St.

Fevzalskaya St.

Spartovskaya St.

Kommunarov St.

Sovietskaya Sq.

Church of the Nativity

Church of the Ascension

Church of the Saviour on the Market

Karl Marx St.

50th October St.

Cathedral of the Dormition

arcade

Kremlin

Rostov and Yaroslavl Museum

Frunze St.

Octyabrskaya St.

Lenin St.

Tolstovskaya Ave.

Lake Nero

Saviour Monastery

Spaso-Yakovlevsky Monastery

Church of the Saviour on the Sands

To Moscow

© The Guidebook Company Ltd

Restaurant. Across from the hotel on Volkov Square is the **Volkov Drama Theater**, founded by Fyodor Volkov, who opened Russia's first professional theater to the public in 1729; he formed his own drama company in 1748.

At the end of Ushinskov Street is a statue of Lenin on Krasnaya Ploshchad (Red Square). Circle back toward the Volga on Sovietskaya Street until it intersects with Sovietskaya Square. Dominating the town's main square is the **Church of Elijah the Prophet**, now a Museum of Architecture. The church is open from May 1 to October 1 from 10:00 to 18:00 and is closed on Wednesdays. Built in 1647, the white-stone church is decorated with ornamental tiles and surrounded by a gallery with chapels and a bell tower. The wooden iconostasis is carved in baroque fashion; the frescoes were painted in 1680 by the Kostroma artists Savin and Nikitin. These murals depict Christ's ascension, his life on earth, the lives of his Apostles, and the prophet Elijah. Prayer benches carved for Czar Alexei (father of Peter the Great) and Patriarch Nikon are also to be found inside.

Behind this church, at 23 Volzhsky Embankment, is a **Branch Museum of Russian Art** from the 18th to 20th centuries, housed in the former governor's residence. It is open from 10:00 to 17:00 and is closed on Fridays. Across the street from the museum is **Nadei's Church of St Nicholas** (1620), a gift to the city from a wealthy merchant named Nadei Sveteshnikov. This church is open from May 1 to October 1 from 9:00 to 17:00 and is closed on Thursdays. Ten churches in Yaroslavl were dedicated to St Nicholas, the patron saint of commerce.

The impressive **Vakhrameyev Mansion** is also next to the water, in the other direction, off Revolution Street. The house was built in the 1780s in the baroque fashion. Members of this wealthy noble family were avid patrons of the arts in Yaroslavl. Behind the mansion (at 17 Volzhsky Embankment) is a small Branch Museum of Local History. It is open from 10:00 to 17:30 and is closed on Mondays.

Walking directly along the Volga, on the Volzhsky Embankment, leads to the two-story building of the **Metropolitan's Chambers** (1690), located in the old Timber Town. It was originally built to accommodate the Metropolitan of Rostov Veliky when he visited. The chambers are now a **Museum of Old Russian Art**, displaying many icons, paintings and ceramic tiles. The museum is open from 10:00 to 17:00 and is closed on Fridays. Of interest is the icon *The Lay of the Bloody Battle with Khan Mamai*, a portrait of Count Musin-Pushkin and a bronze sculpture of Yaroslavl the Wise.

Making your way back toward the Savior Monastery, along the Kotorosl Embankment, leads past three distinctive churches. The first (at 8 Kotorosl) is the simple white cube-shaped **Church of St Nicholas in the Timber** (1695), built by the local shipbuilders who lived in this part of the Timber Town. Next (at number 10) is the **Church of the Transfiguraton in the Marketplace** (1672). It was built from funds collected by the townspeople in the old marketplace of the original Earth Town, where the local merchants and artisans lived. In the summer of 1693, 22 Yaroslavl artists helped paint the interior frescoes. The red-brick **Church of the Archangel Michael** (1658), directly across from the monastery (at number 14), is filled with brightly colored frescoes painted by local Yaroslavl artists in 1730.

Outside the Strelka in the village of Tolchkovo (in the northern part of the city) is the picturesque 15-domed **Church of St John the Baptist** (1671), located at 69 Kotorosl Embankment on the right bank of the river. The five central green domes with a tulip-shaped dome in the middle, gold crosses and ornamental tiles, are prime examples of the architecture of the Golden Age of Yaroslavl. The whole principality of Yaroslavl donated funds to build the church. I n 1694, 15 masters from around Russia painted the frescoes and icons that adorn every part of the interior. The baroque-style iconostasis was carved in 1701. The complex also includes a seven-tiered bell tower. The church is open from 10:00 to 18:00 and is closed on Tuesdays.

Also on the Kotorosl's right bank, but further down the Volga (at 2 Port Embankment), is a delightful architectural ensemble in the **Village of Korovniki**. The most impressive structure is the five-domed **Church of St John Chrysostom** (1649). Its tent-shaped bell tower is known as the 'Candle of Yaroslavl.' The **Church of Our Lady of Vladimir** (1669) was used as the winter church.

If you have time, take a boat ride along the Volga; cruises last about an hour. For an evening's entertainment, book tickets at your hotel for the Yaroslavl Circus (located at 69 Svobody Street across from Truda Square). The Puppet Theater is at 25 Svobody Street.

Each summer, beginning August 1, the Yaroslavl Sunsets Music Festival is held, which usually opens with the overture to Borodin's *Prince Igor.*

VICINITY OF YAROSLAVL

On the Uglich Highway 15 miles (29 kilometers) southwest of Yaroslavl is the **Cosmos Museum**, dedicated to Valentina Tereshkova, the first female cosmonaut. Valentina's flight, in 1963, lasted 70 hours and orbited the earth 48 times. The museum, near the house where she was born in the village of Nikulskoye, displays her space capsule and the history of Soviet space travel. In 1993, a major auction of Soviet space memorabilia was held in New York at Sotheby's. In 1994, history was made when the first Russian cosmonaut flew in the American space shuttle. The museum is open from 10:00 to 17:00 and is closed on Mondays. The Service desk at your hotel may arrange excursions to these places.

About 10 miles (16 kilometers) from Yaroslavl, along the Moscow-Yaroslavl Highway, is the **Nekrasov Estate-Museum** in the village of Karabikha. The famous Russian writer Nikolai Nekrasov (1821–78) stayed on the estate in the summer months; it retains its former appearance. Among his works is the satire *Who is Happy*

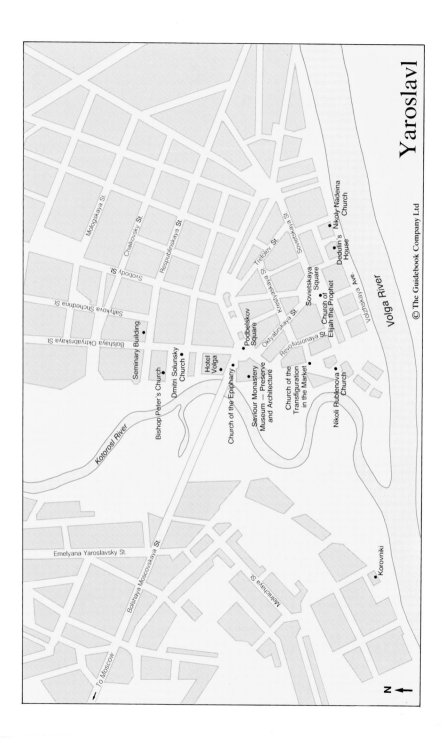

Yaroslavl

© The Guidebook Company Ltd

in Russia? His poems and other works are on display. The museum is open from 10:00 to 17:00 and is closed on Mondays. Each summer there is a Nekrasov Poetry Festival at Karabikha.

Kostroma

Kostroma, 47 miles (76 kilometers) northeast of Yaroslavl, is the only city in Russia which has retained the original layout of its town center; it was founded by Yuri Dolgoruky in the 12th century. Reconstructed in the early 18th century, it is one of the country's finest examples of old Russian classic design; no two houses are alike.

Once a bustling trade center known as the 'Flax Capital of the North,' Kostroma (pronounced with last syllable accented) supplied Russia and Europe with the finest sail cloth. The emblem of this picturesque town set along the Volga River depicts a small boat on silvery waters with sails billowing in the wind. The central mercantile square was situated on the banks of the Volga. The Krasniye, Beautiful, and *Bolshiye*, Large, stalls were connected by covered galleries where fabrics and other goods were sold. Today, the modernized **Arcade** still houses the town's markets and stores. The **Borschchov Mansion** (home of a general who fought in the War of 1812), the largest of the older residential buildings, stands nearby.

The oldest building in Kostroma is the octagon-roofed **Cathedral of the Epiphany** (1592) in the village of Krasnoye-on-the-Volga. The most beautiful structure is the **Church of the Resurrection on-the-Debre**, situated on the outskirts of town. In 1652, the merchant Kiril Isakov built this elaborate red-brick and green-domed church from money found in a shipment of English dyes. When informed of the discovery of gold pieces, the London company told Isakov to keep the money for 'charitable deeds.' Some of the bas-reliefs on the outside of the church illustrate the British lion and unicorn. The towering five-domed church has a gallery running along the sides; at the northwestern end is the **Chapel of Three Bishops**, with a magnificently carved iconostasis. The gates of the church are surrounded by ornamental *kokoshniki*, and the interior is ornately decorated with frescoes and icons from the 15th century.

The real gem of the town is the **Ipatyevsky Monastery**, founded in the 14th century by the Zernov Boyars, ancestors of the Godunovs. This large structure is enclosed by a white brick *kremlin* and topped by green tent-shaped domes. Later, the relatives of Boris Godunov built the monastery's golden-domed **Trinity Cathedral**. While Boris Godunov was czar (1598–1605), the Ipatyevsky Monastery became the wealthiest in the country, containing over 100 icons. The Godunov family had its own mansion (the rose-colored building with the small windows) within the monastery, and most members were buried in the cathedral. The monastery was continually ravaged by internal strife, blackened by Polish invasions, and captured by the second False Dmitri in 1605, who claimed the throne of the Russian Empire. Later, the Romanovs who, like the Godunovs, were powerful feudal lords in Kostroma, got the young Mikhail elected czar after the Time of Troubles. In 1613, Mikhail Romanov left the monastery to be crowned in the Moscow Kremlin. Today, the famous Ipatyevsky Chronicles are displayed here; this valuable document, found in the monastery's archives, traces the fascinating history of ancient Rus.

The **Church of St John the Divine** (1687), which functioned as the winter church, stands nearby. From the monastery's five-tiered bell tower, there is a pleasing view of the countryside and the **Museum of Wooden Architecture**, open daily to the public. Intricately carved old wooden buildings gathered from nearby villages include the **Church of the Virgin** (1552), a typical peasant dwelling, a windmill and a bathhouse.

Other churches on the right bank of the Volga are the **Church of the Transfiguration** (1685), **Church of St Elijah-at-the-Gorodishche** (1683-85) and the beautiful hilltop **Church of the Prophet Elijah**. The Kostroma Hotel, with restaurant, overlooks the Volga (request a room on the riverside with balcony). There are paths along the river and even swimming in summer. Try catching a circus performance in the evening.

Ivanovo

Ivanovo, an industrial and regional center 180 miles (288 kilometers) northeast of Moscow, began as a small village on the right bank of the River Uvod. The River Talka also crosses the town; both rivers flow into the River Klyazma, a tributary of the Moskva. The village of Voznesensk, on the left bank, was annexed by Ivanovo in 1871. In 1561, a chronicle mentioned that Ivan the Terrible presented the village of Ivanovo to a powerful princely family. When, two centuries later, an Ivanovo princess married a Sheremetev, the town passed over to this powerful aristocratic family. In 1710, Peter the Great ordered weaving mills and printing factories built here. Soon the town grew into a major textile and commercial center with little religious significance. Ivanovo calico was famous worldwide; by the mid-1800s, the town was known as the Russian Manchester. Today, almost 20 per cent of the country's cloth is produced in this city of more than half a million people. Ivanovo is nicknamed the 'City of Brides'—80 per cent of textile workers are women, many men come here to look for a wife.

The circus trapeze act backstage

Restoration work

Ivanovo participated actively in the revolutionary campaigns and was called the Third Proletarian Capital after Moscow and the former Leningrad. Major strikes were held in the city in 1883 and 1885; in 1897, 14,000 workers held a strike against the appalling conditions in the factories. The 1905 strike, with over 80,000 participants, was headed by the famous Bolshevik leader Mikhail Frunze, who established the town's first Workers' Soviet, which provided assistance to the strikers and their families during the three-month protest.

Compared to other Golden Ring towns, Ivanovo is relatively new and modern, with only a few places of particular interest. On Lenin Prospekt, the **Ivanovo Museums of Art and History** portray the city's historical events and display collections of textiles, old printing blocks and other traditional folk arts. Off Kuznetsov Street is the **Museum-Study of Mikhail Frunze**. On Smirnov Street is the 17th-century **Shudrovskaya Chapel**; on nearby Sadovaya Street stands the large red-bricked **House-Museum of the Ivanovo-Voznesensk City Council**. Other locations of interest in the city are the circus, puppet theater, a 17th-century wooden church and **Stepanov Park**, with an open-air theater, planetarium and boats for hire. The Zarya Restaurant is on Lenin Prospekt and the Tsentralnaya Hotel on Engels Street.

Palekh

This village lies 30 miles (48 kilometers) east of Ivanovo and is famous for colorfully painted lacquer boxes. After the Revolution, when icon production was halted, it became popular to paint small miniatures on lacquer papier-mâché boxes, which combined the art of ancient Russian painting with the local folkcrafts. Ivan Golivko (1886–1937), the Master of Palekh Folk Art, created many beautiful lacquer scenes drawn from traditional Russian fairy-tales, folk epics and songs; he sometimes lined the box interiors with Russian poetry. The **Museum of Palekh Art** displays a magnificent collection of painted boxes and other lacquer art by the folk artists of Palekh. These include works by the masters Vatagin, Bakanov, Vakurov, Butorin, Zubkov and Golivko. The **Timber House of Golivko**, where he lived and worked, is also open to the public.

Traditionally, the Palekh box was fashioned from birch wood or linden and varnished black on the outside with a red interior. The artists used special tempera paints, and made fine brushes from squirrel tails. After the top of the box was dusted with a special powder, the outline of the painting was sketched on with white paint. After the design was colored in, a series of coats of translucent lacquer was applied, so that the box shone with an unusual brightness. The top was further decorated with gold, silver and mother-of-pearl. A wolf's tooth was used to fine polish the decorative colors.

The 17th-century **Cathedral of the Exaltation of the Holy Cross**, now a museum, stands in the town center. A plaque on the outside of the west wall shows the builder to be Master Yegor Dubov. Local craftsmen carved and painted the baroque-style golden iconostasis inside the church, which is covered with almost 50 colorful icons. For centuries before the Revolution, the highly respected Palekh artists were sent all over Russia to paint beautiful icons and frescoes in the Central Russian style. Today, the artists of Palekh carry on the traditions of lacquer design and over 250 craftsmen are employed at the Palekh Art Studio. Throughout Russia, painted boxes and jewelry are sold in the *Beriozkas*, where Palekh laquerware is widely displayed. The writer Maxim Gorky, who often asked Golikov to illustrate his texts, wrote: 'The masters of Palekh carry on the icon painting traditions through their boxes...and with these beautiful achievements, win the admiration of all who see them.'

Vladimir

Vladimir lies 120 miles (190 kilometers) northeast of Moscow along the M7 Highway. Trains also leave from Moscow's Kursk Station and pass through the cultivated countryside, strewn with collective farms that raise corn and livestock. The same rural scenes of farmers, dressed in embroidered peasant shirts with wide leather belts and *valenki*, black felt boots, plowing the fertile land, were painted by Russian artists such as Kramskoi, Vrubel and Repin over a century ago. It is recommended to spend at least a few days in the Vladimir region. After visiting Vladimir (stay overnight in the Vladimir Hotel), spend the next day in the ancient town of Suzdal, only 16 miles (26 kilometers) to the north. Between these two cities is the historic village of Bogoliubovo and the Church-of-the-Intercession on the River Nerl.

HISTORY

Even though Vladimir is now a bustling city of 325,000 and the administrative head of the region, it is still one of the best preserved centers of 12th- and 13th-century Old Russian architecture. Eight centuries ago, Vladimir was the most powerful town of ancient Rus. Located on the banks of the Klyazma River, a small tributary of the Volga, Vladimir was an important stop on the trade routes between Europe and Asia. Greeks from Constantinople, Vikings from the north, Bulgars from the Volga and Central Asian merchants all journeyed through the Vladimir-Suzdal principality.

Vsevolod, the son of Kievan Grand-Prince Yaroslavl the Wise, first began to settle the area of Vladimir in northeastern Rus while Kiev was being attacked by numerous hostile tribes in the late 11th century. Many Russians, at this time, began to migrate northward; this exodus is described in one of Russia's earliest epic chronicles, *The Lay of Igor's Host*. With the death of his father, Vsevolod became the most powerful prince in all the land. Prince Vsevolod built a small fortress near the village of Suzdal on the road from Kiev. Later, a trading settlement was established around the fort by Vsevolod's son, who also built the first stone church. The town was named after Vladimir Monomakh in 1108. After Monomakh's death in 1125, the Kievan states in the south began to lose their political and economic importance; under Monomakh's son Yuri Dolgoruky, the northern territories began to flourish. Vladimir grew so large and prosperous that it became the capital of northern Rus by the middle of the 12th century.

Dolgoruky's heir, Andrei Bogoliubsky, decided to rule Russia from a more centralized and peaceful area, and transferred the throne of the Grand-Prince from Kiev to Vladimir in 1157, after a vision of the Blessed Virgin directed him to do so. Bogoliubsky (Lover of God) left Kiev under the protection of a holy icon, said to have been painted by St Luke from Constantinople, known as Our Lady of Vladimir. This revered icon became the sacred palladium of the Vladimir region; the prince even took it on his military campaigns. As the protectorate of the city, it became the symbol of divine intervention and power of the grand-princes.

Andrei brought in master artists and craftsmen to recreate the splendors of Kiev in the new town of Vladimir. A crowned lion carrying a cross was the town's coat-of-arms. Under his brother, Vsevolod III (who ruled from 1174 to 1212), the Vladimir–Suzdal principality, with Vladimir as its capital, reached the zenith of its political power.

When the Mongol Tatars invaded in 1238, Vladimir, like many other towns in Russia, suffered extensive damage. For a while, Vladimir retained the seat of the Church Metropolitan, and the grand-princes were still crowned in the town's Uspensky Cathedral. But eventually the princes of Moscovy began governing Russia through the Khans. When Vladimir was annexed to the principality of Moscovy, and Moscow became the capital of the country in the 16th century, its importance slowly declined; by 1668, the population numbered only 990. After the Revolution, the city grew with industrialization and today it is a large producer of electrical machinery. The Vladimiret tractor, sold around the world, once won a Gold Medal at a Brussels Machinery Exhibition.

Sights

To enter the old part of town along the river, pass through the **Golden Gates** (the only surviving gates of the city), built in 1158 by Prince Bogoliubsky, who modeled them after the Golden Gates of Kiev. The oak doors of the now white gates were once covered with gilded copper; the golden-domed structure on top of the gates was the

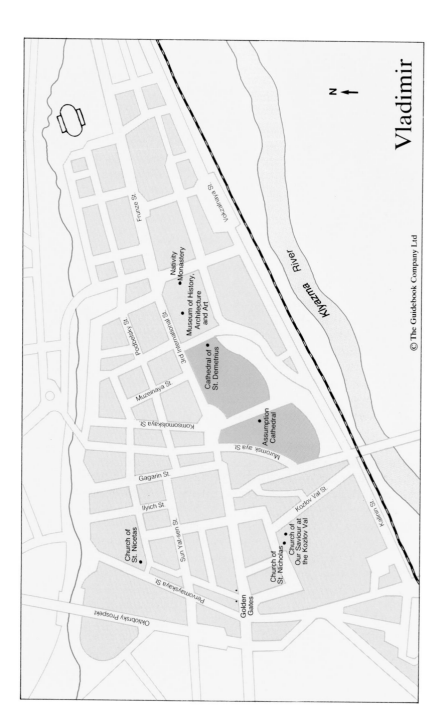

Vladimir

N

Kvyazma River

Vokzalnaya St.

Frunze St.

Nativity Monastery

Museum of History, Architecture, and Art

Podbelsky St.

3'd International St.

Cathedral of St. Demetrius

Muzeinaya St.

Komsomolskaya St.

Assumption Cathedral

Muromsk'aya St.

Gagarin St.

Ilyich St.

Sun Yat-sen St.

Church of St. Nicetas

Kozlov Val St.

Church of Our Saviour at the Kozlov Val

Church of St. Nicholas

Kalinin St.

Pervomayskaya St.

Oktiobrsky Prospekt

Golden Gates

© The Guidebook Company Ltd

Church of the Deposition of the Robe. These gates were used as a defense fortification for the western part of town and also served as a triumphal arch—Alexander Nevsky, Dmitri Donskoi (in 1380) and troops on their way to fight Napoleon in the Battle of Borodino in 1812 all passed through the arch. The gates were damaged many times through the years, and were reconstructed in the 18th century. Today the Golden Gates house the local **Military Historical Museum**. Next to the Gates, in the red-brick building (formerly a church) and the fire observation tower, are the **Museums of Contemporary Artisits and Ancient Town Life**. The latter has many interesting old illustrations and black and white photographs, tracing the history of the region.

The oldest buildings of the city were constructed on the hills by the water, which served as a defensive wall. As you walk through the gates, a cluster of golden-domed white churches come into view. In 1158, Andrei Bogoliubsky brought in master craftsmen from all over Russia and Europe to build the triple-domed *Uspensky Sobor*, the **Assumption Cathedral**. Built to rival Kiev's St Sophia, the cathedral was decorated with gold, silver and precious stones. It was the tallest building in all of Rus. Filled with frescoes and icons, the iconostasis was also the largest of its kind in Russia. A tenth of the Grand-Prince's revenue was contributed to the upkeep of the cathedral. After much of it was destroyed by fire in 1185 (along with 33 other churches), Prince Vsevolod III had it rebuilt with five domes. Since the original walls were encased within a larger structure, the cathedral doubled in size, with an area for a congregation of 4,000 people. The Italian architect Fioravanti used it as his model for the Moscow Kremlin's own Assumption Cathedral. After more fires blackened the walls, the famous iconists Andrei Rublev and Daniil Chorny were sent in 1408 to restore the interior. Frescoes from the 12th and 13th centuries are still evident on the western and northern walls. Rublev's and Chorny's frescoes, including scenes from the *Last Judgment*, decorate two vaults beneath the choir gallery and the altar pillars. The famed icon of the *Virgin of Vladimir*, that once hung by the altar, was transferred in 1380 to Moscow's Assumption Cathedral; it is now in the Moscow Tretyakov Gallery.

This cathedral was one of the most revered churches in Russia; all the Vladimir and Moscow grand-princes were crowned inside it, from the son of Yuri Dolgoruky to Ivan III, in the early 15th century. It was the main center of the Church Metropolitan in the 14th century. The Assumption Cathedral was also the burial place of the Princes of Vladimir, including Andrei Bogoliubsky and Vsevolod III. The three-story belfry was built in 1810. The cathedral has been under continuous restoration during the last century. Mass is celebrated on Saturday evenings, Sundays and Orthodox feast days. Visitors are welcome in respectful attire. Flash photography is not permitted.

A short walk away to the right of the cathedral (with your back to the river) leads to one of the most splendid examples of old Russian architecture, the **Cathedral of St**

Demetrius (1193–97). It was built by Vsevolod III as his court church; his palace once stood nearby. The cathedral, with its one large helmut drum, was named after 'Big Nest' Vsevolod's patron saint (St Demetrius of Thessaloniki) and new-born son Dmitri. (Vsevolod was nicknamed 'Big Nest' because of his large family of 12 children.) It is built from blocks of white limestone and decorated with intricate *kokoshniki* along the doorways and arches. Over 1,300 bas-reliefs cover the outer walls: decorative beasts, birds, griffins, saints, prophets, the labors of Hercules, and many elaborate floral patterns all glorify the might of Vladimir. The friezes of King David and Alexander the Great symbolize Vsevolod's cunning military exploits. At the top of the left section of the northern façade is Prince Vsevolod seated on the throne with his young son; the other sons are bowing to their father. The interior frescoes date back to the 12th century. In 1834, Nicholas I ordered the cathedral restored; it is now part of the local museum complex.

Across from this cathedral at 64 IIIrd International Street is the **Vladimir Museum of Art and Architecture**, with displays of old religious paintings, manuscripts and architectural designs. Directly across the street is the **Museum of History**. A rich collection of artifacts, archeological materials, old fabrics and weapons, princely possessions and the white stone tomb of Alexander Nevsky are on display. Another branch of the museum with lacquered art, crystal and embroidery is located at the end of IIIrd International Street past the Golden Gates. The museums are open daily and closed on Thursdays.

Directly behind this last branch museum is the simple white **Church of St Nicholas** and the **Church of the Savior at the Kozlov Val**, both built in the late 17th century. Across from them, nearer the water, is the **Church of St Nicholas-at-Galeya**, with its tent-shaped bell tower. The church was built by a wealthy citizen of Vladimir in the early 18th century.

At the opposite end of IIIrd International Street toward Frunze Square is the **Nativity Monastery** (1191–96), one of Russia's most important religious complexes up until the end of the 16th century; it was closed in 1744. Alexander Nevsky was buried here in 1263; his remains were transferred to St Petersburg by Peter the Great in 1724. The Nikolskaya Church next door is now the Planetarium.

Next to the Vladimir Hotel (across from the Planetarium on Frunze Street) is the brick and five-domed **Assumption Church** (1644), built from donations given by rich local merchants. At the end of Frunze Street is the Eternal Flame, commemorating the soldiers who lost their lives during World War II.

Directly in front of the Golden Gates on Gagarin Street is the city's main shopping district, the *Torgoviye Ryady*. Across the street is the **Monument to the 850th Anniversary of Vladimir**.

Stroll down Gagarin Street and look out over the old section of Vladimir. In the distance are many old squat wooden houses with long sloping roofs and stone floors. Many of the town's inhabitants have lived in these homes for generations. The people enjoy a simple town life. During the day you may see residents hanging out laundry, perhaps painting the lattice work around their windows a pastel blue-green, chopping wood, or gathering fruits and mushrooms. The children enjoy having their pictures taken. Bring a few souvenirs from home to trade.

At the end of Gagarin Street is the **Knyaginin (Princess) Convent**, founded by the wife of Vsevolod III, Maria Shvarnovna, in 1200. The grand-princesses of the court were buried in the convent's Assumption Cathedral, rebuilt in the 16th century. The cathedral's three-tiered walls are lined with fancy *zakamora* and topped with a single helmet drum. In 1648, Moscow artists painted the colorful interior frescoes. The north and south walls depict the life of the Virgin Mary, and the west wall shows scenes from the *Last Judgment*. Paintings of Vladimir princesses, portrayed as saints, are on the southwest side, and the pillars recount the lives of the grand-princes. The cathedral is the only remaining building of the convent complex and now houses a restoration organization. Next to the convent stands the **Church of St Nicetas** (1762). This green and white, three-tiered baroque church was built by the merchant Semion Lazarev. The interior is divided into three separate churches on each floor. It was restored in 1970. In front of this church is a bust of the writer Gogol. Pervomaiskaya (First of May) Street leads back to the Golden Gates.

At the end of the day, your group tour may stop at the rustic log-hewn Traktir Restaurant for an enjoyable meal of the local cuisine.

VICINITY OF VLADIMIR

The quaint village of Bogoliubovo lies five miles (eight kilometers) from Vladimir. Group tours sometimes stop; if not, a car can be hired in the town. One legend says that when Prince Andrei was traveling from Kiev to Vladimir, carrying the sacred icon of Our Lady of Vladimir, his horses stopped on a large hill and would move no farther. At this junction, by the confluence of the Klyazma and Nerl rivers, Andrei decided to build a fortress and royal residence. He named the town Bogoliubovo (Loved by God) and took the name of Bogoliubsky; he was canonized by the Church in 1702. Supposedly, after the Virgin appeared to him in a dream, he built the **Nativity of the Virgin Church**. This cathedral was still standing in the 18th century, but when one Father Superior decided to renovate it in 1722 by adding more windows, the cathedral collapsed; it was partially rebuilt in 1751. Only a few of the 12th-century palace walls remain, of which chronicles relate: 'it was hard to look at all the gold.' On the staircase tower are pictures depicting the death of Andrei Bogoliubsky— assassinated by jealous nobles in this tower in 1174. The coffins of his assassins were said to have been buried in the surrounding marshes and their wailing cries heard at night. The buildings in Bogoliubovo are now museums, which are closed on Mondays. About one mile southeast of Bogoliubovo on the River Nerl is the graceful **Church of the Intercession-on-the-Nerl**, built during the Golden Age of Vladimir architecture. Standing alone in the green summer meadows or snowy winter landscape, it is reflected in the quiet waters of the river that is filled with delicate lilies. It has come down from legend that Andrei built this church in 1164 to celebrate his victory over the Volga Bulgars. The Virgin of the Intercession was thought to have protected the rulers of Vladimir. With the building of this church, Andrei proclaimed a new church holiday, the Feast of the Intercession.

Suzdal

Suzdal is a pleasant half-hour journey from Vladimir through open fields dotted with hay stacks and mounds of dark rich soil. Vladimir was the younger rival of Suzdal which, along with Rostov Veliky, was founded a full century earlier. The town was settled along the banks of the Kamenka River, which empties into the Nerl a few miles downstream. Over 100 examples of Old Russian architecture attract half a

Market day

Trying to keep a secret

million visitors each year to this remarkable medieval museum. Just outside Suzdal is Kideksha, a small preserved village that dates back to the beginning of the 12th century. On the left bank of the river is the delightful **Suzdal Museum of Wooden Architecture**, portraying the typical Russian life-style of centuries ago. In 1983, the town received the Golden Apple. Awarded by an international jury, the prize symbolizes excellence in historical preservation and local color.

The first view of Suzdal from the road encompasses towering silhouettes of gleaming domes and pinkish walls atop Poklonnaya Hill, rising up amidst green patches of woods and gardens. It is as though time has stopped in this enchanting place—a perfection of spatial harmony. Today, Suzdal is a quiet town with no industrial enterprises. Crop and orchard farming is the main occupation of the residents who still live in the predominant *izba* wooden houses. The scenic town is a popular site for film-making. The American production of *Peter the Great* used Suzdal as one of its locations.

Traveling along the Golden Ring route, you may have noticed that the distances between towns are similar. When these towns were settled, one unit of length was measured by how much ground a team of horses could cover in 24 hours. Most towns were laid out about one post-unit apart. So the distance between Moscow and Pereslavl-Zalessky, Pereslavl and Rostov, or Rostov and Yaroslavl could easily be covered in one day's time. Distances in medieval Russia, from Kiev to the White Sea, were measured by these units; thus, the traveler knew how many days it took to arrive at his destination—from Moscow to Suzdal took about three days.

HISTORY

The area of Suzdalia was first mentioned in chronicles in 1024, when Kievan Grand-Prince Yaroslavl the Wise came to suppress the rebellions. By 1096, a small kremlin had been built around the settlement, which one chronicle already described as a 'town.' As Suzdal grew, princes and rich nobles from Kiev settled here, bringing with them spiritual representatives from the church, who introduced Christianity to the region. The town slowly gained in prominence; Grand-Prince Yuri Dolgoruky named it the capital of the northern provinces in 1125. From Suzdal, the seat of his royal residence, he went on to establish the small settlement of Moscow in 1147. His son, Andrei Bogoliubsky, transferred the capital to Vladimir in 1157.

After the Kievan States crumbled in the 12th century, Suzdal, along with Rostov Veliky, became the religious center of medieval Rus. The princes and *boyars* donated vast sums of money to build splendid churches and monasteries; by the 14th century, Suzdal had over 50 churches, 400 dwellings and a famous school of icon painting. No other place in all of Russia had such a high proportion of religious buildings. The crest of Suzdal was a white falcon within a prince's crown.

Since the town itself was not situated along important trade routes, the monks (and not the merchants) grew in wealth from large donations to the monasteries. The Church eventually took over the fertile lands and controlled the serf-peasants.

Suzdal was invaded many times, first by the Mongols in 1238, then by Lithuanians and Poles. After the Mongol occupation, no new stone buildings were erected until well into the 16th century. When it was annexed to Moscovy in the late 14th century, Suzdal lost its political importance, but remained a religious center.

During the 1700s, Peter the Great's reforms undermined ecclesiastical power and the Church in Suzdal lost much of its land and wealth. Churches and monasteries were mainly used to house religious fanatics and political prisoners. Many barren or unpopular wives were forced to take the veil and exiled to Suzdal's convents. By the end of the 19th century, only 6,000 residents remained, and one account described Suzdal as 'a town of churches, bell towers, old folk legends and tombstones.' But today, this enthralling, poetic spot has been restored to the majesty of its former days. As one 13th-century chronicler observed: 'Oh, most radiant and bountiful, how wondrous art thou with thy beauty vast.'

Sights

Approaching Suzdal from Vladimir, as horse coaches once did, two churches are passed on the right before crossing the Kamenka River. These are the **Church of Our Lady of the Sign** (1749) and the **Church of the Deposition of the Robe** (1777). The former houses the Suzdal Excursion Bureau.

The *kremlin* was well protected on three sides by the river; along the eastern wall ran a large moat. Remnants of the 11th-century earthen walls are still evident today. These ramparts are topped with wooden walls and towers.

A tour of Suzdal begins on the right bank of the river, where much of the old architecture is clustered. Take a moment to gaze out along the fertile plains and meandering waters of the river. The rich arable land in this area first attracted settlers seeking greater freedoms from Novgorod, where pagan priests were still leading uprisings against Kievan attempts to Christianize and feudalize the northern lands. In Old Russian, su*zdal* meant to 'give judgment or justice.' Today, several streets still carry the names of Slavic pagan gods, such as Kupala, Netyoka and Yarunova.

As you cross the river, a simple white church with red outlines, comes into view on the left side of Lenin Street. This was used as the summer church; the slender helmet-domed building behind it was used in winter.

The 13th-century **Korsunsky Gates** lead to the main cathedral and are covered with Byzantine patterns; religious scenes from the New Testament were engraved and etched with acid on copper sheets and then gilded.

Prince Vladimir Monomakh laid the first stone of the town's main **Cathedral of**

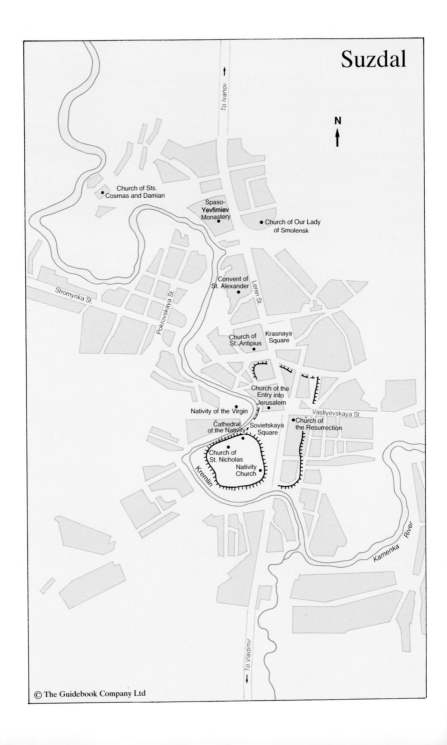

Suzdal

To Ivanov

N

Church of Sts.
Cosmas and Damian

Spaso-
Yevfimiev
Monastery

Church of Our Lady
of Smolensk

Stromynka St.

Pokrovskaya St.

Lenin St.

Convent of
St. Alexander

Church of
St. Antipius

Krasnaya
Square

Church of the
Entry into
Jerusalem

Nativity of the Virgin

Vasliyevskaya St.

Church of
the Resurrection

Cathedral
of the Nativity

Sovietskaya
Square

Church of
St. Nicholas

Nativity
Church

Kremlin

Kamenka River

To Vladimr

© The Guidebook Company Ltd

the Nativity at the end of the 11th century. This structure was rebuilt many times; in 1528, Grand-Prince Vasily III of Moscow reconstructed it from brick and white stone and surmounted it with five helmet-shaped domes. In 1748, the domes were altered to the present blue onion and gold-star pattern.

The southern doors, surrounded by elaborate stone decorations, were the official entrance of the princes. Lions, carved along the portals, were the emblems of the princes of Vladimir. The carved female faces symbolize the Virgin Mary, whose nativity is celebrated. The southern and western doors (1230–33) are made of gilded copper and depict scenes from the life of St George, the patron saint of both Prince Georgi and his grandfather, Yuri Dolgoruky.

Early 13th-century frescoes of saints and other ornamental floral patterns are still visible in the vestry. Most of the other murals and frescoes are from the 17th century. Tombs of early bishops and princes from as far back as 1023 are also found inside. The burial vaults of the early princesses are near the west wall. The octagonal bell tower was built in 1635 by order of Czar Mikhail Romanov and repaired in 1967. Old Slavonic letters correspond to numbers of the face of the clock.

The Archbishop's Palace, now the **Suzdal Museum**, was built next to the cathedral on the bank of the Kamenka between the 15th and 17th centuries. The main chamber of the palace, a large pillarless hall, held important meetings and banquets. In the 17th century, this *Krestovaya* (Cross-Vaulted) Chamber was considered one of the most elegant rooms in all Russia. The museum contains collections of ancient art and traces the evolution of architecture in the Suzdal region.

Enter the palace chamber through the western entrance. In the center stands a long wooden table, covered with a rich red cloth, once used by the archbishop and his clergy. An 18th-century tiled stove stands in one corner. The walls are decorated with many 15th-century icons. Suzdal developed its own school of icon painting in the early 13th century. Its use of lyrical flowing outlines, detailed facial qualities and soft designs in red and gold, were later adopted by the Moscow school, headed by Andrei Rublev. Both the Moscow Tretyakov Gallery and the St Petersburg Russian Museum include Suzdal icons among their exhibits.

Pass through the gateway to the left of the palace to reach another art section of the museum. Here are more displays of icons, paintings, sculptures, ivory carvings, embroideries and other crafts.

In front of the palace by the river is the wooden **Church of St Nicholas** (1766). It represents one of the oldest types of Old Russian wooden architecture and is built from logs into a square frame with a long sloping roof. The early architects used only an ax, chisel and plane to build these designs. No nails were needed; the logs were held together by wooden pegs and filled with moss. The church was transferred from the village of Glotovo in 1960. Beside it, in lovely contrast, stands the red and white-

The Man in the Window

The building stands behind the high red-brick wall known to the entire world. There are many windows in that building, but one was distinguished from all the others because it was lit twenty-four hours a day. Those who gathered in the evening on the broad square in front of the red-brick wall would crane their necks, strain their eyes to the point of tears, and say excitedly to one another: "Look, over there, the window's lit. He's not sleeping. He's working. He's thinking about us."

If someone came from the provinces to this city or had to stop over while in transit, he'd be informed that it was obligatory to visit that famous square and look and see whether that window was lit. Upon returning home, the fortunate provincial would deliver authoritative reports, both at closed meetings and at those open to the public, that yes, the window was lit, and judging by all appearances, he truly never slept and was continually thinking about them.

Naturally, even back then, there were certain people who abused the trust of their collectives. Instead of going to look at that window, they'd race around to all the stores, wherever there was anything for sale. But, upon their return, they, too, would report that the window was lit, and just try and tell them otherwise.

The window, of course, was lit. But the person who was said never to sleep was never at that window. A dummy made of gutta-percha, built by the finest craftsmen, stood in for him. That dummy had been so skillfully constructed that unless you actually touched it there was nothing to indicate that it wasn't alive. Its hand held a curved pipe of English manufacture, which had a special mechanisim that puffed out tobacco smoke at pre-determined intervals. As far as the original himself was concerned, he only smoked his pipe when there were people around, and his moustache was of the paste-on variety. He lived in another room, in which there were not only no windows but not even any doors. That room could only be reached through a crawl-hole in his safe, which had doors both in the front and in the rear and which stood in the room that was officially his.

He loved this secret room where he could be himself and not smoke a pipe or wear that moustache; where he could live simply and modestly, in keeping with the room's furnishings—an iron bed, a striped mattress stuffed with straw, a washbasin containing warm water, and an old gramophone, together with a collection of records which he personally had marked—good, average, remarkable, trash.

There in that room he spent the finest hours of his life in peace and quiet; there, hidden from everyone, he would sometimes sleep with the old cleaning woman who crawled in every morning through the safe with her bucket and broom. He would call her over to him, she would set her broom in the corner in business-like fashion, give herself to him, and then return to her cleaning. In all the years, he had not exchanged a single word with her and was not even absolutely certain whether it was the same old woman or a different one every time.

One strange incident occurred. The old woman began rolling her eyes and moving her lips soundlessly.

"What's the matter with you?"

"I was just thinking," the old woman said with a serene smile. "My niece is coming to visit, my brother's daughter. I've got to fix some eats for her, but all I've got is three roubles. So it's either spend two roubles on millet and one on butter, or two on butter and one on millet."

This peasant sagacity touched him deeply. He wrote a note to the storehouse ordering that the old woman be issued as much millet and butter as she needed. The old woman, no fool, did not take the note to the storehouse but to the Museum of the Revolution, where she sold it for enough money to buy herself a little house near Moscow and a cow; she quit her job, and rumor has it that to this day she's still bringing in milk to sell at Tishinsky market.

Vladimir Voinovich, A Circle of Friends

trimmed **Church of the Assumption** (1732), with its green rounded roof and horseshoe *kokoshniki*.

Farther up the riverbank by Trade Square is the yellow-white brick summer **Church of the Entry into Jerusalem** (1707), surmounted by a half-dome drum and a gilded cross. The white-washed winter **Church of St Paraskeva** (1772) stands next to it.

Many of the local citizens built their own churches. Across the river are four churches constructed between the 16th and 18th centuries with money raised by the local tanners, who lived and worked by the river near the marketplace. The local blacksmiths, who lived at the northern end of town, built the **Churches of Sts Cosmas and Damian**, the patron saints of blacksmiths.

The long trading stalls of the T*org*, marketplace, built in 1806, mark the town's center. During holidays, the grounds were opened to fairs and exhibitions, and were filled with jolly jesters, merry-go-rounds and craft booths. Horses were tied up along the arcade. Today, the colonnade has over 100 stores, where the townspeople congregate, especially around midday.

For a lunch break, try dining at the Trapeznaya restaurant, located in the Refectory of the Archbishop's Palace (closed on Mondays; sometimes advance reservations are needed). Sample the splendors of ancient Suzdalian monastic cooking—the local fish-soup and home-brewed mead are especially tasty. Also try the *medovukha*, an alcoholic beverage combined with honey that is made only in Suzdal. On Lenin Street are the Sokol restaurant and a tearoom. The Suzdal Hotel and Restaurant are near the central square and the Pogrebok (Cellar) Café is on Kremlyovskaya Street.

Behind the trading stalls on Lenin Street is the **Church of the Resurrection on-the-Marketplace**, now a branch of the Suzdal Museum. Here are exhibits of architectural decorations, wooden carvings and colorful tiles used to adorn buildings in the 17th and 18th centuries.

Continuing west along Lenin Street brings you to two other sets of church complexes. Not only did the number of churches in a town symbolize its wealth, but it was also customary in medieval Russia to build twin churches; this added even more to the cluster of religious structures. These twin churches usually stood in close proximity to each other—one cool, high-vaulted and richly decorated was used only in summer; the other, simpler and smaller, held the congregation in winter. The first complex comprises the **Church of the Emperor Constantine** (1707), topped by five slender drum domes, a unique feature of Suzdalian architecture. The glazed green-roofed and white-bricked **Church of Our Lady of Sorrows** (1787), with a large bell tower, was for winter. The next pair consists of the **Church of St Antipus** (1745), recognizable by its unusual multicolored octagonal red-roofed bell tower, and the **Church of St Lazarus** (1667), surmounted with beautiful forged crosses on five domes.

protective citadels for the citizens during times of war. These institutions, besides being religious, became the educational centers of the town. Husbands could also force their wives to take the veil as a quick way to divorce. Fathers would also place daughters in a convent until they were married. In front of the twin churches, by the water, is the **Convent of the Deposition of the Robe**, founded by Bishop John of Rostov Veliky in 1207.

The convent was rebuilt in stone in the 17th century. The white Holy Gates are topped with two red and white octagonal towers covered with glazed tile. The convent's church was built by Ivan Shigonia-Podzhogin, a rich *boyar* who served Czar Vasily III. The citizens of Suzdal erected the 72-meter (312-foot) bell tower in 1813 to commemorate Napoleon's defeat.

The neighboring red-brick **Convent of St Alexander** was built in 1240 in honor of Prince Alexander Nevsky, who defeated the Swedes on the Neva River that same year. After it was burned down by the Poles in the 17th century, the Mother Superior had Peter the Great rebuild it. In 1682, the Ascension Cathedral was constructed from funds donated by Peter's mother, Natalya Naryshkina. The convent closed in 1764, but the church remains open to the public.

Behind this convent and nestled in the former posad is a 17th-century tailor's house with a gabled roof. It now contains a domestic museum with displays of furniture and utensils from the 17th to 19th centuries. The rooms represent a typical peasant hut. Across from the *pechka*, stove, over which the eldest member of the family slept, was the *krasnaya ugol*, beautiful corner, where the family icons were kept. Usually the *gornitsa*, living area, comprised one or two rooms. Here were found a few beds, chairs, tables and a clothes chest. The kitchen was situated in the corner nearest to the kamin, fireplace, or stove. A small storage house was also built into the hut. This house stands next to the summer **Church of Our Lady of Smolensk** (1696) on Krasnaya Square.

The largest architectural complex on the right bank of the river is the **Spaso-Yevfimiev Monastery**, built in 1350 by a Suzdal Prince; the monks eventually owned vast amounts of land and their monastery became the wealthiest in the region. It is enclosed by a massive, mile-long, red *kremlin* that has 20 decorated towers. The **Cathedral of the Transfiguration** was built in 1594. Inside, 17th-century frescoes depict the history of the monastery. Prince Dmitry Pozharsky, hero of the 1612 Polish war and Governor of Suzdal, is buried beside the altar; a monument to him, standing outside the cathedral, is inscribed: 'To Dmitri Mikhailovsky 1578–1642.' Adjoining the cathedral is a small chapel that stands over the grave of the Abbot Yevfimy.

The **Church of the Assumption**, built in 1526, was decorated with *kokoshniki* and a large tent-shaped dome. The Kostroma artists Nikitin and Savin painted the frescoes on the outside southern and western walls. At one point, Catherine the

Great had it converted into a prison to house those who committed crimes against the church and state. The Decembrist Shakhovskoi died in this prison. Leo Tolstoy, excommunicated by the Church, was almost sent here too. The monk cells contain an exhibit of Contemporary Folk Art that includes works by local painters, potters, sculptors and glass blowers.

The large complex across the river is the **Convent of the Intercession**, built by Prince Andrei in 1364. Prince Vasily III built the convent's churches in 1510. The white three-domed Cathedral of the Intercession served as the burial place for Suzdal noblewomen. Vasily exiled his wife Solomonia Saburova to the convent. He wanted to divorce her on the grounds that she was barren; Solomonia accused Vasily of sterility. The Metropolitan granted Vasily his divorce and sent Solomonia to the Pokrovsky (Intercession) Convent to live out her life as a nun. Vasily remarried a Polish girl named Elena Glinskaya. Some time later news reached Moscow that Solomonia had given birth to a son. Fearing for her son's life, Solomonia hid him with friends and then staged a fake burial. For centuries this tale was regarded only as legend, but in 1934 a small casket was unearthed beside Solomonia's (d. 1594) tomb. There was no skeleton, only a stuffed silk shirt embroidered with pearls. The small white tomb and pieces of clothing are on display in the Suzdal Museum. Ivan the Terrible also sent his wife Anna to this convent in 1575. Later, Peter the Great even exiled his first wife, Yevdokia Lopukhina, here in 1698. For a splendid panoramic view of Suzdal, climb the bank of the river in front of the convent.

At the southern end of town on the left bank of the Kamenka is the Suzdal **Museum of Wooden Architecture**. Old wooden villages were brought in from all around the Vladimir-Suzdal region and reassembled at this location on Dmitriyevskaya Hill, to give an idea of the way of life in a typical Russian village. This open-air museum consists of log-built churches covered with aspen-shingled roofs, residential houses, windmills, barns and bath-houses.

At the end of the day, return to your hotel, probably at the Main Tourist Complex behind the Convent of the Intercession. Before dinner, take a walk along the river as the sun sets over the town. Young boys can be seen swimming and fishing in the warmer months or skating in winter. Many small side streets are filled with the local wooden *dacha*, covered with elaborate wood carvings and latticework. Ask your driver to stop by the **House of Merchant Bibanov**, the most lavishly decorated house in town. If you are lucky, a pink full moon will rise above the magical display of gabled roofs and towers, to call an end to the delightful Suzdalian day. Try taking a banya or a dip in the hotel's indoor pool. The hotel also offers *troika* rides in winter.

(preceeding pages) Stark Beauty

VICINITY OF SUZDAL

A few miles to the north of Suzdal is the small **Village of Kideksha**. According to chronicles, in 1015 the brothers Boris and Gleb, sons of the Kievan Prince Vladimir who brought Christianity to Russia, had a meeting here, where the Kamenka River empties into the Nerl. They were later assassinated by their brother, but died defending the Christian faith; they became the first Russian saints. In 1152, Prince Yuri Dolgoruky chose to build his country estate on this spot. Dolgoruky also erected the simple white-stone **Church of Sts Boris and Gleb**, where his son Boris, and daughter-in-law Maria are buried. The winter Church of St Stephan was erected in the 18th century.

A summer's day, Suzdal by the House of Merchant Bibanov

Meeting the Professor

There is absolutely no necessity to learn how to read; meat smells a mile off, anyway. Nevertheless, if you live in Moscow and have a brain in your head, you'll pick up reading will-nilly, and without attending any courses. Out of forty thousand or so Moscow dogs, only a total idiot won't know how to read the word "sausage."

Sharik first began to learn by color. When he was only four months old, blue-green signs with the letters MSPO—indicating a meat store— appeared all over Moscow. I repeat, there was no need for any of them— you can smell meat anyway. But one day Sharik made a mistake. Tempted by an acid-blue sign, Sharik, whose sense of smell had been knocked out by the exhaust of a passing car, dashed into an electric supplies store instead of a butcher shop. The store was on Myasnitsky Street and was owned by the Polubizner Bros. The brothers gave the dog a taste of insulated wire, and that is even neater than a cabby's whip. That famous moment may be regarded as the starting point of Sharik's education. Back on the sidewalk, he began to realize that blue didn't always mean "meat." Howling with fiery pain, his tail pressed down between his legs, he recalled that all over the butchers shops there was a red or golden wriggle—the first one on the left—that looked like a sled.

After that, his learning proceeded by leaps and bounds. He learned the letter "t" from "Fish Trust" on the corner of Mokhovaya, and then the letter "s" (it was handier for him to approach the store from the tail end of the word, because of the militiaman who stood near the beginning of the "fish").

Tile squares set in to corner houses in Moscow always and inevitably meant "cheese". A black samovar faucet over the word indicated the former owner of Chichkin's, piles of red Holland cheese, beastly salesmen who hate dogs, sawdust on the floor, and that most disgusting evil-smelling Beckstein.

If somebody was playing an accordion, which was not much better than "Celeste Aida," and there was a smell of frankfurters, the first letters on the white signs very conveniently added up to the words "no inde...," which meant "no indecent language and no tips." In such places there were occasional messy brawls and people got hit in the face with fists, and sometimes with napkins or boots.

If there were stale hams hanging in a window and tangerines on the sill, it meant...Grr...grr...groceries. And if there were dark bottles with a vile liquid, it meant...Wwhi-w-i-wines...The former Yeliseyev Brothers.

The unknown gentleman who had brought the dog to the doors of his luxurious apartment on the second floor rang, and the dog immediately raised his eyes to the large black card with gold letters next to the wide door with panes of wavy pink glass. He put together the first three letters right away: Pe-ar-o, "Pro." After that came a queer little hooked stick, nasty looking, unfamiliar. No telling what it meant. Could it be "proletarian"? Sharik wondered with astonishment...No, impossible. He raised his nose, sniffed the coat again, and said to himself with certainty: Oh, no, there's nothing proletarian in this smell. Some fancy, learned word, who knows what it means.

Mikhail Bulgakov, Heart of a Dog

Practical Information

Holidays and Festivals

Since the end of 1991, many Russian holidays and festivals have changed, ceased to exist or have even been resurrected. Events relating to revolutions are no longer celebrated, except the failure of the August 1991 attempted coup. Constitution Day (in October), established by Brezhnev to commemorate the adoption of the 1977 Constitution, has naturally been dropped, but other holidays like Orthodox Christmas and Easter have been revived and are openly observed.

The traditional **Subbotnik**, when every citizen worked without pay, supposedly voluntarily, on the Saturday before Lenin's Birthday (April 22) to help clean up their cities, was dissolved with the Soviet Union.

OFFICIAL HOLIDAYS

Jan 1	New Year's Day	The last week in December is quite festive, culminating in New Year's Eve. Presents are given on New Year's Day.
Jan 7	Russian Orthodox	A new official holiday. (The Orthodox Church Christmas still goes by the old calendar, which differs from the Gregorian by 13 days.) Churches throughout the country hold services.
Mar 8	Women's Day	Established after the Second International Conference of Socialist Women in Copenhagen in 1910. Women receive gifts and usually do not have to work.
March/April	Easter, or *Pashka*	Traditional Russian Orthodox holiday.
May 1–2	May Day	Even though no longer celebrated as International Workers Solidarity Day, this event, now known as Labor and Spring Holiday, still has the old festive nature with colorful parades through Red Square (minus the tanks, missiles and leaders standing on Lenin's Mausoleum).

May 9	Victory Day	Parades are held at war memorials, such as the Piskaryovskoye Cemetery in St Petersburg, to celebrate VE Day at the end of World War II.
Jun 12	Russian Independence Day	Another new holiday.

FESTIVALS

Feb 23	Armed Forces Day	Conscription still exists in Russia so most Russian men have spent two years in the Army.
First week in March	Maslenitsa, or *Blini* Day	This day stems from the old Pagan tradition of making *blini*, pancakes, to honor the coming of spring; *blini* represent the sun.

Each spring there are festivals in the major cities and towns to celebrate the end of winter.

Apr 12	Cosmonaut's Day	
May 5–13	Festival of Moscow Stars	
Jun 6	Pushkin's Birthday	Poetry readings at Pushkin monuments.
The last Sunday in July	Navy Day	In St Petersburg, the fleet, including ships, submarines and sailors, is displayed.
June 21	White Nights Festival	While the sun hardly sets, musical concerts, theatrical performances, street events, fireworks and other celebrations happen throughout Moscow, St Petersburg and the Golden Ring area.
Aug 19	Day of the Failed August 1991 Coup	To mark the downfall of Communism and honor those who were killed.
Sept 8	Seige of Leningrad Day	This day marks the end of the 900-day seige of former Leningrad; it features special ceremonies at the Piskarovskoye Cemetery.

Plain walls with Zakomaral gold trim on a Golden Ring church

Sept 19	Moscow Day	A day of merrymaking in the city.
Nov 7–8	Anniversary of the October Revolution	(On the old calendar, the revolution took place on October 25.) A traditional holiday for nearly 75 years, it is no longer an official holiday, but many Russians now celebrate not having to celebrate the 1917 Revolution any more!
Dec 25–Jan 5		Russian Winter Festival. Events are held to celebrate the coming new year especially in Moscow, St Petersburg, Novgorod, Vladimir and Suzdal, where *troika* rides and other traditional Russian folk customs, take place. Because the Soviet Union ceased to exist on December 21, 1991, Christmas week now offers another reason to celebrate.

Many church holidays are celebrated by the Russian Orthodox Church, such as Easter, Christmas, Orthodox New Year (usually in January) and church name days.

Name Days: Many calendar dates have a corresponding name. Russians like to celebrate their own name days.

Moscow and St Petersburg have many other art, music and sports festivals during the year. Every alternate summer, Moscow hosts the **Moscow International Film Festival**. Every August, the **Moscow International Marathon** is run through the city.

Accommodation

HOTELS

Most visitors stay in Russian Intourist or foreign-operated hotels, which have restaurants, cafés, *Beriozkas* (shopping), post offices, money exchanges and, usually, nightly entertainment; most of these hotels need to be prebooked. Bed-and-breakfast and youth hostel opportunities now exist and should also be prearranged. Some agencies rent out apartments or space with families as home-stays. Some of the very expensive hotels charge more than $200 per person, the expensive more than $100, and the moderate still cost more than $50. Hostels, bed-and-breakfasts and home-stays charge from $15 to $85 per day. Prices vary according to season and occupancy—single or double.

Check with a travel agency that deals with Russian travel; they should have price lists and locations. You may need proof of a hotel reservation to get your Russian Tourist visa. Travel agencies can also secure your visas and hotel reservations.

Aerostar
37 Leningradsky Prospekt, Korpus 9
Tel 155-5030
A Russian-Canadian joint venture. Located out of town on the way to the airport. It also offers a set menu Sunday brunch from 11:30 to 14:30. Moderate to expensive. Metro Dynamo.

Akademicheskaya Hotel I
Leninsky Prospekt
Tel 238-0902

Akademicheskaya Hotel II
Donskaya Street
Tel 238-0508.
Adequate Russian hotels outside city center. Moderate.

Baltschug Hotel
1 Baltschug Street
This deluxe hotel was the old Bucharest Hotel, totally renovated in 1992. It is located across the river from Red Square and has beautiful views of the Kremlin churches and St Basil's. Provides three-star quality, along the lines of the Metropole and Savoy hotels. Very expensive. Metro Novokuznetskaya.

Belgrade
5 Smolensky Square
Tel 248-1643
Belgrade I
Next door to the Belgrade. Now called the *Zolotoye Koltso* or Golden Ring Hotel
Tel 248-6734
Both are modern Russian hotels centrally located near the Arbat. Moderate to expensive. Nearest Metro station is Smolenskaya.

Inflotel
A boat-hotel on the *Alexander Blok* docked near the Mezhdunarody Hotel
Tel 255-9278, fax 253-9578

Moderate to expensive, includes breakfast and free saunas. A little noisy with a disco/casino on board, and the Medusa Bar operates until 05:00.

Kosmos
150 Prospect Mira
Tel. 217-0785/8680
Built by the French, it is situated opposite the Park of Economic Achievements, 20 minutes from the city center, and directly opposite Metro station VDNKh. Deluxe hotel with bowling alley, sauna, pool and a popular late-night disco. Expensive.

Intourist
3/5 Tverskaya Street
Tel 203-4008
A first-class Russian hotel right across from Red Square. It has the usual restaurants, bars, shops, and even slot machines. Metro stop Okhotny Ryad is on the corner. Moderate to expensive.

Leningradskaya
21/40 Kalanchovskaya Street
Tel 975-3008/32
As one of the Stalin-era Gothic buildings, this hotel has traditional Russian rooms and atmosphere, along with a casino. Located across the street from Leningrad train station, where trains depart for and arrive from St Petersburg. The center of town is a 15-minute ride away. Moderate.

Marco Polo Presnaya
9 Spiridonyevsky
Tel 202-0381, fax 230-2704
This quaint hotel, formerly the Russian Krasnopresnenskaya, was renovated by a Viennese firm. Now considered a deluxe hotel, it has a restaurant and bar. Near Patriarch's Pond and Pushkin Square, off of Tverskaya, it is just a ten-minute walk to Red Square or the Arbat. Metro Tverskaya. Expensive.

Metropole
1–4 Teatralny Proezd
Tel 927-6000/6096/0002
Considered one of *the* places to stay in Moscow, it was renovated by Finnish interests. The hotel dates from 1903 (Rasputin had his headquarters here) and is lavishly decorated. It has a sauna, restaurants and bars, and every Sunday popular all-you-

can-eat brunches are held in the Metropole Zal with live music (11:30–15:00). It is a short walk to either Red Square or the Bolshoi Theater. Metro Okhotny Ryad. Very Expensive. A superb antique store is on the Teatralnaya side of the hotel.

Mezhdunarodnaya I and II

12 Krasnopresnensky Embankment I
Tel 253-2382, II tel 253-2760/1
The 'International Hotel' or Mezh, as it is nicknamed, is part of the Sovincenter, known as the Armand Hammer Center. This was once the only foreign-owned hotel in the city and was popular with businessmen. Many shops, bars and restaurants, including British, French, Italian and Japanese cuisine; the Vienna café has cappacino. There is also a pharmacy and a food *Beriozka*. The health center (tel 255-6691) on the lobby floor has saunas and a pool. The saunas are segregated, or a private sauna or Presidential-suite sauna can be rented. Open daily from noon to 20:00 and closed the last Monday of each month. Next door in the Sovincenter are foreign businesses, airlines and Federal Express. The hotel is by the Moskva River, about a 20-minute ride to the center. It is not near a Metro station, but plenty of private drivers moonlight by the entrance—bargaining is a must. Expensive

Minsk Hotel

22 Tverskaya Street
Tel 299-1215/1300
A standard Russian-style hotel, centrally located near Pushkin and Red squares. Metro Tverskaya. Moderate.

Molodyozhnaya

27 Dmitrovskoye Shosse
Tel 210-9311/4565
A standard Russian hotel, about a 20-minute drive to the city center. Moderate.

Moscow Palace

Tverskaya Street
Opened in 1993, this deluxe hotel was built by the Austrian Marco Polo chain. Restaurants, bars and health club with sauna. Centrally located near Red Square. Expensive to very expensive.

Moskva

7 Okhotny Ryad
Tel 292-1000/1100

This is another giant Stalinesque building, standing off Red Square. It is a first-class Russian hotel with restaurants and bars (the Spanish Bar on first floor is quite popular), and a nightclub–disco that continues into the early hours. Shops (Christian Dior, Zolotoya Roza and Penguin ice-cream) are located along its sides. Metro Okhotny Ryad. Moderate to expensive.

Mozhaiskaya
165 Mozhaisky Street
Tel 447-3434
A standard Russian hotel, less expensive than most, but located outside of town; also has camping facilities in summer (you must prebook before arriving in the country).

National
14 Okhotny Ryad
Tel 203-6539
Charming, old deluxe hotel that has recently been renovated. Situated opposite Red Square; Lenin lived here after the Revolution. Metro Okhotny Ryad. Expensive to very expensive.

Novotel-Airport
2 Sheremetyevo Airport
Tel 578-9407/8
A typical Western airport hotel. If you are just transiting overnight, it is an ideal place to stay, but if you are touring Moscow, it is much too far from the center. Moderate to expensive.

Orlyonok
15 Kosygin Street
Tel 939-8844/8853
A standard Russian hotel, about a 20-minute drive to the city center. Moderate.

Ostankino
29 Botanicheskaya Street
Tel 219-2880
A Russian-style basic hotel, located outside the city by the Ostankino TV tower. Moderate.

Pekin
Mayakovsky Square
Tel 209-3400

A large Russian-style hotel with a Chinese restaurant. Centrally located near the Arbat and Tverskaya Street. Metro Mayakovskaya. Moderate.

Penta-Olympic
18/1 Olimpisky Prospekt
Tel 971-6101
A German–Russian joint venture that can be booked through Lufthansa. A new upscale foreign-built hotel with restaurants, bars, shops, health center and pool, and a Sunday brunch smorgasbord with live music. Located by the Olympic stadium, it is about a 15-minute journey into town. Metro Prospekt Mira. Expensive to very expensive.

Pullman/Iris
10 Korovinskoye Chaussee
Tel 488-8000/8080
A French–Russian joint venture. As with the Penta, this deluxe foreign-built hotel has all the modern tourist conveniences. About a 20-minute ride into the city. Metro Petrovsko-Razumovskaya. Expensive to very expensive.

Rossiya
6 Varvarka Street
Tel 298-5400/5530
Probably still the world's largest hotel, with accommodation for up to 6,000 people. First-class Russian-style; great location overlooking the Kremlin and St Basil's Cathedral. Has restaurants, cafés, a Baskin-Robbins ice cream, and a large *Beriozka* at the back. Moderate to expensive.

Rus-Hotel
21 Varshavskoye Shosse (near Metro of same name)
Tel 382-0103/0466
A Russian–American joint venture deluxe hotel with restaurant, bar, disco and sauna. Moderate to expensive.

Savoy
3 Rozhdestvenka Street
Tel 929-8500
The Savoy was remodeled from the Hotel Berlin by a Finnish Company. This deluxe hotel has a fine restaurant and bar, where many foreigners gather just to have a burger and watch CNN. Bookings can be made through Finnair. It is located off Lubyanka

Square near the former KGB building; it is within walking distance of Red Square and the Bolshoi Theater. Metro Smolenskaya. Very expensive.

Slavyanskaya/Radisson
2 Berezhkovskaya Embankment
Tel 941-8020
Like the Penta and Pullman, the Slavyanskaya is a new Western-style hotel, built by the Radisson chain. Filled with shops and places to eat. Inside is also the Dialog Bank, one of the few places where you can cash traveler's checks or get money using your credit card. The hotel is located near the Novodevichy Monastery on the way to Moscow University, by the Kievskaya train station (with a Metro stop). It is about a 15-minute Metro ride to the center. Expensive.

Sevastopol
1-A Bolshaya Yushunskaya Street
Tel 110-4659/318-2827/2263
First-class Russian hotel. Not centrally located, but near Metro stop of the same name. Moderate.

Ukraine
2/1 Kutuzovsky Prospekt
Tel 243-3030/2895
First-class Russian hotel in another of Stalin's giant monoliths. Located near the White House, on the Moscow River. About a 10-minute journey to the center. Nearest Metro stop is Kievskaya. Moderate to expensive.

Tsentralnaya
10 Tverskaya Street
Tel 229-8589
A basic Russian-style hotel with a café/restaurant; some rooms have small balconies. Short walk to Red Square. Moderate.

If you need to find a room at the last minute, you can check at:
Rus-Hotel. Tel 382-0586
Spros Joint Venture Hotel. Tel 133-4393/94
Novoye Vremya. Tel 272-4694/1809
These Russian–US joint ventures may also be of help:
Alexander Blok Houseboat. Tel 255-9278
Hotel Vizit. Tel 202-2848.

If you need to find accommodation for a long-term stay, try one of the following rental co-operatives. Laws and prices are changing daily; foreigners need to be registered in the city. For apartment rentals, try:

Astoria 7 Tverskaya. Tel 229-2300
Avangard Byelomorskaya Street. Tel 455-9210
Elex. Tel 932-4969
Express. Tel 227-5827
Jupiter 7 Butyrsky Val. Tel 250-2300
Medservice. Tel 288-5875/281-4805
Raznoservice. Tel 246-9587/328-1377
Rupin Prospekt Mira. Tel 283-1659
Real Estate 23 Bolshaya Molchanovka, Apt 56. Tel 290-1457
Vremya 8 Strastnoi Bulvar. Tel 233-5081, fax 229-3511.

HOMESTAYS AND YOUTH HOSTELS
Most agencies will make reservations and secure visas; some also arrange airlines and other travel. All are inexpensive to moderate.

■ IBV BED AND BREAKFAST SYSTEMS
13113 IDEAL DRIVE, SILVER SPRING, MARYLAND. 20906.
Tel (800) 428-2010/(301) 942-3770
Specializes in stays throughout the former Soviet Union.

■ INTERNATIONAL BED AND BREAKFAST
1010 ARTHUR AVE., HUNTINGTON VALLEY, PENNSYLVANIA, 19006.
Tel (800) 422-5283

■ MOSCOW INTERNATIONAL HOSTEL/GUEST HOUSE
50 Bolshaya Pereyaslavskaya Street, 10th Floor
(Mailing address: PO Box 27, 51 Prospekt Mira, Moscow, 121110.)
Tel/fax (7095) 971-4059, fax 280-7686
A ten-minute walk from Prospekt Mira Metro. This Western-style hostel has English-speaking staff, a kitchen, laundry facilities, a lounge with a TV, phone and fax services, and singles, doubles and rooms for four. It also provides travel services, train tickets and visas. Advance reservations recommended. Inexpensive.

■ RUSSIAN YOUTH HOSTELS (RYH) ST PETERSBURG
3rd Sovyetskaya (Rozhedstenskaya) Street, 28
Tel (7-812) 277-0569, fax (7-812) 277-5102

A five-minute walk from the Moskva Train Station and Nevsky Prospekt. This US–Russian joint-venture in a newly renovated pre-revolutionary building has rooms for three or four, breakfast included. Kitchen facilities and TV room.

Also arranges visas, train travel (including the Trans-Siberian), tours, theater and ballet tickets. Advance reservations recommended. Inexpensive. (Reservations for Moscow and Helsinki hostels can be made here, too.)

■ EUROHOSTEL IN HELSINKI

If you are entering Russia from Helsinki, Finland, Eurohostel is centrally located at 9 Linnankatu, Helsinki
Tel (3580) 664452, fax (3580) 655044
It has single, double and triple rooms with complimentary morning sauna. Also has a café, guest kitchen and laundry facilities. You can make reservations for St Petersburg/Moscow Hostels from here. Inexpensive.

You can also make reservations for the Moscow/St Petersburg/Helsinki Hostels (and Russian visas/travel) in the United States at **Russian Youth Hostels**, 409 Pacific Coast Highway, Bldg 106, Suite 390, Redondo Beach, California, 90277; tel (310) 379-4316, fax (310) 379-8420. In London at: **YHA Travel Store**, 14 Southampton Street, London, England WC2E 7HY; tel (4471) 836-1036.

Useful Addresses and Telephone Numbers

IN THE US

■ RUSSIAN EMBASSY
1115–25 16th Street NW, Washington, D.C. 20036. Tel (202) 628-7551/7554

■ VISA/CONSULAR OFFICE
1825 Phelps Place NW, Washington, D.C. 20009. Tel (202) 939-8913/18/07
The travel advisory line at the US State Department is (202) 647-5225

■ RUSSIAN CONSULATE GENERAL
In New York: 9 East 91st Street, New York, NY 10020. Tel (212) 348-6772
In San Francisco: 2790 Green Street, San Francisco, CA 94123. Tel (415) 202-9800, fax (415) 929-0306

■ AIRLINES

Aeroflot Tel (800) 995-5555
Air France Tel (800) 237-2747
British Airways Tel (800) 247-9297
Delta Tel (800) 241-4141
Finnair Tel (800) 950-5000
KLM Tel (800) 374-7747
Lufthansa Tel (800) 645-3880
SAS Tel (800) 221-2350

■ TRAVEL AGENCIES

American Express Travel Services World Financial Center, 200 Vesey Street, New York, NY 10285-0320. Tel (212) 640-2000
Beverly International Travel 4630 Campus Drive #205, Newport Beach, CA 92660. Tel (310) 271-4116/(714) 474-7582, fax (714) 756-2169
Center for Citizen Initiatives 3268 Sacramento Street, San Francisco, CA 94115. Tel (415) 346-1875. For more information on the work of citizen diplomacy and trips to Russia, write to the above address.
Council on International Exchange (CIEE) 205 East 42nd Street, New York, NY 10017. Tel (212) 661-1414
Cultural Access/Traveling Shoes 4101 Cathedral Avenue NW #808, Washington D.C. 20016. Tel (202) 537-6198 Fax (202) 244-3463. Also at 3731 East Fernwood Avenue, Orange, CA 92669. Tel (714) 288-1603, fax (714) 288-1604. Specializes in educational and specific interest travel to Russia.
Intourist 630 Fifth Avenue, Suite 868, New York, NY 10111. Tel (212) 757-3884/5
Russian Youth Hostels & Tourism (RYH), See Hotels section, page 240.
Tour Designs 616 G Street SW, Washington, D.C. 20024. Tel (800) 432-8687/(202) 554-5820, fax (202) 479-0472
Vega International Travel Service 201 North Wells Street, Suite 430, Chicago, Illinois 60606. Tel (312) 332-7211

■ ADVENTURE TRAVEL

Boojum Expeditions (Horse) Tel/fax (406) 587-0125
Direct Action/Wild World Tel (201) 796-6861
Mountain Travel/Sobek The Adventure Co 6420 Fairmont Avenue, El Cerrito, CA 94530. Tel (800) 227-2384, (510) 527–8100
REI Adventures Tel (800) 622-2236
Zegrahm Expeditions (Arctic) Tel (800) 628-8747 or (206) 285-4000

In the UK

■ RUSSIAN EMBASSY
18 Kensington Place Gardens, London. W8 4QP. Tel (71) 229-6412/727-6888

■ RUSSIAN VISA CONSULATE
5 Kensington Place Gardens, London. Tel (71) 229-3215/16

■ AIRLINES IN LONDON
Aeroflot Tel (71) 355-2233/580-1221
British Airways Tel (71) 897-4000
Finnair Tel (71) 408-1222
KLM Tel (81) 750-9000

■ TRAVEL AGENCIES
Barry Martin Travel Ltd 342/346 Linen Hall, 162/168 Regent Street, London W1 (there is also an office in Russia.). Tel (71) 439-1271
East-West Travel 15 Kensington High Street, London W8. Tel (71) 938-3211
Individual Travel 47–51 Wharfdale Road, London N1. Tel(71) 278-2512 (They have a branch office in St Petersburg called Redmond Travel at 5 Plekhanov Street #20. Tel (812) 311-4586)
Intourist 292 Regent Street/219 Marsh Wall, London W1/E14. Tel (71) 631-1252/580-1221/538-8600
Progressive Tours Ltd 12 Porchester Place, Connaught Square, London W2. Tel (71) 262-1676
Room with the Russians 1–7 Station Chambers, High Street North, London E6; Tel (81) 472-2694
YHA Travel Store See Hotels section, page 240.

In Canada

■ RUSSIAN EMBASSY
285 Charlott Street, Ottawa, K1N8TS. Tel (613) 235-4341

■ CONSULATES
52 Range Road, Ottawa, Ontario K1N8G5. Tel (613) 236-7220
3655 Avenue du Musée, Montréal, Quebéc, H3GE1. Tel (514) 843-5901

■ AIRLINES
Aeroflot Tel Montréal (514) 288-2125

British Airways Tel Toronto (416) 250-1350/Montréal (514) 287-9282
Finnair Tel Toronto (416) 222-0740
KLM Tel Toronto (416) 323-1515/Montréal (514) 939-4040

■ TRAVEL AGENCIES
Intourist Office 1891 McGill College Avenue, #630, Montréal, H3A2N4. Tel (514) 849-6394
Nouvelles Frontières 800 Boulevard de Maisonneuve Est. Montréal, H2L4L8. Tel (514) 288-9942
Travel Cuts 187 College Street, Toronto, M5T1P7. Tel (416) 979-2406

IN HONG KONG
There is currently no Russian consulate in Hong Kong. Visas may be obtained via the travel agency listed.

■ AIRLINES
Aeroflot Tel 537-2611
British Airways Tel 868 0303
Finnair Tel 922-62048
KLM Tel 822-8111

■ TRAVEL AGENCY
Global Union Express HK Ltd, Rm22 2/F New Henry House, 10 Ice House Street, Central, Hong Kong. Tel 868-3231

IN AUSTRALIA

■ RUSSIAN EMBASSY
78 Canberra Avenue, Griffith ACT, Canberra 2603. Tel (06) 295-9474, fax (06) 295-1847

■ CONSULATE
7-9 Fullerton Street, Woollahra, Sydney, NSW 2025. Tel (02) 326-1188, fax (02) 327-5065

■ AIRLINES
Aeroflot has direct flights from Sydney to Moscow. Tel (02) 667-0032
British Airways Tel (02) 258-330
Finnair Tel (02) 326-2999
KLM Tel (08) 222-747

■ TRAVEL AGENCIES
Gateway Travel, 48 The Boulevarde, Strathfield, NSW 2135. Tel (02) 745-3333, fax (612) 745-3237
Intourist, 37 Pitt Street, Sydney NSW. Tel (02) 247-7652/277-652
STA Travel, 1a Lee Street, Railway Square, Sydney 2000. Tel (02) 519-9866

IN NEW ZEALAND

■ RUSSIAN EMBASSY
57 Messines Road, Karori, Wellington. Tel 766-742/766-113

■ AIRLINE
Finnair Tel (09) 303-0070
KLM Tel (09) 309-1782

■ TRAVEL AGENCY
STA Travel 64 High Street, Auckland, Tel (09) 309-0458

IN RUSSIA

■ EMBASSIES IN MOSCOW
Australia 13 Prechistenka Street. Tel 246-5011/12
Austria 1 Starokonushenny Per. Tel 201-7307
Belgium 7 Malaya Molchanovka. Tel 291-6027
Canada 23 Starokunushenny Per. Tel 241-5070
Denmark 9 Ostrovskovo Per. Tel 201-7860
Estonia 5 Sobinovsky Per. Tel 290-5013
Finland 15 Prechistanka Street. Tel 230-2143/44
France 45 Dmitrova Street. Tel 236-0003
Germany 17B Gruzinskaya Street. Tel 252-5521
Italy 5 Vesnina Street. Tel 241-1533
Japan 12 Kalashny Per. Tel 291-8500
Latvia 3 Chaplygina. Tel 925-2707
Lithuania 10 Pisemskovo. Tel 291-1698
Netherlands 6 Kalashny Per. Tel 291-2999/2948
Norway 7 Vorovskovo Street. Tel 290-3872
Spain 50/8 Herzen Street. Tel 202-2610/2161
Sweden 60 Mosfilmskaya. Tel 147-9009
Switzerland 2 Stopani Per. Tel 925-5322

United Kingdom 14 Morisa Toreza Emb. Tel 231-8511/12
United States 19/23 Novinsky (Tchaikovsky) Bulvar. Tel 252-2451-59 (For emergencies, when the embassy is closed call 230-2001/2610)

■ ST PETERSBURG CONSULATES
China 12 Vasilyevsky Island 3-ya Liniya. Tel 218-1721
Finland 71 Chaikovskaya Street. Tel 272-4256, 273-7321/4331
France 15 Moika Emb. Tel 314-1443/312-1130
Germany 39 Furshtatskaya Street. Tel 273-5598/5731
Italy 10 Teatralnaya Square. Tel 312-3217/2896
Japan 29 Moika Emb. Tel 314-1418/1434
Mongolia 11 Seperny. Tel 272-2688 (you may need a transit visa if you are taking the Trans-Siberian)
Poland 5 Sovyetskaya Street. Tel 274-4170/4351
Sweden 11 Vasilyevsky Island 10-ya Liniya. Tel 218-3526/27
United Kingdom 5 Proletarsky Diktatury Square. Tel 312-0072
United States 5 Furshtatskaya (Petra Lavrova) Street. Tel 274-8235/8568/8689

■ AIRLINES IN MOSCOW
Aeroflot Head Office, Znamenka (Frunzenskaya) Emb 4. Tel 241-9947/245-0002
Air France 7 Korovy Val. Tel 237-2325
British Airways Hotel Mezhdunarodnaya II, Krasnopresnenskaya 12, Room 1905. Tel 253-2492/82
Delta Mezhdunarodnaya Hotel II, Room 1102; tel. 253-2658/59
Finnair 5 Proyezd Khudozhestvennovo Teatra/Kamergersky Per. Tel 292-8788
Japan Air Lines 3 Kuznetksy Most. Tel 921-6448
KLM Mezhdunarodnaya Hotel II, Room 1307. Tel 253-2150/51
Lufthansa 3 Kunetsky Most/Hotel Penta. Tel 923-0488/975-2501
SAS 3 Kuznetskty Most. Tel 925-4747

■ AIRLINES IN ST PETERSBURG
Aeroflot Corner of Nevsky and Gogol. For information: Tel 293-9031; International: Tel 310-4581; Arrivals/departures: Tel 314-6943; Domestic: Tel 293-9021
British Airways 36 Herzen Street. Tel 311-5820
Delta 36 Herzen Street. Tel 311-5819/20
Finnair 19 Gogol Street. Tel 315-9736/312-8987
KLM (at airport) Tel 104-3440
Lufthansa 7 Voznesensky (Mayorova) Prospekt. Tel 314-4979/5917

■ TRAVEL AGENCIES

American Express Co 21-A Sadovo-Kudrinskaya Street, Moscow. Tel 254-0671/ 2111 (Open Monday to Friday 09:00 to 17:30, Saturdays 12:30 to 13:30) **Barry Martin Travel** Hotel Mezhdunarodnaya II, Krasnopresnenskaya Emb 12, Room 940, Moscow. Tel 253-2940 **Intourist** Moscow Main Office, 16 Okhotny Ryad, Moscow. Tel 203-6962, tlx 411211. At Airport Sheremetyevo II: Tel 156-9435 (Each Intourist Hotel has a Service desk)

■ MOSCOW AIRPORTS

Sheremetyevo Leningradskoe Shosse. Tel 578-5614 **Sheremetyevo II** (the international airport about 20 miles, 32 kilometers, outside the city) Tel 155-0922 **Vnukovo** Tel 436-2967 **Domodedovo** Tel 323-8652

■ TRAIN STATIONS

Byelorussky Byelorussky Square. Tel 253-4244/4908 (trains to and from Berlin, Warsaw, London, Paris, Vilnius, Minsk, Smolensk and Brest) **Kazansky** Komsomolsky Square. Tel 266-2736/2542 (trains to and from Siberia and Central Asian States) **Kievsky** Kievsky Square. Tel 240-0484/7622 (trains to and from the Ukraine and Eastern Europe) **Kursky** 29 Zemlyanoi Val (Chkalov). Tel 262-8532/266-5652 (trains to and from Vladimir, Armenia, Azerbaijan, the Crimea and the Caucasus.) **Leningradsky** 1 Komsomolsky Square. Tel 262-6038/4281 (trains to and from St Petersburg, Finland, Novgorod, Pskov and Tallinn, Estonia) **Paveletsky** Leninsky Square. Tel 235-3960/4673 (trains to and from the Volgograd region) **Rizhsky** Rizhsky Square. Tel 281-0118/266-1176 (trains to and from the Baltic) **Savyolovsky** Butyrskoi Zastavy Square. Tel 285-1883/9000 (trains to Uglich) **Yaroslavsky** Komsomolsky Square. Tel 266-0301/0595 (trains to and from the Far East. The Trans-Siberian departs daily at 10:00. *Elektrichka* also run to Sergiyev Posad in the Golden Ring area.)

■ ST PETERSBURG

AIRPORTS

Pulkovo II is international, **Pulkovo I** is domestic; they are about five kilometers apart. Another smaller airport, **Rzhevka**, provides flights to northwest Russia.

TRAIN STATIONS
Baltiisky 120 Obvodnov Kanal (trains to and from Petrodvorets and Lomonosov).
Finlandsky 6 Lenin Square (trains to and from Repino and Finland).
Moskovsky 2 Vosstaniya (Uprising) Square (trains to and from Moscow and points south).
Varshavsky Izmailovsky Prospekt (trains to and from Warsaw, Eastern Europe and Berlin).
Vitebsk 52 Zagorodny Prospekt (trains to and from Pushkin and Pavlovsk).

USEFUL NUMBERS
Fire 01
Police 02
Medical Ambulance 03 (In case of medical emergency contact your hotel or embassy for staff doctor)
Local long-distance asstistance 07
Local long-distance line dial 8—wait for tone and then dial city code and number
Ordering an international call Moscow: 8-194, St Petersburg: 3144747—or order through your hotel Service desk.
Information inquiries Business 09; Private 00; Time (Moscow) 100, (St Petersburg) 08; Weather (St Petersburg) 001
Taxi Moscow: 2250000,9270000,457-9005, St Petersburg: 3120022

City Area Codes
Moscow 095
St Petersburg 812
Yaroslavl 0852
Kostroma 09422
Ivanovo 09322
Vladimir 09222
Novgorod 816
Pskov 81122

Restaurants

A boom in co-operative and joint venture restaurantsover the last several years has raised the number of eating establishments in Moscow to well over 9,000. Every Russian or Western-style hotel has several restaurants, cafés and bars; some even offer nightly entertainment. It is advisable to make restaurant reservations in advance, especially in Russian hotels, through the hotel Service desk. The restaurants are usually open for lunch and dinner from 11:00 to midnight, with a few hours' break in the late afternoon. Bars are usually open until midnight or 02:00. More and more hotels are now offering the *Svetsky Stol*, Swedish Table. This smorgasbord-style cafeteria is open for breakfast, lunch and dinner and is an excellent way to get a quick, filling meal, in contrast to the slow service found in many venues. Remember that Russians expect to spend a full evening when dining out in a good establishment (an expensive luxury). Often the service is slow (to stretch out the night), the music can be loud, and other people may be seated at your table. Anticipate a dinner with entertainment to last all evening.

Definitely try to venture outside of your hotel to sample a few of these restaurants and cafés. Even though the menu may be all in Russian, be ready for an adventure and some fun—if you want a chicken, mime one! Take along your phrasebook and enjoy yourself. Many of the co-operatives have delicious regional food, fast service, and some offer floor shows, folk music or dance bands. For the more popular ones, advance reservations are recommended. If the restaurant accepts rubles, the meal will be relatively inexpensive, given the exchange rates. In most Russian-style restaurants, it is acceptable to bring your own alcohol.

Note: Many new Russian-operated and Western joint-venture establishments have opened throughout the city. Check before ordering as to what type of payment is possible and in what currency items are priced, usually in rubles or US dollars. Offically only rubles can be accepted and many establishments now have their own Bureau de Change where hard currency can be exchanged for rubles. Other places may accept foreign cash only (and not credit cards) but still give change in rubles. Some restaurants take only credit cards. Still others may take only rubles, but accept payment in credit cards (food in rubles and drinks in hard currency). Always try to have some rubles, hard cash and a credit card.

Establishments noted as inexpensive will cost less than $5 per person and moderate about $10 (more expensive if ordering liquor). Expensive varies widely, depending on what and how much you order. Very Expensive equates to a high quality restaurant at home.

Russian-Georgian-Asian
Aragvi
6 Tverskaya
Tel 229-3762
An established and popular Georgian restaurant in the center of town. (Winston Churchill once ate here.) Georgian dishes of *shashlik* shish kebab, *lavash* bread, hot *solguni* cheese, *kharcho* spicy meat soup, *satsavi* chicken in coriander sauce, and salads. Georgian wines and Russian champagne are also available. Music and dancing in evenings. Moderate (depending on how much is drunk). Reserve.

Arkadia
3 Teatralny Proezd
Tel 926-9008
Located a few minutes walk from the Metropole Hotel, this co-op is a favorite spot of locals. Tasty and varied Russian menu that includes, *blini*, chicken Kiev, *gribi* mushrooms in sour cream, cucumber salad and local wines, vodka or champage. Inexpensive.

Atrium
44 Leningradsky Prospekt
Tel 137-3008
A Russian co-op serving nouvelle Russian-style food in a Western atmosphere. This cosy restaurant has white marble columns and an elegant modern decor. Food is nicely presented; some served in earthernware pots. Usually serves a fixed menu and alcohol is available. Accepts major credit cards only; moderate.

Baku
The Baku and Livan restaurants are at the same place at 24 Tverskaya Street
Tel 299-8506
Great Azerbaijani food, wine and music, but usually busy and noisy. Try *piti* (lamb and potato soup in a clay pot), *narkurma* (roast lamb with pomegranates), *plov*, *dolma*, *falafels* and *bakhlava*. Moderate. Make a reservation.

Café Margarita
28 Malaya Bronnaya, across from Patriarch's Pond
Tel 299-6539
This small and cosy place is named after Bulgakov's famous book *The Master and Margarita*, which was set in this area. The café serves quick meals of soups, chicken, casseroles and pastries; some alcohol. Inexpensive.

Café Viru
50 Ostozhenka Street (opposite Park Kultury Metro)
Tel 246-6107
A trendy Estonian-style café that serves sandwiches and cakes, coffee and tea. Inexpensive.

Den i Noch
12 Kolomensky Proezd
Tel 112-5092/9425

(following pages) A church in the country

The ex-Kremlin chef cooks at Day and Night. The Russian menu includes meat, chicken and fish. Wine, vodka and champagne are available for hard currency. Evenings have an erotic show, and sometimes even breakdancing. Inexpensive to moderate.

Dom na Tverskoi
12 Gotvalda Street
Tel 251-8419
An old literary haunt with photographs lining the walls. Typical Russian fare with cognac and champagne. Inexpensive.

Druzhba
In the Expocenter at 12 Krasnopresnenskaya Emb
Tel 255-2970
The Friendship Café also doubles as an art gallery and is covered floor to ceiling with paintings. Dinner is reminiscent of a 16th-century Muscovite banquet for Ivan the Terrible—little suckling pigs are served with bowls of cavier and bottles of champagne. Make a reservation. Expensive.

Farkhad
4 Bolshaya Marfinskaya Street
Tel 218-4136
The Azerbaijani idea of the Arabian Nights; colorfully painted interior with comfortable wooden booths. Such dishes as the *gutap* stuffed crepes are delicious. Bring along a bottle of your favorite wine. Make a reservation. Moderate.

Fyodorov's
36 Prechistenka Street
Tel 201-7500
This is Moscow's first co-operative restaurant (formerly Kropotkinsky 36). Downstairs is cosy with a violin player; upstairs is more formal. Serves excellent Russian-style food like *shchi* (cabbage soup), mushroom pie, blini pancakes, and stuffed carp. Sometimes there's even home-made ice cream. Available are a variety of wines— French, Georgian and, at times, even Californian. Moderate to expensive.

Glazur
12 Smolensky Bulvar
Tel 248-4438

This fashionable new co-operative gives a twist to traditional Russian food and serves a great chicken-and-elk stew. Order the *baklazhannaya ikra*, if you like eggplant. Moderate.

Guria
7 Komsomolskaya Prospekt
Tel 246-0378
A diner-like café with filling Georgian food, including *hachapuri* and *satsivi*. Inexpensive.

Hard Rock Café
Gorky Park
Tel 237-0709
Also called the Viktoria Café. Not affiliated with the Western version, this is owned by the rock-star Stas Namin, and serves Russian-Armenian food. It can be difficult to find: Walk through the park to the Zelyoni (Green) Theater; it is in the basement (don't wander around late at night). Mostly a musician's den that gets going later in the evening, perhaps with a performance. Inexpensive.

Kashtan
40 Taganskaya Street
Tel 272-6242
Russian food, like garlic chicken, served in a dark atmosphere. A loud floor show in the evenings. Liquor is available. Moderate.

Karina
1-3 Solyansky Proezd
Tel 924-0369
Styled to look like a Greek taverna, this co-operative offers several fixed menu specials that include soups and meat dishes. You can also order a suckling pig in advance. Alcohol available. Inexpensive to moderate.

Kolkhida
6 Sadovo-Samotechnaya Street
Tel 299-6757
A lively Georgian restaurant, where a canary even sings along with the musical groups. Great food—if you notice other tables have bowls of *khinkali* (steamed dumplings), order them immediately before they run out. Moderate.

Moosh
2/4 Okyabrskaya Street
Tel 284-3670
A small traditional Armenian restaurant, where mutton is a famous dish. Armenian rifles and portraits of Armenian martyrs hang on the walls. Moderate.

Okhotnik
40 Tverskaya Street
Tel 251-4268
The Hunter Café serves traditional Russian food. Inexpensive.

Olimp
On the river embankment behind Luzhniki Stadium—you can't miss it, lights are hung all around it
Tel 201-0148
A large restaurant that serves traditional Russian food such as *pelmeni* dumplings. Alcohol is available. In the evenings, entertainment is provided in the form of musical and singing revues. Make a reservation. Moderate to expensive.

Ordynka
71 Bolshaya Ordynka Street
Tel 237-9905
A Russian tavern that serves hearty meals of pork and potato dishes. Inexpensive to moderate.

Orient
1/9 Nikoloshchepovsky Lane
Tel 241-1078
The former Smolensky Traktir serves tasty fried dishes of fish, pork and potatoes. Good *zakuski* appetizers include caviar and salads. Make a reservation. Moderate to inexpensive.

Pokrovka
4 Chernyshevsky Street
Tel 923-0282
A candlelit bistro that serves mainly *blini* pancakes, *pelmeni* dumplings, chickens and salads. You can bring your own liquor. Credit cards only; moderate.

A day by the river

Praga
On the corner of the old (2) Arbat
Tel 290-6171
One of the oldest restaurants in Moscow, mostly banquets are held here. The Czech and Russian food (like Chicken Kiev) is adequate, but the loud music and dancing make conversation difficult. Moderate. Reservations needed.

Razgulyai
11 Spartakovskaya Street
Tel 267-7613
This colorful cellar-type restaurant provides the usual Russian favorites of soups, dumplings and cutlets. A gypsy group plays music at weekends. Moderate.

Rossiya
In the Rossiya Hotel
Tel 298-2981
One of the few restaurants where the view is better than the food. Look out at St Basil's Cathedral while you eat the usual Russian fare. Wash it down with vodka or champagne. Moderate.

Ruslan
32 Vorontsovskaya Street
Tel 272-0632
Russian-style food and champagne, along with gypsy trios at weekends. Inexpensive.

Russkaya Izba
The Russian House is located in Ilyinskoye Village on the way to Arkhangelsk
Tel 561-4244
About a 40-minute drive outside of Moscow, this pleasant country-style restaurant, built to look like a traditional *Izba* or wooden cottage, serves authenic old Russian food: stews, potatoes, fish, mushrooms and wild berries. Tea is served from a *samovar*. Music by a balalaika band. Alcohol available. Expensive. Reserve a day in advance.

Sedmoye Nyebo
The Seventh Heaven Restaurant is situated at the top of the Ostankino TV tower and rotates once an hour. It offers wonderful views of Moscow when clear. Buy tickets inside the pavilion by the tower. You may need to show a passport or other identification before being allowed up.

Skazka
1 Tovarischevsky Lane
The Fairy-Tale is a dark-wooded restaurant that serves traditional Russian food.
Inexpensive to moderate.

Slavyansky Bazaar
Located in Old Moscow at 13 Nikolskaya Street
Tel 921-1872
This famous spot, where Stanislavsky once spent an 18-hour lunch dreaming up the
Moscow Arts Theater, is worth visiting. Traditional Russian food is served in a 19th-
century atmosphere. Alcohol is available. In the evenings, loud floor shows are on
the first floor; banquet halls can also be rented. Moderate to expensive.

Sorok Cheterie
The '44' café is at 44 Leningradskoye Shosse
Tel 159-9951
Wall booths, mellow jazz, Russian food and Turkish coffee. Inexpensive.

Stoleshniki Café
8 Stoleshniki Per
Tel 229-2050
Tavern atmosphere and Russian food. Inexpensive to moderate.

Strasnoi 7
The same address as its name
Tel 299-049
A quiet place that serves Russian food, some liquor, including beer. Visit the art
gallery next door. Credit cards only; moderate.

Taganka Bar
15 Radishchevskaya Street
Tel 272-4351
Named after the Taganka Theater, this avant-garde tavern serves a hefty selection of
zakuski appetizers, some entrées and liquor. As you walk in, albino frogs croak in the
lobby aquarium. A variety of entertainment in the evenings—you never know quite
what will show up. Moderate to inexpensive.

Taganka Café
76 Zemlyanoi Val

Tel 272-7320
Many actors from the Taganka Theater come here for lunch; dinners are Russian, including *pelmini* dumplings, with beer and champagne. Inexpensive.

Theater Café
Near the Intourist Hotel at 5 Tverskaya
Perfect for a quick snack. Take a tray and choose what you want. You can sign your name on the graffiti wall when leaving. Inexpensive.

Tsentralny
10 Tverskaya Street
Tel 229-0241
The small, but elegant dining area serves Russian food like *blini* with caviar. Floor shows are held in the evenings. Alcohol served. Moderate.

U Kamena
37 Chernyshevskaya Street
Tel 297-0840
Just a few tables, but lots of *zakuski* appetizers. Most of the clientele do not come to eat, but to watch the sex show—the usual topless erotic dancers. Moderate.

U Margarity
9 Ryleyeva Street
Tel 291-6063
At Margarita's serves Russian food in a cosy environment. Moderate.

U Nikitskikh Vorot
Herzen Street, by Suvorovsky Bulvar
Tel 290-4883/4825
This bistro-style restaurant, decorated in wood and red-brick, has special Russian dishes of chicken, mushrooms, cheese, bread and the plat du jour. Inexpensive to moderate.

U Pirosmani
Across from Novodevichy Monastery at 4 Novodevichy Lane
Tel 247-1926
Pirosmani was a famous Georgian painter whose works depicted people merrily eating and drinking; his works, among others, decorate the walls. Delightful white-washed interior with musicians playing the piano and violin at night. Dishes include

tolma with meat and rice in vine leaves, eggplant *chanakh*, chicken *chakhokhbili* and bowls of steaming dumplings. Georgian wine and champagne are also available. Make a reservation. Moderate to expensive.

Vareniki
On the corner of Skaterny and Paliashvilli Lanes
Vareniki means dumplings, the small café's speciality. Also serves Ukrainian-style chicken and *shchi* soup. Order at the counter and take a seat anywhere. Inexpensive.

Uzbekistan
29 Neglinnaya Street
Tel 924-6053
Now popular with large wedding and tourist parties. Uzbek dishes include *lagman* meat-and-noodle soup and *manty* spicy lamp dumplings.

Vyecherni Siluett
88 Taganskaya Ploshchad
Tel 272-2280
The Evening Silhouette restaurant is a popular élite haunt. Elegant décor and white-satin walls. The tasty Russian food includes caviar, chicken, crab and delicious desserts. Moderate to expensive.

The Writer's Union
52 Vorovskaya Street
Tel 291-2169/1515
Well worth a visit, if you can get a reservation. Once a private mansion, it has been renovated in Gothic style, with a wood-panelled interior complete with fireplace,

In the Tikhvin Cemetery

crystal and real silverware. The food is delicious, especially the Chicken Kiev and potato pancakes. A variety of wines is also available. Moderate.

Yakimanka
2/10 Bolshaya Polyanka
Tel 238-8888
This Uzbek restaurant serves dishes like stuffed grape leaves, dumplings and *plov*. A band plays Russian hit songs for dancing. Moderate.

Zaidi i Poprobui
124 Prospekt Mira
Tel 286-8165
The Come In and Taste Restaurant has typical Russian food. The menu changes daily, depending on available food.

Zolotoi Drako
64 Plushchikha Street
Tel 248-3602
Szechuan food.

EUROPEAN AND AMERICAN JOINT-VENTURES
Arlecchino
15 Druzhinnikovskaya Street (off street in the alleyway)
Tel 205-7088
Popular with the foreign community, especially Italians—most of the food is trucked in from Italy. Elegant atmosphere and good service. An excellent selection of pastas, meat, veal and chicken dishes, and a large salad bar with antipasto. Italian wines available too. Serves cappacino and expresso, and fabulous desserts. Make a reservation. Credit cards only; expensive.

Boyarsky
Metropole Hotel, 4th floor
Tel 927-6089
A huge stuffed bear glares at you, while sweet serenades drift down from the overhead balcony. The traditional Russian cuisine is delicious; trout stuffed with caviar, and *pirozhki* smothered in brandy sauce. Alcohol available. Very expensive.

Brasserie
In the Penta Hotel
Tel 971-6101
Decorated like a ship's interior with a folklore show. Has exotic choices like goat cheese, duck breast, moussaka and French pastries. Expensive.

Café Taiga
In the Aerostar Hotel at 37 Leningradsky Prospekt
Tel 155-5030
The Canadians have brought lobster to the Moscow menu, along with other delectable dishes. The café also has a superior Sunday brunch and a fixed-price business luncheon. Moderate to expensive.

Champs Elysées
In the Pullman/Iris Hotel at 10 Korovinskoye Shosse
Tel 488-8000
French restaurant offering asparagus and salmon; desserts include éclairs and apple tarts. Expensive to very expensive.

Delhi
23b Krasnaya Presnya Street
tel 252-1766/ 255-0492
Good Indian food—Tandoori chicken, breads and curries. Moderate to expensive.

El Rincon Español
In the Spanish Bar at the Moskva Hotel by Red Square
Tel 292-2893
Has Spanish-Mexican-style spicy fare. The menu includes paella, fabada, spicy sausage and omelettes, tapas and even Sangria and San Miguel beer. Entertainment with accordians or flamenco dancers at night. Moderate.

Evropeisky Zal
In the Metropole Hotel
Tel 927-6039
One of the best restaurants in the city. Dishes include crab-stuffed crepes and Chicken Kiev. Expresso and pastries for dessert. Expensive to very expensive. Popular all-you-can-eat brunches on Sundays in the Metropole Zal, 11:30–15:00.

The Exchange
In the Slavyanskaya/Radisson Hotel
Tel 941-8333
The menu includes sirloin and porterhouse steaks, barbecued shrimp, and apple pie
with ice-cream for dessert. Expensive.

Galaxy
Near the Exhibition of Economic Achievements at 9 Selskhozyaistveny Lane
Tel 181-2074
A British pub, with saloon food and English beer. A cover charge at night, when there
is dancing. Moderate. (Another British pub is **The Red Lion** in the Mezh Hotel.)

Inflotel
In the boat, *Alexander Blok*, moored by the Mezh Hotel
Tel 255-9278
Serves mainly Greek/American food; the buffet is filled with Greek delights, from
stuffed grape leaves to baklava. Expensive. After dinner go to the **Medusa Café** on
the boat—a nightclub/casino that is open late.

In Vino
Third floor of the Ukraine Hotel
Tel 243-2316
Overlooks the river and serves dishes such as beef stroganov; good selection of wine.
Expensive.

Kuilong
7 Litovsky Boulevard
Tel 425-1111
Vietnamese cuisine with food brought in weekly from Vietnam. Spring rolls, papaya
and lychee nuts. Expensive.

Lasagne
40 Pyatnitskaya
Tel 231-1085
Hearty Italian fare. Credit cards. Moderate.

Mei-hua
2/1 Rusakovskaya Street, next to Rusalka Café
Tel 264-9574
One of the best Chinese restaurants in Moscow. Moderate.

Pekin
In the Peking Hotel at 1/2 Bolshaya Sadovaya
Tel 209-1865
Popular Chinese restaurant for lunch and dinner. Moderate to expensive.

Peter's Place
72 Zemlyanoi Street, near the Taganka Theater
Tel 298-3248
This popular Dutch restaurant is open until midnight, and the bar, with beer and dancing, until 04:00. Russian-European food—salade nicoise to *blini*. Moderate to expensive.

Sakura
First floor of the Mezh Hotel
Tel 253-2894
All food is brought in daily from Japan. Sushi to sashimi. Expensive to very expensive.

Savoy
In the Savoy Hotel
Tel 928-0450
First-class dining. Expensive. The **Savoy Bar** on the first floor offers burgers & CNN.

Stanislavsky 2
At the address of its name
Tel 291-8689
A trendy dining spot, especially with the foreign community. Russian food with classical ensembles. Champagne and wine served. Moderate.

Tren-Mos
21 Komsomolsky Prospekt
Tel 245-1216
This Trenton, New Jersey joint venture provides home-cooked American meals, from burgers to mashed potatoes. (You can also call and preorder take-outs.) Moderate to expensive.

U Yuzefa
11/17 Dubinskaya Street
Tel 238-4646
'The only kosher Jewish restaurant in Russia.' Ethnic music at night. Moderate.

Vienna Café
In the Penta Hotel
Tel 971-6101
Serves buffet-style lunches and dinners, with an excellent salad bar. Popular for Sunday brunch. Expensive.

Villa Peredekino,
In Peredelkino, about a 50-minute drive from Moscow
Tel 435-1478
Peredelkino is the writer's village where Pasternak is buried. An Italian-Russian joint venture with imported food from Italy. Credit cards only; expensive to very expensive.

FAST FOOD

Not only has fast food come to Moscow, some even be delivered to your door.

McDonald's
Off Pushkin Square on Tverskaya Street
Tel 200-1655
Usually long queues, but occasionally they move quickly. It is the largest McDonald's in the world, with more than 700 seats. McDonald's plans to open many more outlets; others are located in the Arbat and Tverskaya (across from the Post Office Buliding).

Pizza Hut
12 Tverskaya Street and 17 Kutuzovsky Prospekt
Tel 229-2013 (Tverskaya) and 243-1727 (Kutuzovsky) to order food in advance for collection. Has both rubles and hard currency sides.

Baku-Livan
Tverskaya Street
If McDonald's is crowded, walk along the street to get a burger or falafel. There is also a counter with pastries and breads.

Pettina
Opposite the Kosmos Hotel
Tel 286-5217 to order in advance; they also deliver daily between 10:00 and 11:00. A foodstand. Finnish burgers, chicken sandwiches, sodas etc.

Russky Pryanik (Russian Gingerbread)
40 Leninsky Prospekt

Russian-Australian Bakery
28/8 Pyatnitksya Street

The Kulinarnaya
Alongside the Praga Restaurant in the Arbat shop
Sells delicious pastries.

Dessert Bar
45 Tverskaya Street
Serves desserts and ice-cream.

Baskin-Robbins Ice Cream
Kutuzovsky Prospekt, in the Rossiya Hotel, the Arbat and at the airport.

Foreign Goods Markets

If you need food or pharmaceutical products a few well-stocked stores have opened
in Moscow. Most take credit cards or hard currency only. Check to see if prices are
marked in rubles, Golden rubles (a different exchange rate) or a foreign currency.

The Irish Store
19 Novy Arbat, second floor
A large grocery store, stocked with food, drink, alcohol. Open Monday to Sunday
from 09:00 to 20:00.

Tina Fontana
Mezhdunarodnaya Hotel, second floor
Foodstore that includes Italian products and alcohol. Open Monday to Saturday from
10:00 to 21:00 and on Sundays from 10:00 to 14:00. Also in the Mezh Hotel, around
the corner on the second floor, is The Pharmacy for prescriptions.

Sadko
16 Bolshaya Dorogomilovskaya, around the corner from Pizza Hut on Kutuzovsky
Well-stocked market with a drugstore section. Open Monday to Saturday from 10:00
to 20:00 and Sundays from 10:00 to 18:00; closed from 15:00 to 16:00.

Stockmann (Kalinka)
4/8 Zatsepsky Val
This Finnish foodstore carries a wide variety of foodstuffs. Credit cards only. Open Monday to Sunday from 10:00 to 20:00.

Recently, many smaller foreign goods stores have opened. In the Patriarch's Pond area are the Dutch **Intermarket** (27/14 Malaya Bronnaya) and the French **Fortcor** with French wines (across the street); both are open daily from 10:00 to 20:00. The German **Intercar** (near the Peking Hotel on 5 Bolshaya Sadovaya) includes cheeses and wursts. Open from 10:00 to 20:00 and on Saturdays and Sundays from 11:00 to 19:00. Also **Yeliseyev's** is at 14 Tverskaya Street. **Novoarbatsky Gastronom** (food store) is at 21 Novy Arbat; others are along Tverskaya.

Shopping Tips

In 1994 all foreign currency payments in Russian stores were banned. Now, unless an establishment can officially accept foreign currency, most Russian stores will accept rubles only. Others accept foreign cash and give change in rubles. When bargaining in the markets anything goes.

The easiest and fastest way to purchase souvenirs is to visit a *Beriozka*. (*Beriozka* stems from the Russian word for Birch tree.) Here you can purchase Russian goods that are sometimes cheaper than in ordinary street shops. Although the Beriozkas are now in open competition with numerous other shops starting up all over Moscow, they are still good for

(opposite and above) GUM Department Store

some bargains such as fur hats and vodka. Most importantly, their merchandise is guaranteed to be genuine. A number of souvenir shops have opened in Moscow, along with other private cooperatives; markets in the Arbat or Izmailovo Park also have a good selection of itms to buy. Each city has large department stores, *Univermag*—an arcade of shops that sells a variety of products for rubles. A number of hard currency stores have opened stocking gifts, Western clothing, cosmetics, electronics, and books. If you have time, take a walk through a shopping district, such as GUM or Tverskaya Street. This will give you an idea of how Muscovites shop and what is available to them.

In most Russian stores, you must first pay a cashier at the *kassa*, then show the receipt to the salesperson, who wraps and hands over the purchase. If something catches your eye outside a *Beriozka*, you should buy it; when you return the next day, it may be gone. Many goods are not available in large supplies; people in long queues can quickly buy all that is available. Most Russian stores will sell items for rubles; most do not accept foreign currency or credit cards—so make sure you have some rubles when shopping about the city. Stores are generally open from 10:00 to 19:00 or 20:00, and close for an hour (around 14:00–15:00) in the afternoon. If you purchase antiques, art (such as expensive paintings and icons) or rugs, official permission may be required to take them out of the country; a duty is often levied. Check before buying; the items could be confiscated at customs.

The main shopping areas of Moscow are located along Tverskaya Street, Novy Arbat, GUM, the Arbat promenade, and the small side streets (including Stoleshnikov, Petrovka and Kuznetsky Most) behind GUM Department Store on Red Square.

Art Export: If you have purchased art from a well-established gallery or shop, they can do the Custom's export paperwork for you. Valuable art pieces cannot be taken out of the country until you have them officially appraised by the Moscow Export Commission at 29 Chekhov Street. It is open on Tuesday from 10:00 to 14:00. Bring two small photographs of the item(s) in question and be prepared to pay a small sum for the appraisal and export permission.

BERIOZKAS

The largest are found at the Rossiya (in the back) and Ukraine (2nd floor) hotels. Others are located in the National, Intourist, Kosmos and Mezhdunarodny hotels. (Every large hotel has some type of *Beriozka* shopping.) Two *Beriozkas* are located opposite the Novodevichy Monastery and at 9 Kutuzovsky Prospekt (near the Ukraine Hotel).

LOCAL DEPARTMENT STORES

GUM, *Glavny Universalny Magazine* (Main Universal Store), Red Square

Built in the 1880s, GUM is the largest shopping center in Moscow. Merchants once rented the long rows of small shopping alcoves, now filled with Russian-made products. Don't let the crowds and lines deter you from strolling inside. (Stores opened for foreign currency credit card purchases include, Botany 500, Escada, L'Oréal, Lego, Samsonite Luggage, Santens Towels of Belgium, Stockman's, United Colors of Benetton and Yves Rocher.) Other shops are for rubles. On the first floor are souvenirs, second floor fur hats and coats. Open Monday to Saturday from 08:00 to 21:00.

TsUM, Central Department Store
2 Petrovka Street
Now filled with private co-ops, so the selection ranges from fur hats and clothes to *samovars* and rugs. Items change depending on stock. Open Monday to Saturday from 08:00 to 21:00.

Moskva Department Store
54 Leninsky Prospekt
Open from 08:00 to 21:00.

Universalny Magazin
9 Tverskaya Street
Department store. Open Monday to Saturday from 08:00 to 20:00; closed from 14:00 to 15:00.

Petrovsky Passage
10 Petrovsky Street
Accepts both rubles and hard currency. Kodak is also on this street, along with a stationery store, Sony, Honda, and shops that are open from 09:00 to 20:00.

Voentorg (Military Goods Store)
10 Novy Arbat near the Kremlin
You cannot buy items such as uniforms unless you have the right coupons or papers. But you can get great paraphenalia like buttons, pins and belts. On the first floor are other clothing and sports items. Open Monday to Saturday from 08:00 to21:00.

KOMMISSIONI (SECOND-HAND STORES)
Kommissioni
16 Tverskaya Street
Used clothes, porcelain, crystal for rubles. Open Monday to Friday from 10:00 to 19:00 and until 20:00 on Saturdays; closed between 14:00 and 15:00. Another Kom

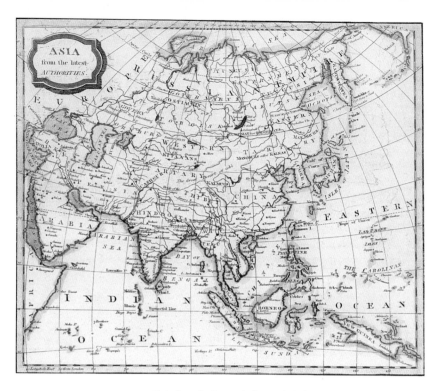

'Asia from the Latest Authorities', 1780

missioni is at 18 Varshavskoye Shosse. Same hours, but on Saturdays it closes at 18:00. It also sells a wide variety of goods, including used carpets.

Other **porcelain, crystal and china shops** are at 32 Arbat, 15/48 Tverskaya, 8 Izmailovsky, 56 Dmitrov, and 36/54 Leningradsky Prospekt. Some of the more popular ones are at 4/2 Myasnitskaya (Kirov) Street and *Farfori Steklo* (Porcelain and Glass) 74 Prospekt Mira. **Furniture and clocks** are sold at 5 Smolensky and 54 Frunze Emb.

Antique Shops
Unisat
5 Vakhtangova Street (off the Arbat)
One room is filled with icons and candelabras, another with paintings, plates and sculptures, others with kitsch. Open Monday to Saturday from 11:00 to 20:00 and Sundays to 19:00.

Art and Icon Sale
6 Arbat

The End of the Line

As usual, Marya Sidorovna Tyutina got up at eight, had oatmeal for breakfast, and cleaned up the dishes after herself and her husband. Then she went off to the corner grocery, a half-flight down from the street, where yesterday they had definitely promised that they would have cod filet in the morning.

Marya Sidoravna didn't bother to get a receipt beforehand. She just took a place in the line at the fish and meat department so they could weigh it out first. After standing there half the day—half an hour, anyway—she finally wound up at the counter, and then the sales girl told her they won't serve you without a receipt. Marya Sidorovna begged her to weigh out half a kilo anyway, for an invalid, because she'd been in line there since they opened, and it was too crowded at the cashier; but the salesgirl didn't even bother discussing it, took a receipt from some man, and turned her back. Someone in line yelled at Marya Sidorovna to stop holding things up—they all had to work; so she went straight over to the cashier without even waiting in line, said she just had to pay a bit extra on her bill and took out several kopeks. But despite the receipt, they wouldn't let her up to the counter because she'd missed her turn, and the filet was almost gone.

When Marya Sidorovna said that she's been standing there, one woman declared that personally she hadn't seen anyone. What people! Marya Sidorovna didn't want to get mixed up in anything, so she went to the end of the line and waited another twenty minutes; but three people ahead of her they ran out of cod.

Nina Katerli, The Barsukov Triangle

Metropole
On the main side of the Metropole Hotel is a marvelous antique shop. Filled with icons, paintings, furniture, crystal, porcelain, *samovars*, books, and more. Open after 11:00 and closed on Sundays.

Bookinist
4 Pushechnaya Street
Filled with old treasures. Open Tuesday to Saturday from 10:00 to 19:00; closed between 14:00 and 15:00.

ARTS AND CRAFTS
Russkiye Souveniry
9 Kutuzovsky Prospekt (along the street from Pizza Hut)
Sells jewelry, *matryoshka* dolls, lacquer boxes etc.

Izmailovsky Park:
Definitely worth visiting on weekends. A giant flea market, feel free to haggle.

Art Salon
24 Kutuzovsky Prospekt and 6 Ukrainsky Boulevard
Pictures, prints etc.

Kabul
7 Sadovaya Kudrinskaya
Souvenirs from Afghanistan.

Podarki
4 and 37 Tverskaya Street, and 29 Vozdvizhenka
Gifts.

Russky Lyon
29 Komsomolsky Prospekt
Sells handicrafts, linens and souvenirs.

Russkiye Uzory (Russian Designs)
16 Petrovka and 15 Stoleshnikov
Even sells balalaikas and chess sets.

Suveniri
12/45 Tverskaya.

Tadzhikistan
52 Tverskaya (Gorky)
Sells wares from this Central Asian nation.

Yantar
14 Gruzinsky Val
The Amber store offers a selection of amber jewelry. Open Monday to Saturday from
10:00 to 19:00; closed between 14:00 and 15:00.

JEWELRY STORES
Almaz, 4 and 37/45 Tverskaya/Gorky and 14 Stoleshnikov.The Diamond shop.
Agat (Agate), 16 Bolshaya Kolkhoznaya.
Biryuza (Turquoise), 21 Sadovaya Spasskaya.
Izumrud (Emeralds), 23 Lomonovsky Prospekt.
Jewelery Salon, 30 Grokholsky Lane.
Lazurit (Azure), 3 Sirenevy Bulvar. Gold, silver and stones bought and sold.
Malakhitovaya Shkatulka (Malachite Box), 24 Vozdvizhenka.
Rubin (Ruby), 78 Leningradsky Prospekt.
Sapfir at 120 Prospekt Mira.
Samotsveti (Semi-Precious Stones), 35 and 11 Arbat.
Topaz, 11 Profsoyuznaya.
Yashma (Jasper), 13 Stoleshnikov.
Zemchug (Pearl), 22 Olimpisky Prospekt.

BOOKSTORES
Dom Knigi (House of Books)
26 Novy Arbat
The largest bookstore in the city; it also sells foreign publications, posters, postcards, and
now icons on the first floor; open Monday to Saturday from 11:00 to 20:00.

Books and Prints
31 Prechistenka Street
A large bookstore that stocks fiction (including books that are difficult to find by
such authors as Pasternak and Akhmatova), art and cultural books, dictionaries, and
so on. Open daily from 09:00 to 20:00.

Moscow Metro

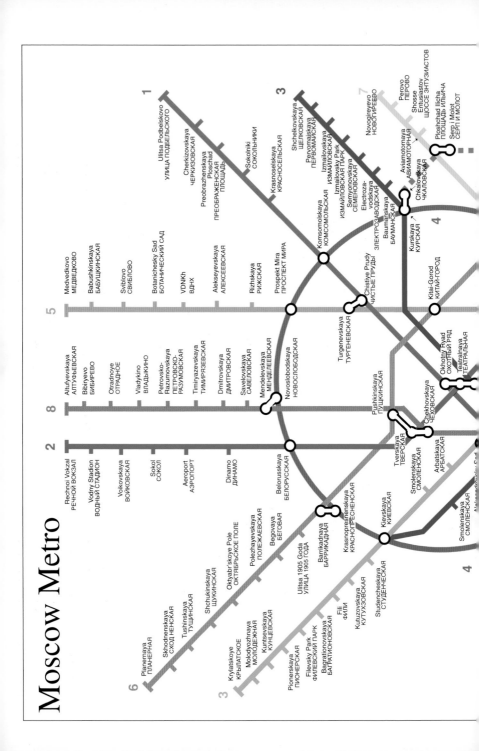

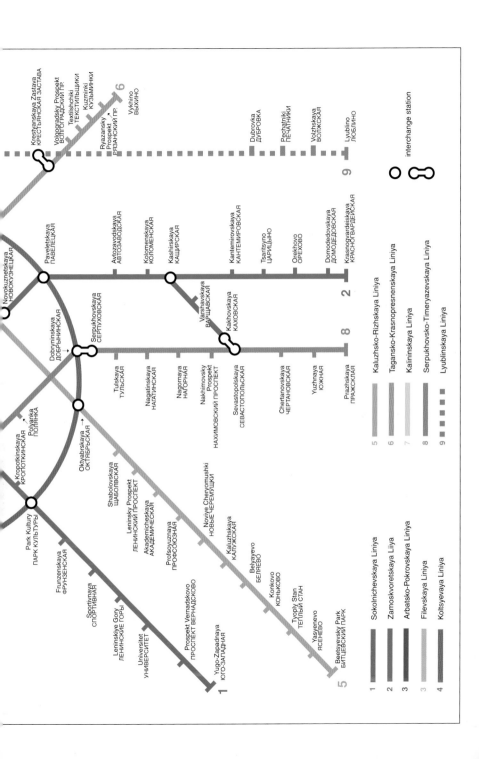

The Poster Shop
4 Arbat
Open Monday to Saturday from 10:00 to 19:00.

Shkolnik (School)
21 Leninsky Prospekt
School supplies (and sometimes Russian flags). Open Mon.-Fri. 10 a.m. to 7 p.m. (Sat. to 6 p.m.)

Inostrannaya Kniga
16 Kachalov Street
Sells foreign books and old engravings, expensive.

The **Atlas Map Store**
10 Kuznetsky Most
Stamps and maps of Russia and Moscow are for sale.

Knigi-Podarki
16 Stoleshnikov Pereulok
Gifts and books. Next door, at number 14, is a **bukinist** (second-hand bookstore), selling used and rare books.

Knizhny Mir (Book World)
6 Myasnitskaya Street
Books, prints, posters and postcards.

Moskva
8 Tverskaya Street
Sells books, maps and postcards.

Planeta
8 Vesnin Street
Foreign-language books, expensive.

Progress
17 Zubovsky Boulevard
Books in foreign languages.

Troika Press
At the kiosk to the right side of the Metropole Hotel (coming from the Kremlin)
Here, you can buy foreign magazines and newspapers. Most hotels also have news-
stands; the best for foreign publications are in the Metropole, Savoy, Penta and
Mezh hotels.

Stockman Fashion and Office Store
GUM (first floor) and 78/8 Leninsky Prospekt
Office supplies that you cannot find anywhere else. Credit cards only. Open daily
from 10:00 to 20:00. On the second floor of the Mezh Hotel is a small stationery store.

ELECTRONIC STORES
Stockman Home and Car Store, 70/1 Lyusinovskaya Street. Items for cars and kitch-
ens, and electronics. Open Mon.-Sat. 10 a.m. to 8 p.m.
Moskva, 31 Kutuzovsky Prospekt.
Fairn and Svanson, 78 Leningradsky Prospekt and the Mezh Hotel.
Star Progress, 30 Fruzenskaya Emb.
Supershop, 5 Astrakhansky Per.
Zigzag, 17 Kuznetsky Most.
AHA, Presnensky Val and Stolyany Per.
JVC Shop, 86 Leninsky Prospekt.

CHILDREN'S STORES
Detski Mir (Children's World), 2 Teatralnaya (next to the former KGB building),
the largest toy store in Moscow.
Dom Igrushki (House of Toys), 8 Kutuzovsky Prospekt.
Mashenka, 10 Smolensky Street. Sells girls' clothing.
Malysh (Little Ones), 8 Kutuzovsky Prospekt. Sells baby clothing. Another large
children's shop is at 56 Tverskaya (Gorky).
Tovari dlya Dyetay (Goods for Children), 97 Prospekt Mira.

COSMETICS AND COLOGNES
Estée Lauder, at 6 Tverskaya, and **Christian Dior** (alongside Moskva Hotel) both
sell cosmetics for rubles (sometimes long queues). Dior also sells in the Mezh Hotel
and Sadko on Kutuzovsky. **Zolotoya Rosa** (Golden Rose), is also alongside the
Moskva Hotel.

THE TRANS-SIBERIAN RAILROAD

Construction of the Trans-Siberian Railroad was started in 1891 and only completed 25 years later in 1916. Linking Chelyubinsk in the Ural Mountains to the Pacific port of Vladivostok, it facilitated the settlement of sparsely populated regions in southern regions of the Soviet Union.

Today, over one hundred years after the first tracks were laid, the Trans-Siberian is one of the cheapest ways of traveling from Europe to Asia. It is also one of the great travel adventures, though at times it can be mind-bogglingly boring—endless stretches of birch forest clacking by.

The main section of the railroad stretches 4,000 miles (9,600 kilometres) from Moscow to Beijing. The five-day Chinese Trans-Mongolian train via Ulan Bator leaves every Wednesday, while the six-day Russian Trans-Manchurian via Manzhouli leaves Friday and Saturday. Starting in Moscow, the departure days are Tuesday and Friday, respectively.

Reservations are essential, and must be made at least two months in advance. The train is heavily booked during the summer, and the wheels of Russian bureaucracy grind slowly all year round. Many travel agencies, including places in Moscow, can book space on the Trans-Siberian. Tourists have the option of reserving a berth in a two-, four- or six-berth compartment, which almost always is in a car set aside for foreigners. If you travel alone, you may be booked into a compartment with Russians. Avoid buying open tickets, as they are virtually impossible to book and expire after two months. Russian and/or Chinese visas are required for both trains, and an additional Mongolian visa is needed for the Trans-Mongolian.

From May to September, trains travel from Moscow all the way to Nakhodka near Vladivostok on the Pacific Ocean, and from there you can take a Russian cruise ship to Yokohama, Japan. You can stop overnight or a few days in Novosibirsk and Irkutsk, and all passengers spend the night in Khabarovsk, where they change trains. On the stretch between Khabarovsk and Nakhodka, the train runs along the Chinese-Russian border, and you can see the lights of numerous mysterious military installations.

Popular connecting destinations to the west include: Berlin, which can be reached, from Moscow, in less than 28 hours; Budapest (34 hours) and Helsinki (14 hours). If you're a real train fanatic, you can extend this journey all the way to Paris on the East–West Express via Berlin and Warsaw. Tickets on the East–West Express can be reserved through Germanrail.

Solo travelers on the Trans-Siberian should try to pay for meals in advance; if you don't, a large tour could eat up all the food and your hunger will be met by shrugs from the waiters. The Russian restaurant car has an impressive menu but a limited supply due in part to selling food stock at high prices on the Siberian black market. All travelers should note that the food is basic stock and alcohol is not available on the train nor in the stations along the way. Bring your own stock of snacks and booze, along with lots of books!

FARES DECEMBER 1994

Moscow to Irkutsk
First class 2 berth: US$390
Second class 4 berth: US$220

Moscow to Khabarovsk
First class: US$665
Second class: US$343

Moscow to Vladivostok
First class: US$686
Second class: US$364

Moscow to Beijing
Hard Class (two- to four-berth)
First class: US$726
Second class: US$546

Soft Class
First class: US$940
Second class: US$761

Add about US$50 during the peak season (May to September)

Train restaurant carriage

FURS

Fur Kommissioni: At 30 Pushkinskaya Street, it has fur coats and hats for rubles. Fur coats and hats can also be found at 13 Stoleshnikov Lane. Along the street at number 5 is a used fur store. A *mekha* (fur) shop is also at 13 Pyatnitsky Street. Most of the large *Beriozkas* and hotels stock fur coats and hats at foreign currency prices. Try GUM, the Arbat and Izmailovsky Park for ruble prices.

MUSIC STORES

Melodiya at 40 Novy Arbat (by Dom Knigi) is one of the largest record stores. Others are at 24 Herzen Street and 6 Arbat. Russian records, tapes and CDs can also be found in *Beriozkas*.

Russiya Muzika, at 4 Sadovaya Triumfalnaya, is filled with Russian folk, pop and national music. At 14 Neglinny Street. (second floor) is **Noty**, which sells sheet music, opera scores, children's songs, etc.

Terms For Local Stores

Learn the Russian alphabet to recognize these store signs on the street:

aptyeka	pharmacy
bukinist	second-hand bookstore
bulochnaya	bakery
chasy	watches and watch repair
galanteriya	clothing, fabrics and lingerie
gastronom	food store
khozyaistvenny magazin	hardware and kitchen supplies
khudozhestvenny	art gallery
kiosk	small stand
kino	movie cinema
knizhny (knigi) magazin	bookstore
kommissiony magazin	second-hand store
konditerskaya	confectionery—sweets and tea
kulinariya	small take-out delicatessens
magazin	store
mekha	fur shop
moloko	milk, dairy products
morozhenoye	ice cream
myaso-riiba	meat and fish

oboof	shoe store
odezhda	clothing store
ovoshchi-frukti	vegetables and fruit
podarki	gifts
produkti	produce
remont	repair shop
rinok	farmers' market
shkolnik	school and office supplies
tabak	cigarettes and tobacco
tkani	sewing, fabrics, perfumes
tsvyeti	flowers
univermag	department store
viictavka	exhibit
yarmarka	string of small outdoor kiosks
Gedye' magazeen'?	Where is the shop?
Pakazhee'te	I would like to see. . .
Oo vas yest?	Do you have?
Droogoi' raz'mair?	Another size?
(Raz'mair) bol'she/men'she	(Size) smaller-larger
Deshe'vlye/daro'zhe	Cheaper/more expensive
Droogo'va tsvet'a?	Another color?
Skol'ka e'to stoi'yeet?	How much does it cost?
Mozh'na primyer'eet	Can I try it on?
Menye' e'to (ne) nrav'eetsa	I (don't) like it.
Ya e'to kooplyoo'	I'll buy it.

Farmers' Markets (*Ri'nok*)

Here people sell their fresh vegetables, fruits, flowers and other wares. Bring a few bags to carry your provisions. Markets are open from 07:00 to about 18:00, but a better selection is found in the morning.

Arbat is one long market. Take hard currency as well as rubles. Bargaining is all part of the fun.

Cheryomushkinsky Rinok is at 1 Lomonovsky Prospekt. Along with the food, this market also sells homemade crafts.

Kalitnikovsky is the pet market and is a sight in itself. It is held on weekends at 42a Kalitnikovsky Street. Here also is the **Ptichi Rinok**, the Bird Market. Animals for sale include dogs, cats, rabbits, and an assortment of birds and fish. Try to get here in the morning; it opens from 08:00 to about 14:00.

Kiosk Markets now line the streets of Moscow, selling a wide variety of goods and souvenirs for rubles and hard currency.

Izmailovsky is in Izmailovsky Park (near Metro stop of the same name). It is the best flea market to go to on weekends. Thousands of people selling everything imaginable.

Tsentralny is at 15 Tsvetnoi Boulevard, near the Old Circus, Metro Tsvetnoi Bulvar; one of the best-stocked food markets in Moscow.

Theaters

Army Academic Theater, 2 Kommuny Square. Tel 281-5120
Bat Cabaret, 3 Bolshoi Gnezdikovsky Per. Tel 229-8661
Bolshoi Opera and Ballet Theater, 1 Teatralnaya Square. Tel 292-0050
Cabaret Fliedermaus, 10 Bolshoi Gnezdikovsky Per. Tel 229-8661
Central Children's Theater, 2/7 Teatralnaya Square. Tel 292-0069
Chamber Musical Theater, 71 Leningradsky Prospekt. Tel 198-7204
Chekhov Theater, 8 Sheremetyevskaya Street. Tel 289-7985
Children's Musical Theater, 5 Vernadsky Prospekt. Tel 130-5243/930-7021
Durov Animal Theater, 4 Durov Street. Tel 281-2914/7222
Gogol Drama Theater, 8a Kazakova Street. Tel 261-5528
Hermitage Theater, 3 Karetny Ryad. Tel 209-6742/299-9645
Kremlin Palace of Congresses, The Kremlin (entrance through the Borovitsky Gate). Tel 227-8263
Komsomol Theater, 6 Chekhov Street. Tel 299-9668
Lencom Theater, 6 Chekhov Street. Tel 299-0708
Maly Academic Theater, 1/6 Teatralnaya Square. Tel 923-2621
Maly Theater Branch, 69 Bolshaya Ordynka. Tel 237-4472/3181
Mayakovsky Theater, 19 Hertzen Street. Tel 290-6241/4658
Mayakovsky Theater Branch, 21 Khmeleva Street. Tel 925-3070
Moscow Academic Art Theater, 22 Tverskoi Boulevard (new building); 3 Proyezd Khudozhestvennovo Teatra (old building).
Moscow Detective Theater, 13 Lubyanka Square. Tel 222-5213

Moscow Drama Theater, 4 Malaya Bronnaya Street. Tel 290-4093
Moscow Puppet Theater, 26 Spartakovskaya Street. Tel 261-2197
Moscow Theater of Mimicry and Gesture, 39/41 Izmailovsky Boulevard.
Tel 163-8130
Mossoviet Theater, 16 Bolshaya Sadovaya. Tel 299-2035
Musical Comedy Theater, 6 Pushkinskaya Street. Tel 292-0405
Novy Drama Theater, 2 Prokhodchikov Street. Tel 182-1977
Obraztsov Puppet Theater, 3 Sadovo Samotechnaya (with the puppet clock on
building). Tel 299-3310
Pushkin Drama Theater, 23 Tverskoi Boulevard. Tel 203-8582
Romany Gypsy Theater, 32/2 Leningradsky Prospekt. Tel 250-7334/290-6262
Satire Theater, 2 Mayakovsky Square/18 Bolshaya Sadovaya Street. Tel 299-9915
Satiricon Theater, 8 Sheremetyevksky Street. Tel 289-7844
Sovremennik Theater, 19a Chistoprudny Boulevard. Tel 921-6473
Spartacus Theater, 9/1a Spartakovskaya Square. Tel 261-1030
Stanislavsky Drama Theater, 23 Tverkaya Street. Tel 299-7621/7224
Stanislavsky and Nemirovich-Danchencko Musical Theater, 17 Pushkinskaya
Street. Tel 229-8388
Taganka Drama and Comedy Theater, 76 Zemlyanoi Street. Tel 272-6300
Variety Theater, 20/2 Bersenevsky Embankment. Also known as the Estrada.
Vernissage Theater, 5 Begovaya Street. Tel 945-3245
Yermolova Drama Theater, 5 Tverskaya Street. Tel 203-9063/7952
Vakhtangov Drama Theater, 26 Arbat Street. Tel 241-0728

Cinemas

Moscow has more than 100 cinemas; here are a few of them:

Espace Mir, French–Russian joint venture offering French films, on Tsvetnoi Bulvar
next to the Old Circus. Tel 924-9647

Kosmos, 109 Prospekt Mira.

Mir, 11 Tsvetnoi Boulevard
Moskva, 2/2 Mayakovsky Square.
Oktyabr, 42 Novy Arbat (*Gone With the Wind* was premiered here.)
Time-Warner is planning to build a multicinema theater.
Tsircorama, At Exhibition of Economic Achievement complex.
Zaryadye, Rossiya Hotel.
Zvezdny, 14 Vernadsky Prospekt.

Concert Halls

Central Concert Hall, 1 Moskvoretskaya Emb. Tel 298-1124
Church of the Intercession in Fili, 6 Novozavodskaya Street. Tel 148-4552
Glinka Concert Hall, 4 Fadeyev Street. Tel 251-1066
Gnesin Institute Concert Hall, 30/36 Vorovsky Street. Tel 290-6737
House of Artists Concert Hall, 10 Krymsky Val. Tel 238-9634
House of Scientists Concert Hall, 16 Prechistenka Street. Tel 202-5455
House of Unions, 1 Pushkinskaya Street. Also known as the Hall of Columns.
Izmailovo Concert Hall, 71 Izmailovskoye Shosse. Tel 166-7837
Luch Concert Hall, 71 Varhavskoye Shosse. Tel 110-3758
Olympic Village Concert Hall, 1 Pelshe Street. Tel 437-5650
Rachmaninov Hall, Herzen Street.
Tchaikovsky Concert Hall, 4/31 Mayakovsky Square. Tel 299-3487
Tchaikovsky Conservatory, 13 Herzen Street. Tel 299-7412
Znamensky Monastery Concert Hall, 8 Varvarka Street. Tel 298-3398

Circuses

Durova Zoo Circus, 4 Durov Street. Tel 281-2914/7222
New Circus, 7 Vernadsky Prospekt in the Lenin Hills. Tel 130-2815
Old Circus, 13 Tsvetnoi Boulevard. Tel 200-0688
Tent Circus, Gorky and Izmailovsky Parks (summers only).
Performances of the **Moscow Ice Ballet** and the **Circus on Ice** are held throughout the year.

Sports Facilities

The **Aquatic Sports Palace**, 27 Mironovskaya Street.
The **Central Chess Club**, 14 Gogolevsky Boulevard.
The **Central Stadium**, At Luzhniki, Metro Sportivnaya. Tel 201-1632/0955
The **Chaika Sports Palace**, 3/5 Prechistenka Street. Tel 202-0474/246-3521. Has a fully equipped gym, pool, sauna, tennis courts, massage facilities, restaurant and bar. Open from 07:00 to midnight.

Banyas

Nothing gives a better glimpse into the Russian character than a few hours in a Russian banya. This enjoyable sauna tradition has been a part of Russian culture for centuries. Traditionally, each village had its own communal bathhouse where, at different times, males or females would stoke wood-burning stoves and spend hours sitting, sweating and scrubbing. The Greek historian Herodotus reported from Russia in the fifth century BC: 'They make a booth by fixing in the ground three sticks inclined toward one another, and stretching around them wooden felts, which they arrange so as to fit as close as possible; inside the booth a dish is placed upon the ground, into which they put a number of red hot stones; then they take some hemp seed and throw it upon the stones; immediately it smokes, and gives out such a vopor that no Grecian vapor can exceed; they are immediately delighted and shout for joy, and this vapor serves them instead of a water bath.' Later, many homes even had their own private banyas and during winter, naked bodies could be seen rolling out in the snow after a vigorous sweat. Today the banya is still a much favored pastime.

Banya complexes are located throughout Moscow. Some of the most popular are the Sandunovsky and the Tsentralny banyas. For a minimal price, the bather can spend many a pleasurable hour in the company of fellow hedonists. No banya is complete without a bundle of dried birch branches, usually sold outside. Birch has always been a popular symbol of Russia, which claims more birch than any other country in the world. (Foreign currency shops throughout the country are called Beriozka, after the birch tree.)

Many older banyas are housed in splendid pre-revolutionary buildings; marble staircases, mirrored walls and gilded rooms, though somewhat faded, are filled with steam and cold pools. There are three main parts of the banya: the sitting and changing room, the bathing area, and the sauna itself. The bathing area is usually one immense room filled with large benches. Buckets are filled with warm water and birch branches. Here you scrub and rinse, and then carry the wet branches into the hot sauna. The custom is to hit the body lightly with the birch branches; this is believed to draw out toxins and circulate the blood. It is also traditional to hit each other with the branches; since you'll easily blend in like a native, you may find your banya buddy asking if you'd like your back lightly swatted! An old Russian folk-saying claims that 'the birch tree can give life, muffle groans, cure the sick and keep the body clean'. Cries of *oy oy, tak khorosho* (how wonderful) and *slyokim parom* (have an enjoyable sweat) emanate from every corner. When someone, usually one of the *babushki* (grandmothers) or *dedushki* (grandfathers), gets carried away with flinging water on the heated stones, moans of *khvatit* (enough) resound from the depths and bodies come racing out of the red-hot steamy interior. Back in the washroom, the bather rinses alternately in warm and cold water or plunges in the cold pool and then uses a loofa for a vigorous rubdown. Wrapped in a crisp, white towel, the refreshed figure returns to the sitting room to relax and sip tea, water, or even beer or vodka. With the skin glowing and rejuvenated, it is time to take an invigorating walk about the city.

The **Dynamo Stadium**, 36 Leningradsky Prospekt. Tel 217-7092
Dynamo Sports Palace, 32 Lavochkina Street, Metro Rechnoy Vokzal. Tel 454-6155
Izmailovo Sports Palace, 10/3 Tolbukhina, Metro Kutuzovskaya. Tel 448-8777
Krylatskoye Sports Complex, 10 Pyataya Krylatskaya. Tel 141-2224
Moskva Open-Air Swimming Pool, 37 Prechistenka Street. Tel 202-4725
Olympic Sports Complex, 16 Olympisky Prospekt, Metro Prospekt Mira. Tel 288-3777
Sokolniki Sports Palace, 1 Sokkolnichesky Val, Metro Sokolniki Park. Tel 268-6958
Spartak Sports Palace, 23 Maly Oleny Lane, Metro Sokolniki. Tel 268-8013
Hippodrome Race Course, 22 Begovaya Street, Metro Begovaya. Tel 945-4516.
Races are on Wednesday, Saturday and Sunday.
Horseback Riding, 35 Leningradsky Prospekt. Tel 135-8255. The Hippodrome also
rents horses. Tel 945-5872. The Bitsa Complex at 33 Balaklavsky Prospekt also
rents. If you are good, try the Stallion Factory no. 1 outside town, 15 kilometers from
the Russkaya Izba Rest. Tel 592-3644

Banyas

Most have birch brances outside for sale during warmer months. The first two below
have private *banyas* for groups, featuring sauna, small pool and lounging room.

Krasnopresnenskaya at 7 Stolyarny Lane. Tel 255-5306
Sandunovskiye, 1a 1st Neglinny Lane. Tel 925-4631
Tsentralnaya, 4 Okhotny Ryad (across from Metropole Hotel). Tel 925- 0888
Most of the Western hotels in Moscow have a health center. The Mezdunarod-
naya Hotel's Health Club is on the ground floor with sauna and pool. Open from
noon to 20:00 daily. Tel. 255-6691.
Call to find out what days are closed.

Golf Courses

Moscow Country Club in Nahabino (outside Moscow). This was the first golf course
built in the Soviet Union, designed by Robert Trent Jones II. Opened in 1993. Tel
561-2975
Tumba, Russian–Swedish joint-venture. Near Moscow University at 1 Dovzhenko
Street. Tel 147-6254

Parks and Gardens

Alexandrovsky Garden, The Kremlin.
Botanical Garden of the Academy of Sciences, 4 Ostankino-Botanicheskaya Street.
Tel 218-0649
Druzhba Forest Park, 90 Leningradskoye Highway. Tel 456-1048
Fili Recreation Park, 22 Bolshaya Filevskaya Street. Tel 142-2795
Gorky Central Recreation Park, 9 Krymsky Val. Tel 237-0964
Hermitage Garden, 3 Karetny Ryad. Tel 299-0849
Izmailovo Recreation Park, 17 Narodny Prospekt, Metro Izmailovo Park. Tel 166-7909
Kolomenskoye Preserve Museum Park, 39 Andropov Street. Tel 115-2768
Kuskovo Forest Park, 40 3rd Muzeinaya Street. Tel 370-0750
Moscow University Botanical Gardens, Lenin Hills on Mendeleyev Street. Tel 939-3509
Old Botanical Gardens, 28 Prospekt Mira.
Sokolniki Park, 62 Rusakovskaya Street, Metro Sokolniki. Tel 268-5430
Tsaritsyno Park, 4 Radialnaya Street, Metro Tsaritsyno. Tel 321-6733
Zoological Gardens, 1 Bolshaya Gruzinskaya Street.

Places of Worship

Russian Orthodox services are now held in most Russian Orthodox churches in the city. The Uspenskaya Church in the Novodevichy Convent and the Yelokhovsky Cathedral, at 15 Spartakovskaya Street, both have services. Services at the Yelokhovsky are held on Sundays and holidays from 07:00 to 10:00, Monday and Saturday at 08:00 and 18:00.
Catholic: Chapel of Our Lady of Hope, 7/4 Kutuzovsky Prospekt, Kor 5, Ent 3, 3rd Floor, Room 42. Tel 243-9621. The St Louis de Français at 12 Malaya Lubyanka has masses in Latin on Sundays at 08:00 and 11:00 and 18:00. On Monday and Saturday at 08:00 and Friday and Saturday at 18:00. On Sundays at the US Commercial Office, at Sadovaya Chaikovskaya, masses are held in English at 10:00 and in French at noon.
Anglican: St. Andrews, 9 Stankevicha Street. Services are held every second and fourth Sunday at 10:00.
German Evangelical: German Embassy. Services are held twice a month. Tel 238-1324
Mormon: Church of Jesus Christ of Latter-day Saints. 37 Domskaya. Services are held every Sunday at 10:00. Metro Shalbolovskaya. Tel 240-6332

Protestant: UPDK Hall at 5 Olafa Palma Street, behind the Swedish Embassy. Sunday school and adult Bible reading at 10:00. Tel 143-3562
Muslim: Mosque at 7 Vypolzov Per. Largest service is on Friday at 13:00.
Jewish: Synagogue is at 8 Arkhipova Street. Services on Friday at sunset and on Saturday at 09:00. Tel 923-9697

Medical

DOCTORS, MEDICAL FACILITIES

Embassies usually treat only their own staff. If an illness occurs, try contacting any of the following, unless in dire emergency.

The **American Medical Center** is a Western-style medical facility. They have 24-hour emergency care, an on-call doctor, laboratory facilities and a pharmacy. The clinic (regular hours: Monday to Friday from 08:30 to 18:00) is near the Mezh Hotel at 3 Shmitovsky Proezd. Tel 256-8212/8378
The **Sana Medical Clinic**, with foreign and Russian doctors (a French joint-venture), is at 65 Nizhnaya Pervomaiskaya Street. Tel 464-1254/2563/4654, fax 464-4563. It is open Tuesday to Saturday from 10:00 to 21:00, and Sunday from 10:00 to 17:00.
The **International Health Clinic** (French–Russian) is located at 3 Gruzhinsky Lane, Kor 2, Polyclinic 6, open Monday to Friday from 09:00 to 18:00. Tel 253-0703. If there is a serious emergency, these places can also arrange evacuations out of Russia. If you need an ambulance, dial 03 in Moscow. To trace somebody in hospital, dial 924-3152.
Other **pharmacies** are **The Medicine Man** (Swiss) at 4 Cherniakovskaya Street. Tel 155-7080/8788. **Unipharm** is at 13 Skaterny Per. Tel 202-5071. All these accept hard currency, service prescriptions, and have other Western pharmaceutical products.
The **Apteka** on Tverkskaya Street has some items for hard currency too. At the **Mezh Hotel**, second floor, is a pharmacy with an assortment of Western products for hard currency.

DENTISTS

Swiss Medical Interline is located at the Intourist Hotel, 5 Tverskaya, Rm 2030. Open Monday to Saturday from 09:00 to 20:00. Tel 203-9496/8631. This is a Belgian–Hungarian–Swiss–Italian joint-venture.
Intermed (German-Russian) is at 26 Durov Street, Kor 5. Open from 09:00 to 20:00.

Tel 288-9679, 284-7403. Both have all Western equipment—for hard currency. It is not recommended to try a Russian dentist.

OPTICAL

The **Sana Medical Group**, as listed above, offers eye tests, lenses and frames. At 30 Arbat is the American joint-venture **Optic Moscow**, open from 10:00 to 19:00. Tel 241-1577. They can also help with soft lenses; they also stock cleansing materials.

Miscellaneous

COURIERS

Most of these have pick-up and delivery services and accept credit cards:

DHL. Tel 201-2585, 202-8090

Federal Express, Ground Floor, Sovincenter, next to the Mezh Hotel. Tel 253-1641

TNT Express Worldwide. Tel 156-5760/5771

United Parcel Service. Tel 430-7069/6373

Western Union, 4 N-238 Novodevichy Pereulok, 5-1a Yunost Street, or 6 Kuznetsky Most. The main telephone number is 374-6886. Money can be wired from any Western Union office to Moscow. If you receive in foreign currency and not rubles, a 3 to 6 per cent commission will be charged at the Moscow end.

FILM DEVELOPING

If you cannot wait to develope pictures until you are home, try the second floor at the **Mezh Hotel**, where there is a Kodak kiosk. Tel 252-0640. The **Fuji Film Center** is at 25 Novy Arbat (one-hour service available), open Monday to Saturday from 10:00 to 21:00. Tel 203-7307. You can also buy film in most major hotels and *Beriozkas*.

CLOTHING AND SHOE SIZE CONVERSION

Women's Dress Sizes

Russia	44	46	48	50
US	6	8	10	12
European	34	36	38	40

Women's Shoes

Russia	34	35	36	37
US	4	5	6	7

Men's Suits

Russia	48	50	52	54	56
US	37–8	39–40	41–42	43–44	45–46

Men's Shoes

Russia	38	39	40	42	44
US	6 1/2–7	7 1/2–8	8 1/2–9	9 1/2–10	10 1/2–11

CONVERSION TABLE

1 inch	=	2.54 centimeters
1 foot	=	.304 meters
1 mile	=	1.6 kilometers
1 kilometer	=	.6214 miles
1 ounce	=	28.35 grams
1 pound	=	.45 kilograms
1 kilo	=	2.2 pounds
1 pint	=	.57 litres
1 litre	=	1.75 pints
1 quart	=	.946 litres
1 US gallon	=	3.785 litres
1 hectare	=	2.47 acres

To compute centigrade temperatures, subtract 32 from Fahrenheit and divide by 1.8. To go the other way, multiply centigrade by 1.8 and add 32.

Recommended Reading

CITY DIRECTORIES
The Traveller's Yellow Pages for Moscow, and St Petersburg.
The first comprehensive business telephone book for these cities is now sold in many stores and hotels in Moscow and St Petersburg. For a copy, also call in the United States, InfoServices International. Tel (516) 549-0064, fax (516) 549-2032 **Moscow Magazine** and **St Petersburg News**, available in hard currency stores in each city, has many listings of current events, along with interesting articles.

General History and Current Affairs

Billington, James, *The Icon and the Ax: An Interpretive History of Russian Culture* (Vintage)

Burlatsky, Fedor, *Khrushchev and the Russian Spring: The Era of Khrushchev Through the Eyes of his Advisors* (Charles Scribner's Sons, 1988)

CNN Reports: 7 Days that Shook the World and the Collapse of Soviet Communism (Turner Publishing, 1991)

de Jonge, Alex, *The Life and Times of Gregory Rasputin* (Dorset Press, 1987)

Gorbachev, Mikhail, *Perestroika: New Thinking of Our Country and the World* (Harper and Row, 1987)

Hayward, Max, *Writers in Russia: 1917–1978* (Harvest, 1984)

Kagarlitsky, Boris, *The Thinking Reed: Intellectuals and the Soviet State, 1917 to the Present Day* (Verso, 1988)

Kalugin, Oleg, *The First Directorate*, (on the KGB), (St Martin's Press, 1994)

Lenin, Vladimir, *What Is To Be Done?* (Written 1902, published by Penguin, 1988)

Massie, Robert, *Peter the Great* (Ballantine, 1980); *Nicholas and Alexandra* (Atheneum)

Massie, Suzanne. *Land of the Firebird: The Beauty of Old Russia* (Simon and Schuster, 1980); *The Living Mirror: Five Young Poets from Leningrad* (Doubleday)

Medvedev, Roy, *Let the People Judge* (Alfred Knopf, 197); *A Question of Madness* (W W Norton, 1979)

Medvedev, Zhores, *Gorbachev* (Blackwell, 1987)

Morrison, John, *Boris Yeltsin: From Bolshevik to Democrat* (EP Dutton, 1991)

Moynahan, Brian, *Comrades: 1917 Russia in Revolution* (Little Brown & Co, 1992)

Oakley, Jane, *Rasputin: Rascal Master* (St Martin's Press, 1989)

Pozner, Vladimir, *Parting with Illusions* (Avon Books, 1991)

Reed, John, *The Ten Days That Shook the World* (Written 1919, published by International, 1967)

Remnick, David, *Lenin's Tomb: The Last Days of the Soviet Empire* (Random House, 1993) Winner of the Pulitzer Prize 1993.

Riasanovsky, N, *A History of Russia* (Oxford University Press, 1984)

Riehn, Richard, *1812: Napolean's Russian Campaign* (McGraw Hill, 1990)

Salisbury, Harrison, *Nine Hundred Days: The Seige of Leningrad* (Avon, 1970)

Service, Robert, *The Russian Revolution: 1900–1927* (Macmillan, 1986)

Sobchak, Anatoly, *For a New Russia: The Mayor of St Petersburg's Own Story for the Struggle for Justice and Democracy* (Macmillan, 1992)

Smith, Hedrick, *The New Russians* (Random House, 1991) (Also *The Russians*)

Thomas, Bill, *Adventure Capitalism in the New Russia* (Dutton, 1992)

Ulam, Adam, *The Communists: The Story of Power and Lost Illusions 1948–1991*, (Charles Scribners Sons, 1992); *Stalin: The Man and his Era* (Beacon Press, 1989); *The Bolsheviks* (Macmillan)

Yeltsin, Boris, *Against the Grain* (Summit Books, 1990)

PICTURE BOOKS, AND ART AND CULTURE

A Day in the Life of the Soviet Union (Collins, 1987)

A Portrait of Tsarist Russia (Pantheon, 1989)

Before the Revolution: St Petersburg in Photographs 1890–1914 (Harry Abrahms, 1991)

Bird, Alan, *A History of Russian Painting* (Oxford, London, 1987)

Chamberlain, Leslie, *The Food and Cooking of Russia* (Penguin, London, 1983)

Feigan, Leo, *Russian Jazz and the New Identit* (Quartet, 1985)

Konchalovsky, Andrei, *The Inner Circle: An Inside View to Soviet Life Under Stalin* (based on his film, New Market Press, 1991)

Gray, Camilla, *The Russian Experiment in Art 1863–1922* (Thames & Hudson, 1984)

Pokhlebkin, William, *A History of Vodka* (Verso, 1993)

Prince Michael of Greece, *Nicholas and Alexandra: The Family Albums* (Tauris Parke, 1992)

Rudnitsky, Konstantin, *Russian and Soviet Theater 1905–32* (Harry Abrams, 1988)

Robinson, Harlow, *Sergei Prokofiev: A Biography* (Paragon, 1988)

Russian Fairy Tales (Pantheon, 1973)

Russian Masters: Glinka, Borodin, Balakirev, Mussorgsky, Tchaikovsky, (W W Norton, 1986)

Saved for Humanity: The Hermitage During the Seige of Leningrad 1941–44 (Aurora, St Petersburg, 1985)

Shead, Richard, *Ballets Russes* (Wellfleet Press, 1989)

Skvorecky, Josef, *Talking Moscow Blues* (Ecco Press, 1988)

Snowman, Kenneth, *Carl Fabergé: Goldsmith to the Imperial Court of Russia* (Crown, 1983)

Strizhenova, Tatiana, *Soviet Costume and Textiless 1917–45* (Flammarion, 1991)

Tamarov, Vladislav, *Afghanistan: Soviet Vietnam* (Mercury House, 1992)

Troitsky, Artemus, *Children of Glasnost* (1992); *Back in the USSR: The True Story of Rock in Russia* (Faber & Faber, 1987)

Volkogonov, Dmitri, *Lenin: A New Biography,* The Free Press, 1994

NOVELS AND TRAVEL WRITING

Akhmatova, Anna, *The Complete Poems of Anna Akhmatova, Vol. I & II,* Translated by Judith Hemschemeyer and Edited by Roberta Reeder (Zephyr Press, 1990)

Also by Zephyr Press *GLAS: New Russian Writing,* A Literary Journal–4/yr

To order a subscripion write to: Zephyr, 13 Robinson Street, Sommerville, Massachusetts, USA 02145. Tel (617) 628-9726, fax (617) 776-8246

Akhmtova, Anna, *My Half Century, Selected Prose* (Ardis, 1992)

Absyonov, Vasily, *In Search of a Melancholy Baby* (1985) and *Generations of Winter* (Random House, 1993)

Dostoevsky, Fyodor, *Crime and Punishment* (Bantam, 1982)

Finder, Joseph, *The Moscow Club* (Signet, 1992)

Gogol, Nikolai, *Dead Souls* (Penguin)

Hansson and Liden, *Moscow Women* (Random House, 1983)

Leningrad in Literature: The Complete Prose Tales of Alexander Sergeyevitch Pushkin (W W Norton)

Mochulsky, K, *Dostoevsky: His Life and Work* (Princeton University Press)

Morris, Mary, *Wall to Wall* (Penguin, 1989) (A trip from Beijing to Berlin across Russia on the Trans-Siberian)

Pasternak, Boris, *Dr Zhivago* (Ballantine, 1988)

The Portable Chekhov (Viking, Penguin)

The Portable Tolstoy, and *War and Peace* (Penguin)

Radzhinsky, Edvard, *The Last Tsar: The Life and Death of Nicholas II* (Doubleday, 1991)

Rutherford, Edward, *Russka: The Novel of Russia* (Crown, 1991)

Rybakov, Anatoly, *Fear* (Little, Brown & Co, 1992); *Children of the Arrbat* (Dell,1988)

Salisbury, Harrison, *Moscow Journal* (University of Chicago Press)

Solzhenitsyn, Alexander, *One Day in the Life of Ivan Denisovich* (Bantam); *The First Circle,* and *The Gulag Archipelago* (Harper & Row); *The Red Wheel* (1994)

Theroux, Paul, *The Great Railway Bazaar* (A trip across Russia on the Trans-Siberian)

Thubron, Colin, *Where Nights are Longest* (Atlantic Monthly Press, 1983)

Tolstoya, Tatyana, *On the Golden Porch* (1988); *Sleepwalker in a Fog* (1992)

Turgenev, Ivan, *Fathers and Sons* (Penguin)

Ustinov, Peter, *My Russia* (Little, Brown & Co, 1983)

Van Der Post, Laurens, *Journey in Russia* (Penguin, 1965)

Voinovich, Vladimir, *Moscow, 2042* (Harcourt Brace Jovanovich, 1987)

Wilson, A N, *Tolstoy Biography* (Ballantine, 1988)

Films and Videos Available for Rental or Purchase

National Geographic's *Inside the Soviet Circus,* 1988 and *Voices of Leningrad* (1990)

ABC Kane's World of Discovery: *Powers of the Russian Psychics* (1993); *Survive Siberia* (1992); *Trans-Siberian: The Red Express* (1991)

Abuladze's *Repentance* (Russia, 1987)

Alexander Nevsky (Russia, 1938)

Back in the USSR (20th Century Fox/Largo, 1991)

Backstage at the Kirov (1984)

Basic Russian by Video

Coup! Take Two: The Movie (1992)

Crime and Punishment (1993)

Durrell in Russia

Eisenstein (Russia, 1958); Eisenstein's *Potemkin* (Russia, 1925)

HBO's *Stalin* (with Robert Duvall) (1992)

Ivan the Terrible (Russia, 1946)

Kanchalovsky's *The Inner Circle* (1991)

Maya Plisetskaya Dances (Russia)

Menshov's *Moscow Doesn't Believe in Tears* (Russia, 1980)

Moscow on the Hudson (1984)

October: Ten Days that Shook the World (Russia, 1927)

Petrov's *Peter the First: Parts I, II,* (Russia, 1937)

Pichul's *Little Vera* (Russia, 1988)

Pudovkin's *Mother* (Russia, 1926)

Rasputin and The Empress (MGM, 1932, starring Lionel, John and Ethel Barrymore)

Reds (1981)

Tarkovsky's *Andrei Rublev* (Russia, 1965)

Taxi Blues (Russia, 1990)

The End of St Petersburg (Russia, 1927)

Yertov's *The Man with the Movie Camera* (Russia, 1928)

Yevtushenko's *Stalin's Funeral* (1991)

Yeliseyev's

This store, whose nickname was also the Temple of Gluttons, has a long and scandalous history. It was originally built as a mansion by the State Secretary of Catherine the Great, Prince Kozitsky, for his beautiful wife, the heiress of a Siberian goldmine. The mansion was the largest and grandest in the city.

In the 1820s, their granddaughter, Princess Volkonskaya, turned the drawing room into one of Russia's most prestigious salons. All the great literary figures gathered here, including Pushkin, who presented his latest poems. But in 1829, when the princess left for Italy, the mansion fell into other hands.

By the mid-1850s, the dreaded Princess Beloselskaya-Belozerskaya, a relative of Volkanskaya, was living in the mansion, which is all she did for she was a recluse and only left it to go to church on Sundays. She was not popular at home since she had her servants beaten every Saturday, a common practice in that era to single out a few for reprimanding. Not surprisingly, some of these serf-servants ran away and banded together in a house across the street, living a life of crime to survive. During this time, many Muscovites believed the dark house to be haunted, claiming to see devils and ghosts there, and would not walk by the mansion at night. The bandit-servants decided to lend credence to this belief. One night they dressed up like ghosts and spooked the old princess right out of her house. Some time afterwards, an animal trainer took up residence in the mansion; his black panther lived with him.

A number of years later, Grigory Grigoryevich Yeliseyev bought the vacant building. Grigory's serf father had won his freedom when his master released him for producing strawberries in winter. He later made a fortune as a trader in St Petersburg. His son, Grigory, opened a popular food emporium in St Petersburg, where they even made their own chocolate. Since it was quite well known, throngs of people turned out for the Moscow Yeliseyev's grand opening in 1899. There was one unexpected hitch, though—the liquor department turned out to be less than 50 yards from the neighboring church, which contravened the sacred law. So, builders had to do a quick restructuring and move the department 51 yards away. The popular writer Vladimir Gilyarovksy, who lived in the area, wrote in *Moscow and Muscovites*: 'Passers-by stared at the mountains of imported fruits which looked like cannon balls, a pyramid of coconuts each the size of a child's head, bunches of tropical bananas so large you could not get your arms around them and unknown inhabitants of the ocean depths. Overhead, electric stars on tips of wine bottles flashed in the enormous mirrors, the tops of which were lost somewhere up in the heights...' The store was a huge success.

Shortly afterwards, Grigory, a grandfather himself, fell in love with the wife of a local jeweler. Grigory's broken-hearted wife attempted suicide, finally succeeding on her third attempt. When World War I broke out, Grigory married his lover and fled to France. After this magnificent scandal, Yeliseyev's sons renounced their heritage, which included the store. This was probably just as well, since the family would have lost everything anyway in the Bolshevik Revolution, which broke out soon after.

The saga does not end there. Under Brezhnev, the director of Gastronom #1 was Yuri Konstantinovich Sokolov. As a friend of Brezhnev's daughter Galya, Sokolov was quite well-connected. At the store, he invented quotas and took a lot of the food himself, writing it off as spoiled and selling it on the black market or keeping choice picks for himself. Sokolov became wealthy and popular, and threw great parties. But when Brezhnev died in 1982 and Andropov took over, the glorious days of stagnation were numbered for Sokolov. Andropov was determined to crush corruptive influences. The head of Moscow Trade received a sentence of 15 years, the director of another Gastronom six years, and Sokolov was sentenced to death. He was executed by firing squad in 1984. The police supposedly found gold, jewelry and huge bundles of rotting rubles in his backyard.

Today, the new owners of the shop have renamed it Yeliseyev's, hoping to capitalize on its intriguing past. A bust of Grigory Yeliseyev stands in the entrance hall, put up in 1989 to celebrate the store's 90th anniversary. Pictures of the Yeliseyev family are also on the walls. Many of the people in the store will be there just to look since the luxury goods, such as Ameretto and garlic sausages, are far too expensive for ordinary Muscovites to afford.

Yeliseyev's can be found at 14 Tverskaya Street.

Index

Notes